Race and Sports

Recent Titles in the
CONTEMPORARY WORLD ISSUES
Series

Books in the **Contemporary World Issues** series address vital issues in today's society such as genetic engineering, pollution, and biodiversity. Written by professional writers, scholars, and nonacademic experts, these books are authoritative, clearly written, up-to-date, and objective. They provide a good starting point for research by high school and college students, scholars, and general readers as well as by legislators, businesspeople, activists, and others.

Each book, carefully organized and easy to use, contains an overview of the subject, a detailed chronology, biographical sketches, facts and data and/or documents and other primary source material, a forum of authoritative perspective essays, annotated lists of print and nonprint resources, and an index.

Readers of books in the Contemporary World Issues series will find the information they need in order to have a better understanding of the social, political, environmental, and economic issues facing the world today.

Race and Sports

A REFERENCE HANDBOOK

Rachel Laws Myers

An Imprint of ABC-CLIO, LLC
Santa Barbara, California • Denver, Colorado

Library of Congress Cataloging-in-Publication Data

Names: Myers, Rachel Laws, author.

Title: Race and sports : a reference handbook / Rachel Laws Myers.

Description: Santa Barbara : ABC-CLIO, 2021. | Includes bibliographical references and index.

Identifiers: LCCN 2020033720 (print) | LCCN 2020033721 (ebook) | ISBN 9781440862823 (Hardcover : acid-free paper) | ISBN 9781440862830 (eBook)

Subjects: LCSH: Racism in sports—United States. | Discrimination in sports—United States. | Sports—Social aspects—United States. | United States—Race relations.

Classification: LCC GV706.32 .M96 2021 (print) | LCC GV706.32 (ebook) | DDC 796.089—dc23

LC record available at https://lccn.loc.gov/2020033720

LC ebook record available at https://lccn.loc.gov/2020033721

ISBN: 978-1-4408-6282-3 (print)
   978-1-4408-6283-0 (ebook)

25 24 23 22 21   1 2 3 4 5

This book is also available as an eBook.

ABC-CLIO
An Imprint of ABC-CLIO, LLC

ABC-CLIO, LLC
147 Castilian Drive
Santa Barbara, California 93117
www.abc-clio.com

This book is printed on acid-free paper ∞

Manufactured in the United States of America

Contents

Preface

Sports are special in U.S. society. There are a number of nations that do not send athletes—or send very few—every four years to compete in the global Olympic Games. However, many nations and citizens have deemed sport special enough to build an entire industry around it *and* infuse a variety of sports into the foundational years of generations to come. The United States is a clear example of a nation that has lifted sports into a realm beyond friendly competitions based on athleticism and polished skills. In the United States, some organized youth sport opportunities start before children have mastered reading and writing in school.

On the one hand, sports in the United States have had the luxury of being strongly supported financially by the public and private sectors, which, in turn, has created jobs for citizens, leisurely activities for communities, and a pathway for professional athletic advancement for many athletes. On the other hand, those who have had a hand in building the foundational structures of organized sports have also shaped the societal culture around how sport should be consumed. That is to say that those in power within sport have often tainted—whether consciously or unconsciously—what *should* be an equitable space, based on merit, with individual biases, values, and opinions that have caused the reality of a truly diverse, inclusive, and equitable sporting landscape to stall. Race and racism, as experienced at individual and institutional levels, have been—and continue to be—two of the most splintering and unifying catalysts within the realm of sport. This is due to the fact that despite the presence of—and in some cases, predominance of—people of color in sport, dominant racial ideologies are often mirrored and reinforced.

In concluding my book chapter, "More Than One: What Happened When Multiple Black Female Athletes Excelled in Predominantly White Sports at the Rio Olympics," in *Women in Sports: Breaking Barriers, Facing Obstacles,* I emphasized that changes should be made along the lines of race and sport—particularly among predominantly White sports—because data supports the relation between racial diversity and athletic success:

> Changes to organizational efforts to increase participation among people of color and a shift in the way these athletes are presented by the media . . . can cause major shifts in the athletic landscape for generations to come, but also shift the place and value of Whiteness in the racial hierarchy. (Myers, 2017, 72)

It's likely that the U.S. gymnastics team selected for competition at the 2016 Rio Olympic Games (five of whom are pictured on the cover of this reference volume) is the most racially and ethnically diverse squad chosen to represent the country in its history. The all-round winning gold medalist, five-member U.S. women's gymnastics team included two African Americans (Gabby Douglas and Simone Biles), one Latinx American (Laurie Hernandez), and two White Americans (Aly Raisman, who is also ethnically Jewish, and Madison Kocian). In addition, of the three alternates selected to the 2016 Rio Olympics with the U.S. women's gymnastics team, one identifies as Native American (Ashton Locklear), and two identify as White Americans (MyKayla Skinner and Ragan Smith). That's 50 percent self-identified gymnasts of color and 50 percent self-identified White gymnasts. According to the NCAA Demographics Database, over the ten-year span between 2008 and 2018, the percentage of college gymnasts of color increased from 19 to

30 percent. In a sport that has historically been viewed as a White-dominated realm, the 2016 Olympic U.S. women's gymnastics team could certainly be viewed as an example of sport serving as a tool for shifting the place and value of Whiteness in the racial hierarchy of society and the future of the sport an example of race as a unifying catalyst.

This reference volume seeks to discuss how race and racism continue to be enmeshed in sport, despite decades of racial integration in the United States. This volume also examines race and sports and connected issues, from the integration of professional sports to the present day. It includes an exploration into the history of minority involvement in sports at every level: the key issues and barriers broken, the stereotypes that have been shattered, and the difficulties that have been endured. In the opening chapter, a background on the topic of race and sports is offered through a shortened review of the history and an introduction to its theoretical aspects. The first chapter is followed by a chapter discussing the controversies, problems, and possible solutions in the realm of race and sport. Essays from seven contributors in the third chapter showcase different aspects of race and sports, while the remaining chapters of this work are dedicated to reference material—such as biographical sketches of key individuals and organizations relevant to race and sports, a data and documents chapter that discusses race and sports at the youth, collegiate, and professional levels, an extensive annotated bibliography, a chronology, and a glossary of key terms—helpful in further study of the topic.

Acknowledgments

I'd like to thank the team at ABC-CLIO—Catherine LaFuente and Robin Tutt, in particular—for their uplifting of this important topic and their trust in me to be the author to carry out the creation of this reference volume on race and sport. I also want to thank my family, my loving partner, and my dear friends for their support of my completion of this project; they always asked me, "How's the book coming?" exactly when I needed to hear it most. My students and former colleagues at the Hotchkiss School were the best cheerleaders imaginable; I am grateful for their support. A special thank-you goes out to the seven contributors who wrote very personal essays for the "Perspectives" chapter of this volume; your lived experiences and voices are invaluable to the conversation on race and sport. Finally, I have to especially thank and dedicate this work to my son, Wallace. Mommy promises to make up for all the lost playtime together—I hope you fall in love with sports as much as I have, but if you don't, I hope you'll still be proud of what I've done here.

References

Myers, Rachel Laws. 2017. "More Than One: What Happened When Multiple Black Female Athletes Excelled in Predominantly White Sports at the Rio Olympics." In *Women in Sports: Breaking Barriers, Facing Obstacles*, edited by Adrienne N. Milner and Jomills Henry Braddock II, 59–75. Santa Barbara, CA: ABC-CLIO.

Race and Sports

Understanding Race and Sports through Historical and Theoretical Frameworks

To understand the connection between race and sport, it is first important to understand the concept of White supremacy, as White supremacy establishes the hierarchical power dynamic regarding race. Race alone is simply a passive means of categorizing groups of people who share a distinct lineage. For example, someone who is not of Asian ancestry in the United States may choose to categorize someone they know of Asian ancestry who was born in the United States as Asian American based on ancestral geography alone. It is when race is viewed through the lens of White supremacy that things become complex—and many times problematic—in society as a whole and in sport specifically. George Fredrickson states in *White Supremacy: A Comparative Study in American and South African History*, "white supremacy refers to the attitudes, ideologies, and policies associated with the rise of blatant forms of white or European dominance over 'nonwhite' populations. . . . It suggests systematic and self-conscious efforts to make race or color a qualification for membership in the civil community" (Frederickson, 1981, xvii). Through the White supremacist system of U.S. segregation and the White supremacist beliefs

Native American athlete Jim Thorpe, during a football practice in 1920. Thorpe was an All-American football player at Carlisle Indian Institute and excelled in track & field and baseball too. He was voted the greatest athlete of the first half of the 20th century. (Library of Congress)

that remain after its legal dismantling, Frederickson brings readers to the conclusion that the United States has, over long periods of time, manifested a tendency to push the principle of differentiation by race to its logical outcome—a society in which non-Whites, regardless of their numbers or efforts to assimilate, are treated as outsiders.

The periodization of various racial groups' history in the United States varies slightly and has much to do with racial politicization. Generally speaking, racial segregation in the United States spanned the years from 1865 until 1965. According to historian Pero G. Dagbovie, "the years from 1865 until 1965 were marked by African Americans' struggles for basic civil and human rights" (2006, 70). Within this timeframe, since the battle of Wounded Knee in 1890, where several hundred Lakota Indians were massacred by the U.S. Army, the legacy of the Native American experience is marked with violent colonization, forced migrations, and numerous treaty violations. For Asian Americans, look to the Naturalization Act of 1870, which limited naturalization to White persons and persons of African descent, effectively excluding Chinese and other Asian immigrants from naturalization. Anti-Asian racism manifested in the United States through things like segregation, barriers to education, and exclusion bans on immigration and citizenship for people from all or parts of Asia between 1882 and 1965. The formation of the term "Asian American" during the 1960s civil rights movement era was not only an act of resistance against orientalism, it also reflected a self-determined commitment to engage in coalitional work and a means to establish anti-racist political power (Bhangal and Poon, 2020). For those who identify racially under the Latinx American umbrella, the years 1898, 1901, and 1902 are of particular importance:

In 1898, the United States acquires Puerto Rico through war and claims it as a territory; In 1901, under the Platt Amendment, the United States limits Cuban independence as written into the Cuban Constitution. The United States reserves the right to build a naval base on Cuba and enforces that Cuba cannot sign treaties with other countries or borrow money unless it is deemed agreeable to the United States . . . [and] in 1902, the Reclamation Act is passed, dispossessing many Hispanic Americans of their lands. (PBS.org, 2013)

It is these dates, among others, that help to demonstrate how people of color in the United States have been legally treated by Whites.

In terms of sporting history, the periodization can be broken up into youth, college, and professional sports racial integration. At the youth sporting level, public school education was racially integrated in 1954 with the ruling in *Brown v. Board of Education of Topeka* establishing segregation in public schools as a violation of the Fourteenth Amendment. However, each state's government took varying measures and lengths of time to see that integration actually progressed. For example, significant racial integration didn't take place in the Texas public high school system until 1967 (Luberto, 1994). The complete integration of college sport took place in 1971 when the University of Mississippi finally integrated its football team. According to scholar Renford Reese, "money and competition were the two major factors that drove the complete integration of teams" (Wills, 2017), rather than a dismantling of White supremacist ideology. At the professional level, most major professional sporting organizations became integrated in the late 1940s and early 1950s. African American football stars from UCLA, Woody Strode and Kenny Washington, integrated the National Football League (NFL) in 1946. One year later, in the 1947–1948 season, baseball's Brooklyn Dodgers had signed African American second baseman Jackie Robinson, integrating major league baseball. African Americans, Nat "Sweetwater" Clifton and Chuck Cooper integrated the NBA in 1950; Clifton played for the New York Knicks and Cooper for the Boston Celtics. The United States Tennis Association's major tournaments became integrated with the rise of Althea Gibson in the 1950s and Arthur Ashe in the 1960s. Thus, the periodization for the majority of this volume will span 1940 through the present, although certain events, athletes, or organizations may take readers to earlier dates.

With the large gap in time from when systemic racism began to be established to when sports started to become integrated, racism had time to develop and seep into every aspect of U.S. society. Racism should be understood as one race of people believing that they are inherently superior to another race. Usually, this belief is based on one or more of the following reasons: sweeping generalizations, power and privilege, or false science. According to Dr. Camara Phyllis Jones, there are three different types of racism: internalized, personally mediated, and institutionalized:

> In this framework, *institutionalized racism* is defined as differential access to the goods, services, and opportunities of society by race. Institutionalized racism is normative, sometimes legalized, and often manifests as inherited disadvantage. It is structural, having been codified in our institutions of custom, practice, and law, so there need not be an identifiable perpetrator. . . . Institutionalized racism manifests itself both in material conditions and in access to power . . . it is because of institutionalized racism that there is an association between socioeconomic status and race in this country. *Personally mediated racism* is defined as prejudice and discrimination, where prejudice means differential assumptions about the abilities, motives, and intentions of others according to their race, and discrimination means differential actions toward others according to their race. This is what most people think of when they hear the word "racism." Personally mediated racism can be intentional as well as unintentional, and it includes acts of commission as well as acts of omission. It manifests as lack of respect (poor or no service, failure to communicate options), suspicion (shopkeepers' vigilance; everyday

avoidance, including street crossing, purse clutching, and standing when there are empty seats on public transportation), devaluation (surprise at competence, stifling of aspirations), scapegoating, and dehumanization (police brutality, sterilization abuse, hate crimes). *Internalized racism* is defined as acceptance by members of the stigmatized races of negative messages about their own abilities and intrinsic worth. It is characterized by their not believing in others who look like them, and not believing in themselves. It involves accepting limitations to one's own full humanity, including one's spectrum of dreams, one's right to self-determination, and one's range of allowable self-expression. It manifests as an embracing of "whiteness"; self-devaluation; and resignation, helplessness, and hopelessness. (Jones, 2000, 1212–13)

In applying Jones's types of racism with the sport industry, one should make important connections about the historical and current realities and controversies within sport related to race. If "institutionalized racism manifests itself both in material conditions and in access to power," then is it truly surprising to learn that while the NFL's athletes are majority people of color (72.6%), but its vice presidents of color (11.7%) and general managers of color (12.5%) are so few in number? (See TIDES Racial and Gender Report Card by Lapchick, 2018, 15.) Why aren't more athletes of color team owners, managers, and head coaches in sports where they are majority represented as players? And does race play a factor in which sports youth have access or choose to play? In thinking about personally mediated racism and sport, one should think about what Colin Kaepernick and other athletes are advocating for and that many critics of athletes-of-color protesters are quick to label the athletes as ungrateful, unpatriotic, and out of line. Finally, in linking internalized racism to the realm of sport, one should question the resignation, helplessness, and hopelessness that has been experienced by some athletes of color who endured racism without speaking up and wonder about the fates of some athletes of color who spoke up about racism and were punished for it.

In his work *Glory Bound: Black Athletes in a White America*, David Wiggins asserts that "the differences between participation patterns of black and white athletes are primarily a consequence of different historical experiences that individuals and their particular racial group underwent" (1997, 177), but the same could be said of all athletes of color in the United States, beyond Black and White. In the United States, racial segregation and exclusion set the parameters for Black athletes' participation in different sports. Black athletes often pursued athletic aspirations through YMCAs and YWCAs, independent Black clubs, church leagues, and community recreation programs. Basketball and track emerged as the top sports of choice in the Black community, but baseball and tennis also gained popularity in Black communities.

Latinx—a gender neutral/nonbinary alternative term for Latino or Latina—Americans in urban communities in the United States have coexisted with other marginalized races for a long time. Yet, these same community neighbors from marginalized racial groups have very different participation rates in certain sports like professional baseball, basketball, and football. With professional baseball, light-skinned Latinx who could pass for White gained access to the major leagues, whereas darker-skinned Latinx played in the Negro leagues. The actual color of one's skin meant more than where one was from or what one's particular heritage was, so "a layer of heroes were able to be developed strictly on the basis of the fact that they were able to show that they were able to achieve in the context of a racist society" (Young et al., 2013). Currently in major league baseball, the Latinx representation is more global than domestic because the MLB "found that they could develop talent on the cheap by investing tens of millions of dollars into specifically the Dominican Republic, but also Venezuela and Puerto Rico as well" (Young et al., 2013). *Rolling Stone* journalist Juan Vidal explains that there are also differing cultural and educational pathways that have impacted Black and Latinx Americans' participation in sports like basketball and football:

> One factor that differentiates the black and Latino experience as it relates to athletics is that historically black colleges and universities have recruited top prospects in several mainstream sports for decades. And while HBCUs have struggled over recent years to compete with larger schools offering handsome scholarships, there have been a host of notable athletes—from NBA stars Charles Oakley and Ben Wallace to NFL greats like Walter Payton and Jerry Rice—who are products of those efforts. Over the years, a pipeline was built by HBCUs that, though not as deeply felt as it once was, still carries into the present day. According to an analysis published [in July 2016] by Pew Research Center, U.S.-based Latinos are making big strides when it comes to college enrollment, with 35 percent of students ages 18 to 24 enrolled in college in 2014. But almost half of them are attending two-year community colleges, which typically don't have sports teams . . . [in addition] Latinos consistently dominate in contact sports like boxing and MMA, where college participation is not a requirement. Generally, in many Latino communities, and especially in immigrant households . . . sports are not viewed as something to seriously pursue. And Latinos may be some of the most bombastic, spirited fans, the fact that we don't see ourselves reflected more on the court, the football field, nor, dare I say, the hockey rink, can frustrate some from trying to reach the next level. But this is slowly changing, with NCAA basketball seeing a huge spike in Latino players ready to make their mark. (Vidal, 2016)

Vidal's brief commentary on the Black and Latinx experience as it relates to athletics helps to demonstrate that cultural and systemic differences can greatly affect how sport is experienced for racial groups in the United States, where, at the university level, sport is incredibly competitive, structured, and financially lucrative. If Latinx Americans as a racial group have historically been absent from sports and colleges that do not affiliate with the National Collegiate Athletic Association (NCAA), chances are slim that Latinx Americans will be present in professional sports that draw primarily from the collegiate sports pipeline. Vidal also points out, however, that the college sports pipeline is growing in its inclusion of Latinx athletes. For example, according to the NCAA Demographics Database, the percentage of "Other" [read: non-Black and non-White] racially identifying men's basketball players across all divisions has increased from 7 to 16 percent between 2008 and 2018.

The White Puritans who settled in New England during the 1600s did not support athletics, but in the Southern colonies like Virginia, North Carolina, and South Carolina, horse racing rose in popularity and organization. Horse racing became the "most important American sport from the colonial era well into the nineteenth century . . . [as] sports became a way the colonies formed an independent—white—identity apart from Britain" (Zirin, 2008, 5). After the Revolutionary War, sports participation among Whites began to shift based on class, with the working class taking part in more brutal games than those who belonged to the wealthy class. As the 1830s arrived, so too did calculated racism and genocide from Whites to Native Americans and enslaved African-Americans. For Native Americans, their historical and present-day participation patterns in certain sports is absolutely connected to culture:

> Native Americans played far more than lacrosse. They also took part in what we would recognize as forms of wrestling, football, racing, and hunting. . . . Sports were a method of community training in agricultural or military skills. They also formed part of religious ceremony. (Zirin, 2008, 2)

However, the White U.S. government effectively decimated Native Americans numerically with forced removals, disease, and bloody battles. In 1820, 120,000 Indians lived east of the Mississippi, but by 1844, less than 30,000 remained (Zirin, 2008, 11). For many of the Native Americans who survived these forced removals, a familiar, yet intensified challenge awaited them.

White settlers were convinced early on that education was an effectual way to assimilate Native Americans into European culture. The 1870s, however, marked the most successful effort to educate Native Americans. Education, according to the White reformers, would speed up the process of assimilation and would most efficiently teach Native Americans the more "civilized" virtues of White society (Fields, 2008, 243). Two kinds of schools were made available to Native Americans between the 1880s and 1950s: on-reservation day schools and off-reservation boarding schools. The day schools were run by the federal government's Bureau of Indian Affairs (BIA), privately funded Christian missionaries, or occasionally the tribal leaders themselves. The off-reservation boarding schools were based on a U.S. Army lieutenant's Indian prisoner of war model. Native Americans were taught to speak English, worship according to Christianity, learn a trade, and participate in sports to promote physical health and build moral character. Native Americans in boarding schools also wore uniforms and had their hair cut. Carlisle Indian Industrial School in Pennsylvania was one such boarding school with a mission to "kill the Indian and save the man," and it became a model for Indian education (Fields, 2008, 243). Sport became very significant in these Indian boarding schools for both Native Americans and Whites, and scholars have made attempts to analyze the social meanings of these athletic contests:

> Benjamin Rader examined the 1926 Homecoming Game at Haskell Institute in Lawrence, Kansas, when the school's football team beat the Bucknell College team 36-0 in its

new 10,500-seat stadium. Rader argues that the event, which featured traditional *powwow* experiences in addition to the football game, allowed the Indians to revisit their cultural identities and to demonstrate symbolically their resistance to white society. John Bloom's book, *To Show What an Indian Can Do* (2000), supports this notion that sport provided Native American students with an opportunity to subtly resist their school leaders' assimilationist efforts. Bloom explored how sport provided students with a sense of community, dignity, and accomplishment. . . . Linda Peavy and Ursula Smith described the success of a girls' basketball team from Fort Shaw Indian Boarding School in western Montana when they traveled to St. Louis for the 1904 World's Fair and lived in the Model School, playing any team who cared to challenge them. Peavy and Smith maintain that the girls' presence and decorum at the fair helped show fairgoers that Indians were not "savages." . . . Superintendent Pratt of Carlisle School, in particular, championed the belief that sport was an opportunity to show the white community that Native Americans were more than savages and were capable of being good sportsmen and competitive with white people at their own games. . . . The Fort Shaw Superintendent seemed to share the conviction that if white people could see his students at games . . . they would learn that the products of Indian boarding schools had been assimilated into white culture. (Fields, 2008, 244–45)

The research of these scholars reveals that pride was felt among Native American athletes in these boarding schools through their athletic successes, and the pride of these collective groups of Native Americans athletes wasn't just about competition. This pride was a shared racial and ethnic pride that went counter to the claims by White Indian boarding school educators who were positive that their boarding schools were assimilating Native Americans into White culture.

During this same time, the racism provided by Whites against athletes of color through sporting regulations was usually racially binary: White and Black. For example, professional baseball officials held that Whites could compete and Blacks could not. This binary color line meant ambiguity regarding aboriginal players. In the United States, racial classification is rooted in the individually recognized racial difference of White and Black—and these roots often show themselves today when people ask U.S. residents of seemingly racially ambiguous heritage the question, "What are you?" while trying to discern whether the person identifies more with Black or White identity. The fear surrounding the racial mixing and mingling of Blacks and Whites in society led to White supremacists in power establishing racial categorization practices that equated to a "one-drop rule." The "one-drop rule" is the practice of labeling someone as Black because they have even a single drop of "Black blood." Essentially, it means that racially mixed people should be assigned the status of the subordinate (read: non-White) group. Yet, Whites have been procreating with non-Whites in the United States since they arrived, with and without consent from their sexual partners. Thus, a White person in the United States is merely someone who *appears* to have European lineage. The word *appears* is used because some people of color can "pass" for White. Professor of American History Sarah Trembanis explains how this "one-drop" ideology impacted Native American athletes:

> For some aboriginal athletes, their appearance was sufficiently white (or at least non-Black) to allow them entrance into the (all) white world of American sports . . . members of Virginia's aboriginal population claimed "whiteness" for themselves and for their children, thus ensuring their children would have access to public schools. At the same time, other aboriginals were denied not only the privileges of whiteness but also of status within the federally designated category of "American Indian." Because of their

physical features, geographical location, local folk tradition, and the 1924 Racial Integrity Act, these aboriginal people were re-raced and classified as African-American. As such, they were subject to the strictures of Jim Crow. (Trembanis, 2008, 281)

This means that for Native American athletes seeking the highest levels of athletic performance, there has always been a historical negotiation of their Indigenous ethnic and racial identities.

As for Asian Americans—specifically Chinese Americans who had settled on the West Coast after the transcontinental railroad was completed in 1869—cultural reasons kept them away from sports participation. Confucian tradition, which shuns physical competitions, was a reason that the early Chinese did not adopt Western sports. Sociologist Rose Hum Lee has observed: "[A] robust physique was equated with a peasant background. . . . The absence of competitiveness between groups and individuals on an impersonal basis, rather than kinship ties . . . resulted in the lack of emphasis on . . . man-to-man and team-to-team contests" (Lee, 1960, 139). With various legislative acts affecting the immigration of Asians into the United States, public school, sports, and recreation activities were used by Asian Americans to bring about a cultural link. Chinese and Japanese Americans organized their own leagues and competitions in the sports of baseball and basketball. In addition, the establishment of YMCAs and YWCAs in Asian American communities helped to provide opportunities for participation in sports like table tennis, softball, baseball, basketball, tennis, football, golf, and boxing. At the national and international levels, Japanese American basketball player named Wataru Misaka became the first non-White NBA player in 1947, the same year Jackie Robinson integrated professional baseball for the first time. A year later, in 1948, a Korean American diver became the first Asian American to win an Olympic gold medal for the United States. And in a combination of Olympic and Pan American Games competitions, Japanese American weightlifter Tommy Kono was gold medalist in 1952, 1955, 1956, 1959, and 1963.

Even with the success of Asian American athletes at the national and international levels, however, there exists a limited "common knowledge" of Asian American athletes before the 1990s. One reason for a lack of knowledge about Asian American athletes specifically that often comes up when discussing race and Asian Americans is the *model minority myth*. Sociologist William Petersen's 1966 article titled, "Success Story, Japanese-American Style," in the *New York Times Magazine* was the first mainstream media article praising Asian Americans' supposed cultural characters and their achievements in American society as a racial minority group (Osajima, 2008). The assumption of this discourse is that Asian cultural values of education and hard work are the key to Asian Americans' economic success in U.S. society. The stereotype has been used to denigrate other racial groups like Black and Latinx Americans and as an example of why calls for economic and political reformation that benefit people of color should be ignored by the majority White racial group in the powerful position to change systemic conditions. The model minority myth also puts immense pressure on Asian American youth to live up to the seemingly positive stereotypes about Asian American superiority in intelligence, work ethic, and family structure, and it dangerously causes some Asian Americans to act against other communities of color in order to "secure their own humanness by strengthening white dominance" (Bhangal and Poon, 2020; e.g., supporting White supremacists against affirmative action). With Whites and other racial groups viewing Asian Americans through the lens of the model minority myth, it creates the presumption that Asian Americans as athletes is something that emerged in the last thirty 30 years, rather than existing at the same time other racial groups, like African Americans, had gotten involved in sports.

Another reason for limited common knowledge about the sporting histories and present experiences of people of color beyond Black and White racial categories is American multiculturalism. The concept of *American multiculturalism* that first emerged in the 1970s and was popularized in the 1980s helped to create a barrier against claims of remaining White supremacist structures in the United States being to blame for continued inequalities for communities of color. With American multiculturalism, people tend to attribute social inequality to culturally different attributes of different cultural groups, rather than to existing structural inequities. While appearing to celebrate cultural diversity, American multiculturalism's "tendency to shift attention from racial contexts to cultural terrains" (Chae, 2007, 2) effectively obscures the vision of pervasive structural and institutional inequalities. For example, the American multiculturalism paradigm would support a rationale of low percentages of participation of Latinx and Native Americans in the sport of golf because those two groups don't have a cultural interest in golf, rather than place causation on systemic failure to provide access to and programming for golf in those respective communities of color. This American multiculturalism concept is similar to a kind of rationalization social anthropologist Gerard Schutte found White Afrikaners made when challenged about their beliefs and treatment of Black South Africans. In *What Racists Believe: Race Relations in South Africa and the United States*, Schutte refers to this rationalization as the *rationalization of common sense* and describes it as presented in this way:

> Real-life examples of the incompetence of blacks, their inferiority, and a host of other negative characteristics were given by informants. The informants never regarded these as prejudice or interpretation; they were facts. The anecdotes had the ring of truth because they were not only produced by persons predisposed to see blacks negatively but they were formulated as accounts in the interactional field of people sharing those beliefs and experiences about blacks. (Schutte, 1995, 243)

In simpler terms, White Afrikaners were making generalizations about Black South Africans overall based on their limited face-to-face experiences with them, rumors, anecdotes, and gossip they heard. People who take an American multiculturalism framework can make these same kind of generalizations without "regarding these as prejudice or interpretation . . . [just] facts" related to culture and never race. For example, former professional baseball player–turned-journalist Larry Colton encountered this American multiculturalism from a number of Whites living in community with Crow Indians in Montana while gathering information for *Counting Coup* (2000). Colton is actually taken aback when the mother of a White basketball player on a high school team comprising Native American and White players admits her thinking is prejudicial because "it's the first time [he's] heard anybody in Hardin actually admit to being prejudiced" (Colton, 2000, 299).

The *theory of racial formation*, as defined by sociologists Omi and Winant, takes into account the social and structural representation of race. For Omi and Winant, race is a social construct and therefore fluid, rather than something fixed based on one's biology and upbringing. Omi and Winant describe their racial formation theory, first published in 1986, as follows:

> We define racial formation as the sociohistorical process by which racial categories are created, inhabited, transformed, and destroyed . . . racial formation is a process of historically situated *projects* in which human bodies and social structures are represented and organized. . . . From a racial formation perspective, race is a matter of both social structure and cultural representation. . . . *A racial project is simultaneously an interpretation, representation, or explanation of racial dynamics, and an effort to reorganize and redistribute resources along particular racial lines.* (Omi and Winant, 2006, 236)

Under this framework, one could see how the model minority myth, American multiculturalism, rationalization of common sense, and even the individual forms of racism described by Dr. Jones don't quite account for the full complexity of race, racism, and how they function among society. For example, one has to understand that although it could be true that Native Americans prefer to live among other Native Americans for cultural reasons (i.e., American multiculturalism framework), it's also a fact that where Native Americans have settled in the United States among their racialized group is connected to the racial dimension of social structures (i.e., state and federal policies) they had no choice or voice in creating. And in connecting racial formation theory to sport, one should consider that athletes of color and what they choose to say or do on and off the field are "racial projects" that the rest of society often looks to form their views about race (and many other social identifiers).

Within the last decade, a number of race and sport scholars have been connecting *critical race theory* (CRT) to studies of race and sport, attempting to confront the systems and infrastructure at play in the experiences of athletes. CRT was first developed and popularized in the mid-1970s by law professor Derrick Bell and other scholars as a derivative of critical legal studies. CRT examines legislative doctrines that marginalize people of color in order to challenge dominant notions of race and racism. Therefore, CRT centers race and racism at the fore of discussions with marginalized people and groups and seeks to (a) identify its function in educational and social institutions and (b) assist in the eradication of oppressive practices (Bell, 1980; Delgado, 1989; Delgado and Stefancic, 2001; Carter-Francique & Richardson, 2016). Carter-Francique and Richardson expound that:

> CRT recognizes that racism is endemic and woven into the fabric of society; and thus, manifest in varying contexts (i.e., K–20 education, sports, media) and in varying

ways (i.e., access discrimination, inequitable hiring practices, negative stereotypes). Yet, CRT also has the potential transform race relations with policies, practices, and power. Ergo, CRT is not just a theoretical framework, it is a social movement in which scholars attempt to redress social injustices through its use of a number of tenets to illuminate racist acts. (Carter-Francique and Richardson, 2016, 12)

Sports scholars employing CRT to the experiences of athletes of color are looking to develop theoretical practices, reform, and advocacy for college athletes; assessing the athletic representation and leadership opportunities available for athletes of color; and combing CRT and other social theories and concepts to create change and awareness of the experiences of athletes of color.

The Sociology of Race and Sport as Field of Study

It's important to set a foundational understanding of how the way society reacts to and cultivates racialized social constructs within sport led to the establishment of the specialized subdiscipline, sociology of sport, within the field of sociology generally. Arguably the most important figure in the establishment of focus on race within the sociology of sport as consequential academic discipline is Dr. Harry Edwards (see the detailed profile on Edwards in chapter 4). Edwards's 1969 work, *The Revolt of the Black Athlete*, is one of the first focused on race and sport in the United States. *The Revolt of the Black Athlete* was published on the heels of the iconic 1968 Olympics protest by track and field athletes John Carlos and Tommie Smith, an iconic protest that Edwards helped to orchestrate as scholar-activist in the Olympic Project for Human Rights (OPHR). Around this same time, the sociology of sport began to be incorporated into the curricula of collegiate American physical education and sociology departments was encouraged by the publication of four major anthologies by U.S. authors: *Sport, Culture and*

Society (1969) edited by John Loy and Gerald Kenyon; *Sport and American Society* (1970) edited by George H. Sage; *Sport in the Socio-Cultural Process* (1972) by M. Marie Hart; and *Games, Sport and Power* (1972) by G. Stone. Harry Edwards followed up his first book in 1973 with *Sociology of Sport*, one of the earliest introductory textbooks to the field. And with that, the scholarly publications toward the sociology of sport began to swell. Between 1973 and 1978, the publication of eleven additional books designed especially for classroom use did much to foster the integration of the field into American university courses (Talamini and Page, 1973; Ibrahim, 1975; Ball and Loy, 1975; Nixon, 1976; Yiannakis et al., 1976; Coakley, 1978; Eitzen and Sage, 1978; Snyder and Spreitzer, 1978; Coakley, 1987, 65). As the number of scholarly books began to increase, the creation of a number of scholarly journals began to emerge as a means of encouraging new research and writing. The *Journal of Sport History*, the *Journal of Sport Psychology*, *Arena Review*, and the *Journal of Sport Behavior* are just a few publications established in the 1970s; more were founded in the 1980s.

According to professor Ben Carrington and his essay, "The Critical Sociology of Race and Sport: The First Fifty Years," there are two discernible periods within the sociology of race and sport: the 1960s to the mid-1990s and the mid-to-late 1990s to the present. Another way to classify these two periods within the sociology of race and sport would be to label the 1960s through mid-1990s as quantitatively focused while labeling the scholarship produced from the mid-to-late 1990s through the present more qualitatively focused. The sociology of sport, since its emergence as a discrete field of study and formal institutionalization in the late 1960s (Coakley and Dunning, 2000), has been committed to examining questions of socialization and stratification within sport; tracing its social significance and meaning for individuals and communities; and the complex relationship between sport and other social institutions such as the family, education, health, and the criminal justice system (Carrington, 2013, 388). In addition, sport sociologists have sought to diagram the relationship between racial ideologies, systems, and sport.

The scholarship of the 1960s through the mid-1990s focused primarily on measuring racism using survey methodologies, meaning scholars were looking at statistical differences to present and make sense of racism. These studies almost exclusively focused on the Black-White racial binary, although there was occasionally work on Native American communities during this time. As intersectionality had yet to be established until the early 1990s; there was very limited inclusion and discussion of gender, sexual orientation, disability, or class into these studies. Overall, this early period was "marked by a number of studies that showed, for example, employment discrimination within professional male sports; these studies demonstrated that black athletes in particular were paid lower salaries than their white counterparts for similar performance and were more likely to be released earlier than whites for downturns in performance" (Carrington, 2013, 389). Scholarship also revealed discrimination in employment practices for head coaching positions, with preferential opportunities being given to White coaches and managers and Black coaches more likely to be fired earlier in their careers than their White counterparts (see Frey and Eitzen, 1991, 513–16; Washington and Karen, 2001, 191–96).

A shift in the scholarship from quantitative to more qualitative began taking place in the 1990s. In recognizing some of the shortfalls and untapped potential of the scholarship that was being produced by other sports sociologists, Susan Birrell published an essential article in 1989 entitled "Racial Relations Theories and Sport: Suggestions for a More Critical Analysis," and it may have been the catalyst current and emerging sports scholars needed in shifting their approaches. In this article, Birrell calls for a move away from atheoretical approaches to the study of racism in sport and a dissolved reliance on assimilationist models of race relations. Instead, she encourages her fellow scholars to take a cultural studies approach that blends culturalist, materialist, and class-based theories in an effort to move toward the goal of developing a comprehensive model for analyzing the complex relations of dominance and subordination related to race, gender, and class in sport.

Research since the mid-1990s has taken on a broader range of experiences and identities within sport. Rather than focusing simply on the racism experienced by professional African American male athletes, broader questions have been broached that reflect a more critical stance within race theory (Carrington, 2013, 389). These studies have taken a perspective where sport is a site where racial ideologies can be challenged, reinforced, shifted, or even diminished. Contemporary scholars are also looking to the sectors of sport outside of just players and coaches to see how spectators, families, policies, marketing, and much more plays a role in the realm of race and sport. In addition, within the last several years, scholarship is thinking more critically about Whiteness, rather than on non-White racial identities. Since 2000, there have been just over 100 articles directly addressing questions of race and racism within the three journals—the *Sociology of Sport Journal*, the *Journal of Sport and Social Issues*, and the *International Review for the Sociology of Sport*—alone (Carrington, 2013, 389–90). Of course there have been more articles published since 2013 that also address questions of race and racism within those three journals and many others. A number of books have also been published since the 1990s that expand the sociology of race and sport discipline. A few examples of books that are outside of the Black-White racial lens include *Outside the Paint: When Basketball Ruled at the Chinese Playground* (2009) by Yep; Burgos's *Playing America's Game: Baseball, Latinos and the Color Line* (2007); *Mexican Americans and Sports: A Reader on Athletics and Barrio Life* (2006) by Iber and Regalado; and *Native Americans and Sport in North America: Other People's Games* (2008) by C. Richard King. Additional works to explore can be found in chapter 6, "Resources."

Intersectionality and Race and Sport

The brief racial histories of various groups in the United States and theories presented reveal that there is an immense complexity to conversations and experiences related to race and sport. Dave Zirin, a political sportswriter and author, says in the film *Race, Power & American Sports* that "everyone has a stake in understanding racism and how it operates in our society, and has a stake in understanding how race and sports intersect" (Young et al., 2013). Other layers of identity (e.g., ethnicity, education level, socioeconomic status, gender, etc.) often intersect with experiences of sport and race, too, and much of the contemporary scholarship being produced explores these intersections. Some of these intersections will be broadly presented here in chapter 1 and throughout this volume but will not be focused upon in immense detail, because race is the overarching focus of this reference work.

In 1991, Kimberlé Crenshaw first coined the term *intersectionality* because, from Crenshaw's viewpoint, race-based and gender-based bodies of work lack the ability to capture the experiential complexities of people who live at the intersections of marginalization (e.g., a Black person who is also female and/or also a lesbian). Intersectionality acknowledges that racism is exacerbated and manifested in differing ways at the intersections of a person's gender, social class, sexual orientation, religion, and culture (Crenshaw, 1991). Similar to Omi and Winant's claim of race being a social construct, intersectionality discerns that knowledge is socially constructed. Socially constructed knowledge promotes the belief that there are multiple truths; truths that are more often than not a counter-narrative to the truth perpetuated by dominant (e.g., White, heterosexual, Christian, male, etc.) society. Thus, intersectionality exposes experiences that are "social and systemic what was formerly perceived as isolated and individual" (Crenshaw, 1991, 1241–42). The expanded research into these intersections is for readers of this volume to go out and consume or, even better, produce themselves to add to bodies of work related to race, sport, and U.S. society.

The American Sports Media as Conduit of
Socially Constructed Knowledge

A central avenue for knowledge and experiences of race and racism that play out in sport has been through the media. Today, American consumers of sports and sports culture can get their sporting communications as often or as infrequently as they want to. Social media has given athletes, coaches, owners, and sporting industry leaders a way to communicate directly and in real time with enamored and vitriolic viewers and patrons alike. Social media and the internet have also given sports journalists far more airtime and readership as broadcasts can be streamed live, recorded, and shared with the click of a computer, phone, or tablet. Historical forms of media—that is, newspapers, magazines, film, and television—have always held the power to shape the narrative around race and sport. Sometimes that narrative around race and sport can be positively transformative, and other times it can work to reinforce racism and other forms of social identity–related oppression.

The media has tended to reinforce racist messaging through its language use, imagery, and overall framing of experiences of people of color. One frequent narrative in which the media continues to frame the experience of athletes of color is the tragedy-to-triumph story. The tragedy-to-triumph narrative is one in which the media grounds its story of an athlete of color in some sort of tragic experience the athlete has had first and then proceeds to emphasize how a particular athletic talent is what completely changed that athlete's life—a sort of "sports saved their life" takeaway for readers. And although it is true that a number of exceptional athletes of color do have tragedy-to-triumph stories to be told, White athletes do, too, yet those are infrequently shared via mass media platforms.

This author has found that one of the best examples of how the media can also incorrectly force a tragedy-to-triumph narrative on athletes of color is the case of U.S. gymnast Simone Biles and her journey and success at the 2016 Rio Olympics. In the build-up to the Games in Rio, the majority of the media attempted to center Biles's life around the fact that her biological mother struggled with drug addiction and that she was adopted. Even when Biles makes it clear that she has never known suffering or hardship in her childhood because she was five years old when her biological grandfather, Ron, and his wife, Nellie, adopted Biles and her younger sister, the media leads with a tragedy-to-triumph narrative:

> [I]n a detailed piece on Biles and the transformation of the point system in gymnastics, *People* magazine used the headline "How Gymnast Simone Biles Overcame Being Given Up by Her Mother to Become an Olympic Gold Hopeful" to capture readers' attention. *People* magazine's choices to use the word "overcame" and the phrase "given up" in the title of their piece on Biles is laced with insidious racial stereotypes. When one overcomes something, one must have a struggle or difficulty to successfully deal with. Yet, the author of this *People* piece does not mention Biles' difficulty with anything and simply quotes Biles saying of Ron and Nellie that "my parents make sure we have everything we need so that we compete to the best of our abilities." Chances are high that any other Rio Olympic gymnast in the world with parents would have said the same of their own parents. Tom Leonard, a writer for the U.K. publication *Daily Mail*, chose an even more tragic headline for his August 12, 2016 piece on Biles: "Awesome Triumph: How the 4ft. 8in Smiling Girl Who's Set the Olympics Alight Overcame an Appalling Childhood." Yet Biles doesn't view her childhood as "appalling" or that she had to "overcome" being raised by her adopted parents rather than her biological mother. In fact, Biles told

the *Daily Mail*, "When I was younger, I thought every kid was adopted . . . I didn't understand why people made it such a big deal. To me it's just normal." In placing emphasis on her family structure—which is by all means stable and healthy—the media are clearly attempting to place Biles in the tragedy to triumph narrative that a number of successful Black athletes fall into due to socioeconomic hardship; the problem is that Biles doesn't fit into this box at all. (Myers, 2017, 64)

In fact, Biles is so far from this narrative that it seems most of the media simply assumed Biles's narrative *had* to mirror the family and socioeconomic struggle of Rio Olympic teammate and London 2012 Olympic All-Around champion, Gabby Douglas. After all, up until Biles's domination of the sport over the last eight years, the racial hierarchy in gymnastics held White gymnasts as the archetype and U.S. gymnasts of color as tokens. Currently, Simone Biles is the greatest American gymnast of all time—male or female—and appears to be the only Black gymnast known to have a family-owned and -operated gym to train in via the World Champions Centre in Spring, Texas.

Although the Biles example is one in which media used the tragedy-to-triumph narrative to try and force a racist and economically impoverished background on an athlete, the media's use of this narrative can also work to completely ignore the narrative of successful athletes of color who grew up in stable households. Another example from the Olympics, in the sport of women's track and field, helps to demonstrate how this media snubbing can impact an athlete and their future. In the 2008 Beijing Olympics, biracial women's hurdler Lolo Jones was the U.S. favorite for the 100m hurdles, but she fell in the final heat and didn't medal. Her darker complexioned African American teammate, Dawn Harper, went on to win the 2008 Olympic gold medal in the 100m hurdles. Four years later, in the buildup toward the 2012 London Olympics, media chose to focus on Lolo Jones again, opening up her *SEC Storied: Lolo Jones* documentary by referring to her as a "sex symbol" (Karpf, 2012) and proceeding to replay her tragedy-to-triumph story—a story that includes honing in on her troubled childhood with her White mother and sometimes absentee Black father, bouts of homelessness, stealing food, and ultimate "saving" by her White male college track and field coach. In addition to this documentary, Lolo was featured in numerous commercials, on billboards, and on talk shows, and she was lauded for her physique in the highly coveted annual *ESPN: The Body Issue* magazine in 2009 (Myers, 2016, 333). 2008 Olympic gold medalist Dawn Harper received no media attention or endorsements. Harper, along with another African American teammate, Kellie Wells, would go on to win silver and bronze, respectively, in the 2012 Games for 100m hurdles. Jones did not medal again. Even now, as athletes prepare to qualify for the 2021 Olympics in Tokyo, Lolo Jones is more significant to the public than medalists Wells and Harper. On the social media platform Instagram, Jones boasts 467,000 followers, while Harper and Wells have 20,100 and 18,700 followers, respectively. This may not seem particularly important to most, but "the majority of female Olympic track and field athletes cannot afford to live off of running alone [and] therefore, national media attention to a female runner's life story and Olympic medal aspirations can lead to change in socioeconomic status—access to a better life in society" (Myers, 2016, 328). This is not to say that Harper and Wells don't have good lives or that Jones didn't work hard to get to the Olympics. What is evident, however, is that what choices the media made—and will make in leading up to the Tokyo 2021 Olympics for athletes in nonlucrative sports like track and field—matter greatly to the future financial standing of athletes. If media use a racist lens to decide which athletes are "worthy" of their attention, athletes of color are more likely to suffer.

A final example here to demonstrate the power of the media in discussions of race, sport, and intersectionality has to do with nationalism. With a national history of legally denying racial groups citizenship in the United States, some current media continues to subtly reinforce a nationalist "othering" in the level of patriotism held by athletes of color. Most often, this subtlety comes through media word choice in framing instances where a White person and a person of color have acted similarly. The "Other" is a nondominant person or group in society that is marginalized based on dominant ideologies and oppositional binary categorizations such as those found in racial categorization (e.g., White/Black), gender categorization (e.g., male/female), and social class categorization (e.g., upper class/lower class). A known nonsports-related example of this "othering" was highlighted during the weeks following the devastation of Hurricane Katrina in New Orleans in 2005:

> [W]hen the survivors were white, news programs displayed descriptions such as "Hurricane Survivors Searching For Supplies." But when the people on the screen were African American, the chyron read things such as "Katrina Refugees Looting Clothes."

This type of disparity was even more blatant if you flipped to Fox News (Adams, 2018).

A singular word makes all the difference: "looting" versus "searching." Choosing to use the word "looting" with visuals of African Americans upholds racist stereotypes about African Americans being deviant and dangerous, whereas using "searching" paired with White hurricane victims connotes that what White people are doing isn't wrong and must be done to survive. How this plays out in the sports realm with nationalism (e.g., patriotic/unpatriotic) can also be just as subtle.

Another Olympic example that works incredibly well to showcase this subtle media, race, and nationalism relationship involves gymnast Gabby Douglas again and White swimmer Michael Phelps. After the U.S. women's gymnastics team won the team all-around gold in the Rio Games, the team took the podium and stood at attention for the national anthem. While Gabby Douglas stood at attention with her arms down to the sides, each of her teammates stood with their right hands over their hearts. Critics were harsh on the social media platform, Twitter. Although Douglas did have a number of supportive tweets, she still had to deal with reading tweets from others who felt her poor hand placement was "shameful" and suggested that she "move somewhere else" (Yee, 2016). Meanwhile, some of the American news media did little to invalidate claims of Douglas's being unpatriotic. For example, on August 10, 2016—one day after the medal ceremony—the headline of an article for the *San Diego Union-Tribune* read "Was U.S. gymnast national anthem stance 'unpatriotic'?" and an article from *The Los Angeles Times* the same day proclaimed "Gymnast Gabby Douglas Resurrects the Debate over How to Act During the National Anthem." Meanwhile, when White U.S. men's swimmer Michael Phelps took the podium to accept his gold medal for the 200m butterfly, he began laughing uncontrollably during the anthem because some of his friends from Baltimore, Maryland in the audience began to sing "OOOOOOOOO" when the lyrics of the anthem got to "Oh say does that. . . ." There was no criticism of Phelps's laughter. On August 10, 2016, some media headlines about Phelps' podium incident read "The Reason Michael Phelps Was Laughing During the National Anthem will Make You Smile" (*Time*) and "Here's Why Michael Phelps Laughed During the National Anthem" (*HuffPost*). With the Gabby Douglas headlines, the media validates that Gabby Douglas has done something wrong or questionable. With the Michael Phelps headlines, media protect Phelps's behavior from questioning by readers and even put the alleged proper reaction to his laughter—to smile—in readers' minds before beginning to read about what happened. The White male remains patriotic, even while laughing during the anthem, while the Black woman's patriotism is questioned, and she's made to feel she has no other choice but to apologize to everyone in the United States for leaving her hands at her sides during the anthem.

To be clear, this media power of "othering" racial groups of color further through intersections of nationalism can certainly come out in overt ways, too. The overt instances tend to result in national controversy, with weeks, months, and even years of ridicule shown toward athletes—athletes whom sportswriter Howard Bryant refers to in his latest book as upholders of "the Heritage." Referring to Black athletes—Black *male* athletes specifically—Bryant describes those who uphold the Heritage as "being the Ones Who Made It [that took up] the responsibility to speak for the people who had not made it, for whom the road was still blocked" (Bryant, 2018, x) at great cost to their own livelihoods. These are athletes like Paul Robeson, Muhammad Ali, John Carlos, Tommie Smith, Curt Flood, and, most recently, Colin Kaepernick. Each of these Black male athletes is discussed in greater detail in chapter 4, "Profiles." More than ever, scholars, sports fans, players, and industry leaders need to call out the media when they present racially divisive narratives about athletes. Fortunately, it appears that more people are noticing discrepancies in coverage and treatment of athletes of color.

Gender and Sexual Orientation

Two critically important identity intersections within the historical and contemporary conversations and scholarship of race and sport are gender and sexual orientation. In 1972, the status of U.S. female athletics changed significantly. The United States Congress signed the Education Amendments of 1972 into law, which included a section addressing the issue of sex discrimination: Title IX. Section 1681 of Title IX states, "No person in the United States shall, on the basis of sex, be excluded from participation in, be denied the benefits of, or be subjected to discrimination under any educational programs or activities receiving federal financial assistance" (U.S. Department of Education, 2000). Title IX put an end to legal gender discrimination and called for full equality between men and women in all institutions. Title IX legislation expanded college opportunities for women athletes, increasing access to college sports and education for women of all racial identities. By the end of the 1970s, the number of women competing in inter-collegiate sport had doubled, many of them assisted by athletic scholarships (Cahn, 1994, 254).

Title IX had an effect on female athletic participation at all levels, though, including youth sports. In the first thirty years of the legislation's establishment, between 1972 and 2002, the number of females participating in high school sports grew from around a few hundred thousand to a few million. Many women of all races who desired to have access to competitive athletics in the same ways that their male counterparts did were electri-fied at the potential created by the Title IX legislation. For ath-letes of color in particular, this access to sport also meant that they could now also have an institutionally supported outlet for dealing with racialized oppression, in addition to the oppres-sion they experienced due to their gender. For example, a 2000 study focused on the college level revealed that "Black female athletes outpace Black female non-athletes in graduation rates (62 percent to 42 percent) and tend to reflect a sense of satis-faction with their lives, despite ongoing navigation of racialized and gendered norms" (Boyd and Shropshire, 2000, 6). Scholar Ange-Marie Hancock explains that "Black female athletes are victims of both sexism and racism, possessing what feminist theorists conceptualize as a 'both/and identity': both Black and female" (Hancock, 2008, 4). This same dual oppression can be applied to other racial identity groups of women that are often marginalized due to the way race and gender has been socially constructed in the United States. When female athletes of color succeed publicly, it can have positive effects on shifting the ways in which those women of color are depicted and per-ceived in a broader social context. For example, Native Ameri-can female basketball players Jude and Shoni Schimmel—who are discussed in depth in chapter 4, "Profiles"—have helped to show that Native American girls can excel in sport outside of reservations *and* maintain the pride and practices of their Indigenous culture. While there have been significant scholarly publications related to the experience of Black female athletes (see the review of literature in Laws, 2012), more scholarship needs to be produced related to the experiences of other female athletes of color and how race is or is not a factor within the experiences of White female athletes.

An even larger gap in research exists related to race, sport, and gender, particularly in relation to *transgender* identity. People who identify as transgender are individuals whose assigned gender at birth (based on the visible external genitalia) does not align with their gender identity. People who experience a congruence between assigned gender at birth and gender identity are *cisgender*. The majority of scholarship in the realm of race and sport focuses on cisgender athletes, yet there have been critically important policies created and implemented that apply to transgender athletes. In the article, "Sport and Transgender People: A Systematic Review of the Literature Relating to Sport Participation and Competitive Sport Policies," the authors conducted a review of eight research articles—the oldest published in 2004 and the most recent in 2015—and came to important conclusions:

> Within competitive sport, the athletic advantage transgender athletes are perceived to have appears to have been overinterpreted by many sport organisations around the world, which has had a negative effect on the experiences of this population . . . it is only transgender female individuals who are perceived to potentially have an advantage as a result of androgenic hormones. Within the literature, it has been questioned as to whether androgenic hormones should be the only marker of athletic advantage or, indeed, if they are even a useful marker of athletic advantage. Given the established mental and physical health benefits of engaging in physical activity

and sport, the barriers transgender people experience are a significant limitation to the promotion of healthy behaviours in transgender individuals . . . several areas of future research required to significantly improve our knowledge of transgender people's experiences in sport, inform the development of more inclusive sport policies, and most importantly, enhance the lives of transgender people, both physically and psychosocially. (Jones et al., 2017, 714)

One such "area of future research required" is that of the experience of transgender people of color's experiences in sport. The Human Rights Campaign's (n.d.) resource titled "Violence against the Transgender Community in 2019" states that "lethal violence disproportionately affects transgender women of color, and that the intersections of racism, sexism, homophobia, biphobia, transphobia and unchecked access to guns conspire to deprive them of employment, housing, healthcare and other necessities, barriers that make them vulnerable." What does this mean in terms of access to sport and sporting experiences at the youth, college, and professional levels? Does participation in sport act as a deterrent against frequency of violence for transgender athletes of color? These questions are just a couple of examples of how one might set about starting a research study into race, sport, and transgender identity.

The Need for Expanded Scholarship

As scholars of race and sport continue to unveil buried histories and conduct intersectional research, the hope for the dismantling of White supremacist structures and value within the realm of sport increases. However possible, a more collective and inclusive analysis of the experiences of people of color—beyond Black and White—needs to continue in order to achieve a racially equitable experience for all constituencies that comprise the realm of sport. A key way White supremacy sustains itself is through narrative scarcity, which keeps us ignorant about our many stories that can tell us more about complex racial dynamics and systemic racism (Bhangal and Poon, 2020). The intersections to be researched and analyzed within the realm of race and sport are seemingly limitless, and the academic and athletic infrastructures exist—and have the potential for expansion—to support this work. Let this reference volume serve as a starting point and not the finish line.

References

Adams, Joshua. 2018. "What Hurricane Katrina Taught Me about News Framing." *Medium* (October 13).

Ball, D., and J. Loy. 1975. *Sport and Social Order*. New York: Longman.

Bell, D. 1980. *Brown vs. Board of Education* and the Interest-Convergence Principle. *Harvard Law Review* 93 (3): 518–533.

Bhangal, Naseeb, and Oiyan Poon. 2020. "Are Asian Americans White? Or People of Color?" *yes! Magazine* (January 15).

Boyd, Todd, and Kenneth Shropshire. 2000. *Basketball Jones*. New York: New York University Press.

Bryant, Howard. 2018. *The Heritage: Black Athletes, a Divided America, and the Politics of Patriotism*. Boston, MA: Beacon Press.

Burgos, Adrian, Jr. 2007. *Playing America's Game: Baseball, Latinos, and the Color Line*. Berkeley: University of California Press.

Cahn, Susan K. 1994. *Coming on Strong: Gender and Sexuality in Twentieth-Century Women's Sport*. Cambridge, MA: Harvard University Press.

Carrington, Ben. 2013. "The Critical Sociology of Race and Sport: The First Fifty Years." *Annual Review of Sociology* 39 (1): 379–398.

Carter-Francique, Akilah R., and F. Michelle Richardson. 2016. "Controlling Media, Controlling Access." *Race, Gender & Class* 23 (1–2): 7–33.

Chae, Youngsuk. 2007. *Politicizing Asian American Literature: Towards a Critical Multiculturalism*. New York: Routledge.

Coakley, Jay. 1978. *Sport in Society: Issues and Controversies*. St. Louis, MO: Mosby.

Coakley, Jay. 1987. "Sociology of Sport in the United States." *International Review for the Sociology of Sport* 22 (1): 63–79.

Coakley, Jay, and Eric Dunning. 2000. *Handbook of Sports Studies*. Thousand Oaks, CA: SAGE Publications.

Colton, Larry. 2000. *Counting Coup: A True Story of Basketball and Honor on the Little Big Horn*. New York: Warner Books, Inc.

Crenshaw, Kimberlé. 1991. "Mapping the Margins: Intersectionality, Identity Politics, and Violence against Women of Color." *Stanford Law Review* 43 (6): 1241–1299.

Dagbovie, Pero G. 2006. *Black History: "Old School" Black Historians and the Hip Hop Generation*. Troy, MI: Bedford Publishers, Inc.

Delgado, R. 1989. "Storytelling for Oppositionists and Others: A Plea for Narrative." *Michigan Law Review* 87 (8): 2411–2441.

Delgado, R., and J. Stefancic. 2001. *Critical Race Theory: An Introduction*. New York: New York University Press.

Eitzen, Stanley, and George H. Sage. 1978. *Sociology of American Sport*. Dubuque, IA: Wm. C. Brown.

Fields, Sarah K. 2008. "Representations of Sport in the 'Indian School Journal.'" *Journal of Sport History* 35 (2): 241–259.

Frederickson, George M. 1981. *White Supremacy: A Comparative Study of American and South African History*. New York: Oxford University Press.

Frey, James H., and Stanley Eitzen. 1991. "Sport and Society." *Annual Review of Sociology* 17: 503–522.

Hancock, Ange-Marie. 2008. "Black Female Athletes." In *African Americans and Popular Culture Volume 2: Sports*, edited by Todd Boyd. Santa Barbara, CA: Praeger.

Human Rights Campaign. n.d. "Violence against the Transgender Community in 2019." https://www.hrc.org /resources/violence-against-the-transgender-community- in-2019.

Iber, Jorge, and Samuel O. Regalado. 2006. *Mexican Americans and Sports: A Reader on Athletics and Barrio Life*. College Station: Texas A&M University Press.

Ibrahim, H. 1975. *Sport and Society: An Introduction to Sociology of Sport*. Long Beach, CA: Hwong Publishing.

Jones, B. A., J. Arcelus, W. P. Bouman, et al. 2017. "Sport and Transgender People: A Systematic Review of the Literature Relating to Sport Participation and Competitive Sport Policies." *Sports Medicine* 47 (4): 701–716. https://doi.org /10.1007/s40279-016-0621-y.

Jones, Camara Phyllis. 2000. "Levels of Racism: A Theoretical Framework and a Gardener's Tale." *American Journal of Public Health* 90 (8): 1212–1215.

Karpf, Rory. 2012. *SEC Storied: Lolo Jones*. Netflix, Bristol, CT: ESPN Films.

King, C. Richard, ed. 2008. *Native Americans and Sport in North America: Other People's Games*. 1st ed. New York: Routledge.

Lapchick, Richard E. 2018. "2018 Racial and Gender Report Card." In *The Institute for Diversity and Ethics and Sport: Making Waves of Change*, edited by Lee Bowman, Brittany Barber, Meaghan Coleman, Yeehang Fan, Nate Harvey, Daniel Martin, Miranda Murphy, William Thomas II, and David Zimmerman. Orlando, FL: University of Central Florida.

Laws, Rachel Gayle. 2012. "South African & U.S. Black Female Athletes Compared: A Critical Ethnography Focused on Image, Perceptions, and Narratives." Doctor of Philosophy Thesis, African American & African Studies, Michigan State University.

Lee, Rose Hum. 1960. *The Chinese in the United States of America*. Oxford: Oxford University Press.

Luberto, D. Keith. 1994. "The Integration Movement: Texas High School Athletic and Academic Contests." *Journal of Sport & Social Issues* 18 (2): 151–168.

Myers, Rachel L. 2016. "African American Female Athletic Image: What We Should Take Away from the London 2012 Olympic Games." In *Race Still Matters: The Reality of African American Lives and the Myth of Postracial Society*, edited by Yuya Kiuchi, 321–341. Albany: State University of New York Press.

Myers, Rachel Laws. 2017. "More Than One: What Happened When Multiple Black Female Athletes Excelled in Predominantly White Sports at the Rio Olympics." In *Women in Sports: Breaking Barriers, Facing Obstacles*, edited by Adrienne N. Milner and Jomills Henry Braddock II, 59–75. Santa Barbara, CA: ABC-CLIO, LLC.

Nixon, H. 1976. *Sport and Social Organization*. Indianapolis, IN: Bobbs-Merrill.

Omi, Michael, and Howard Winant. 2006. "Racial Formation." In *Social Class and Stratification: Classic Statements and Theoretical Debates*, edited by Rhonda Levine, 233–242. Lanham, MD: Rowman & Littlefield Publishers, Inc.

Osajima, Keith. 2008. "Asian Americans as the Model Minority: An Analysis of the Popular Press Image in the 1960s and 1980s." In *A Companion to Asian American Studies*, edited by Kent A. Ono, 215–225. Malden, MA: Blackwell.

PBS.org. 2013. *Latino Americans: Timeline of Important Dates.* PBS.org: WETA, Washington, D.C., and Latino Public Broadcasting.

Schutte, Gerard. 1995. *What Racists Believe: Race Relations in South Africa and the United States.* Thousand Oaks, CA: SAGE Publications, Inc.

Snyder, E., and E. Spreitzer. 1978. *Social Aspects of Sport.* Englewood Cliffs, NJ: Prentice-Hall.

Talamini, J., and C. Page. 1973. *Sport and Society.* Boston, MA: Little, Brown.

Trembanis, Sarah. 2008. "Research Note: Defining 'Aboriginal' in a Historical and Sporting Context." *Journal of Sport History* 35 (2): 279–283.

U.S. Department of Education. 2000. *Title IX of the Education Amendments of 1972.* Edited by U.S. Department of Justice. Washington, D.C.: U.S. Department of Justice.

Vidal, Juan. 2016. "Why Does American Sports Have a Latino Problem?" *Rolling Stone* (September 16).

Washington, Robert, and David Karen. 2001. "Sport and Society." *Annual Review of Sociology* 27: 187–212.

Wiggins, David. 1997. *Glory Bound: Black Athletes in a White America.* 1st ed. Syracuse, NY: Syracuse University Press.

Wills, Matthew. 2017. "The Uneasy History of Integrated Sports in America." *JSTOR Daily* (September 28).

Yiannakis, A., T. McIntyre, M. Melnick, and D. Hart. 1976. *Sport Sociology: Contemporary Themes.* Dubuque, IA: Kendall Hunt Publishing Company.

Yee, Lawrence. 2016. "Gabby Douglas Criticized for Not Placing Hand over Heart during Olympic Medal Ceremony." *Variety.*

Yep, Kathleen S. 2009. *Outside the Paint: When Basketball Ruled at the Chinese Playground.* Philadelphia, PA: Temple University Press.

Young, Jason, Jeremy Earp, and Sut Jhally. 2013. *Race, Power and American Sports.* Northampton, MA: Media Education Foundation.

Zirin, Dave. 2008. *A People's History of Sports in the United States: 250 Years of Politics, Protest, People, and Play.* New York: The New Press.

2 Problems, Controversies, and Solutions

The sports industry is just like any other industry that relies heavily on employer-employee relationships, consumerism, and marketing. Sometimes, problems arise among these various constituencies, and solutions need to be made. The increased complexity of the sports industry, however, arises from three reasons: (1) the celebrity of its employers and employees, (2) the financial strength of its power brokers, and (3) the personal emotions and values individuals attach to it. Thus, seemingly small problems in the sports industry can quickly become local, national, and even global controversies.

This chapter presents some of the most controversial incidents concerning race and sports at the youth, college and professional level that have occurred since 1940. These incidents have been categorized into three subheadings: Race, Sports, and Politics; Race and the Sports Industry; and Race, Sports, and Representation. After the incidents and actions that have taken place to prevent the problems from reoccurring are presented, a discussion of solutions is offered for each subheading category.

A statue of 1968 Olympic medalists Tommie Smith and John Carlos in their iconic silent podium protest. The statue resides on the campus of San Jose State University, where Smith and Carlos attended college. The statue was dedicated in 2005 and constructed by the artist Rigo 23. (Ken Wolter/ Dreamstime.com)

Race, Sports, and Politics

Even with government supported desegregation and all of the Civil Rights legislation that passed in the 1950s and 1960s in the United States, the treatment of individuals based on race did not suddenly become universally positive. Depending on individual values and beliefs, as well as the "politics of location—those places and spaces we inherit and occupy, which frame our lives in very specific and concrete ways, which are as much a part of our psyches as they are a physical or geographical placement" (Borsa, 1990)—athletes of all races continued to be put into situations where remaining silent and allowing the political status quo to remain intact became impossible. The following problems and controversies all occurred due to athletes' personal conflicts with various politics at state and national levels. And although sometimes these athletes' words and actions in conflict with politics are about their own personal situations, more often than not, they are about the political well-being of entire groups of marginalized people.

Refusing Service to the Boston Celtics' Black Players (1961)

Before the 1961–1962 NBA regular season kicked off, the Boston Celtics traveled to Lexington, Kentucky for an October 17 exhibition game against the St. Louis Hawks. The four Black players on the Celtics—Bill Russell, K.C. Jones, Satch Sanders, and Sam Jones—and their white teammates were staying at the Phoenix Hotel at the height of Jim Crow and segregation in the South. While in the hotel café, Sam Jones was refused service. When Bill Russell found out, he organized a boycott of the game with his Black teammates and Black players from the Hawks team. Russell then told his coach, Red Auerbach, who responded with full support of his players' decision. The incident garnered much attention in the press and continues to be cited as a significant event in Bill Russell's lifelong commitment to the dignity of all people (Brackney, 2014).

Muhammad Ali's Refusal of U.S. Army Induction (1966)

In early March of 1965, the United States entered the Vietnam War. Initially, there was little public opposition to the war. Boxing world champion Muhammad Ali was classified as draft eligible in 1966, and he was indeed selected in the draft to serve in the army. Surrounded by news reporters, Ali boldly stated, "Man, I ain't got no quarrel with them Vietcong." It seemed as though the entire country erupted publicly with hostility and anger. In response to the antiwar sentiments Ali had helped to bolster among Americans—particularly college youth and people of color—the sports and political worlds offered Ali a number of pathways to renege on his earlier statements against the war:

> Ali was given every opportunity to recant, to apologize, to sign up on some cushy USO gig boxing for the troops and the cameras, to go back to making money. But he refused. This refusal was gargantuan, considering what was bubbling over in U.S. society. There was the Black revolution on the one hand, draft resistance and the antiwar struggle on the other, and the heavy weight champ with one foot planted in each. (Zirin, 2005, 65)

Ali's refusal remained gargantuan, as support built up for him. By 1967, religious and civil rights leader Martin Luther King Jr. also came out against the war and in support of Ali. Ali's refusal to fight in Vietnam was front-page news internationally as well, which may have added to the severity of punishment placed on Ali from the boxing world, sports industry, and U.S. government.

On June 19, 1967, an all-white jury sentenced Ali to five years in prison and ordered his passport be confiscated. The boxing world stripped him of his title despite his undefeated record and went on to exile him from the ring for the next three and a half years. Less than two weeks earlier, a meeting held in Cleveland—widely known as the Cleveland Summit—was organized by boxing promotor Bob Arum to bring a number of well-known Black male athletes together with Ali to convince Ali to change his mind and take the deal to box for money while enlisted:

> Several of the men in Cleveland were military veterans. Some believed Elijah Muhammad's separatist ideology was racist and, if followed through, would lead to an American apartheid. They arrived intent on challenging Ali. (Eig, 2017)

With pressure coming at him from all of these different entities, Ali still remained firm in his antiwar stance on Vietnam. Ali was released on bail in 1968 and in 1970, and with intensifying antiwar sentiments among even the Supreme Court justices, Ali's sentence was struck down and he returned to boxing.

Tommie Smith and John Carlos's Gloved Fists and Shoeless Feet (1968)

The peaceful visual protest that Tommie Smith and John Carlos were captured in while on the track and field podium at the 1968 Olympic Games in Mexico City is arguably the biggest controversy that has happened in the relationship between race, sports, and politics. Their gesture—"As the U.S. flag began rising up the flagpole and the anthem played, Smith and Carlos bowed their heads and raised their fists in a Black power salute . . . [they] also wore no shoes, to protest black poverty, and beads, to protest lynching" (Zirin, 2005, 76)—was planned and seen by millions across the world. Since the fall of 1967, Smith and Carlos had been involved in the Olympic Project for Human Rights (OPHR), a group of organized amateur Black athletes that were genuinely concerned with protesting racism and oppression in the United States and globally. The world in 1968 quite simply seemed set on stifling protest: Czech youth were challenging the Stalinist Soviet Union; the Mexican government had murdered hundreds of students who occupied the National University in Mexico City; the injustices of South African apartheid were on the rise; France saw the largest general strike in world history; and the United States was trying to suppress the mass revolts that followed the assassination of MLK Jr. and the growth of the Black Panther Party. Thus, rather than attempting to allow Smith and Carlos an opportunity to discuss what their intentions were, the two sprinters were immediately punished and condemned. Smith and Carlos were immediately stripped of their medals—a gold and bronze respectively—and expelled from the Olympic Village to return back to the United States. The head of the U.S. Olympic Committee at the time, Avery Brundage, justified their punishment by citing one of the principles of the Olympic games: "that politics play no part whatsoever in them" (Zirin, 2005, 76).

When Madison Square Garden Dropped the National Anthem . . . for a Day (1973)

On January 16, 1973, the *New York Times* ran a brief story on the front page entitled "Garden Track Meet Will Drop U.S. Anthem to Avoid Incidents." The relatively new Garden location had opened in 1968 and already "housed more than 500 athletic contests, from the roller derby to wrestling" (Eskenazi, 1973, 1). Since World War II, it had become tradition to play the anthem at Madison Square Garden (MSG), but the chairman of the Olympic Invitational—an event scheduled for a month later in February 1973—decided to do away with the playing of the anthem. While the chairman of the Invitational, Edwin H. Mosler Jr., stated that he "decided as long as a month ago to do away with the playing of the anthem . . . [and] the black factor crossed our minds . . . but it wasn't the key factor [in the decision]" (Eskenazi, 1973, 1), race most certainly was a significant factor. Just two days earlier, at the Knights of Columbus track meet in Uniondale, New York, an incident occurred during the playing of the national anthem between Black athletes from Eastern Michigan and spectators. At the time, it was tradition for the national anthem to be played before the mile race; during the playing of the anthem at the Knights of Columbus meet, three Black members of the mile relay team continued to stretch. "Some fans hooted and cursed and, after a delay, Jim Foley, the meet referee, summoned the games committee to the floor and a decision was made to disqualify the team" (Eskenazi, 1973, 1). In addition to the "black factor," race officials and MSG officials were attempting to find a solution to the national anthem problem during the anti–Vietnam War social climate. Attempting to keep sports and politics separate was the solution reached by race and MSG officials on January 16, 1973. However, the very next morning, the front page of the *New York Times* published a small article entitled "Garden to Hear Anthem at Track Meet, after All." In less than twenty-four hours, pressure from the public and private realms forced Olympic Invitational and MSG officials to recant their removal of the anthem from the Invitational set for February 1973:

> The reversal [from meet officials] came after the Garden management had announced that "The Star-Spangled Banner" would be played at all its future sporting events, thus nullifying contrary policy decisions by promoters of meets. It also came after the United States Olympic Committee had been deluged with "irate calls from all over the country" protesting plans to drop the anthem from the meet. (Amdur, 1973, 1)

The article goes on to discuss how some local politicians also engaged with the debate over the playing of the anthem, which ultimately became an argument of "rights of New Yorkers to hear the national anthem" being more important than "the wishes of a handful of athletes" (Amdur, 1973, 1). Presently, MSG continues to play the national anthem at all its sporting events. In fact, there's immense prestige and attention given to those who are invited to sing or perform the national anthem at MSG.

Craig Hodges's Letter to the President (1991)

The Chicago Bulls teams of the 1990s are best known because of their NBA titles and superstar players Michael Jordan and Scottie Pippen. One of the lesser known Bulls players of the early nineties is Craig Hodges, a two-time NBA champion and three-peat winner of the All-Star Weekend three-point contest. Hodges had been outspoken about issues related to racial injustice and politics long before he entered the NBA, but the success of his team allowed him a wider audience. After the 1991 NBA title was clinched, Hodges's wider audience included then-president of the United States, George H. W. Bush. As has become customary, the championship team was invited to the White House that October in 1991. Hodges arrived to the White House dressed in a white dashiki and handed President Bush an eight-page letter that he'd written addressing a number of issues related to politics, racial discrimination, and economic discrimination. According to a reporter from the Chicago Tribune, parts of Hodges' letter stated the following:

> The purpose of this notice is to speak on behalf of poor people, Native Americans, homeless and most specifically, African-Americans who are not able to come to this great edifice and meet the leader of the nation where they live. Being a descendant of African slaves, I feel it is very important our plight be put on the list of priorities.
>
> It must be clear . . . that the African-American community is unlike any other. We have a sector of our population that is being described as an endangered species, that is the young black man, and the inner cities are in a state of emergency because of the violence we inflict on one another. In studying this condition, we must look at low self-esteem, which is often due to lack of jobs and not understanding who we are.
>
> This letter is not begging the government for anything . . . but 300 years of free labor has left the African-American community destroyed. It is time for a comprehensive plan for change. Hopefully this letter will help become a boost in the unification of inner-city youth and these issues will be brought to the forefront of the domestic agenda. (Smith, 1991)

The former President never responded back to Hodges's letter encouraging a "comprehensive plan for change" from the government. Hodges himself speculates whether former President Bush "got past page one . . . if he even read it" (McRae, 2017). Hodges's letter was eventually leaked to the media, and he got a lot of attention for it; the racially politicized attention is what Hodges feels led the NBA to respond to his voice by effectively "blackballing" him from the league at age 32. Hodges was informed that he wouldn't be contracted with the Bulls 25 days after winning a second straight NBA title in the 1991–1992 season, and no NBA team would return his calls or offer him a tryout. He filed a federal lawsuit four years later, charging the NBA with racial discrimination, but the claim was eventually dismissed as the judge ruled that the statute of limitations in the case was only two years. If the solution of those in power in the NBA was to silence Hodges's problematic voice by taking away his career, they surely succeeded.

Mahmoud Abdul-Rauf Stops Standing for the National Anthem (1996)

Only a few years after Craig Hodges's NBA career ended prematurely, another NBA player, Mahmoud Abdul-Rauf, saw his career end peculiarly. Abdul-Rauf, who entered the NBA after only two years of college basketball at Louisiana State University, was drafted by the Denver Nuggets in 1990 under the name Chris Jackson. Shortly after, he converted to Islam and changed his name to Mahmoud Abdul-Rauf. In his 1995–1996 season— a season in which he excelled—Abdul-Rauf chose to stop standing for the national anthem before the start of games. Similar to former NFL quarterback Colin Kaepernick, no one seemed to really notice until the media inquired with him about it directly.

Abdul-Rauf explained that standing for the Anthem conflicted with his Muslim faith. The NBA responded to the Nuggets team-high points and assists man overtly and then covertly:

On March 12, 1996, the NBA suspended Abdul-Rauf for one game, citing a rule that players must line up in a "dignified posture" for the anthem. It cost him almost $32,000 of his $2.6 million salary. The players union supported Abdul-Rauf, and he quickly reaching a compromise with the league that allowed him to stand and pray with his head down during the anthem. But at the end of the season, the Nuggets traded Abdul-Rauf to the Sacramento Kings. His playing time dropped. He lost his starting spot. After his contract expired in 1998, Abdul-Rauf couldn't get so much as a tryout with any NBA team. He was just 29 years old. (Washington, 2016)

The monetary fine and the one-game suspension from his employer made an overt statement about the role of the national anthem in the NBA and about who has the power over the physical actions of the athletes. It was with "the players union support" that a compromise was reached, rather than through Abdul-Rauf confronting the NBA on his own. Yet, one could argue that the NBA was not satisfied with a result of compromise over Abdul-Rauf's personal and religious views. Abdul-Rauf was facing jeers from Nuggets fans in the arena and "death threats by mail and phone" (Washington, 2016) outside of the arena.

Trading Abdul-Rauf and slowly dropping his playing time placed all of the cause and responsibility of his eventual unemployment with the NBA squarely on Abdul-Rauf's athleticism and not his character. There could be no real grounds for legal battle with the NBA, as Abdul-Rauf's decline in stardom came in a more calculated manner than Hodges's did. After he was ousted by the NBA, Abdul-Rauf spent the rest of his competitive athletic career playing on various teams overseas.

Toni Smith Turns Her Back to the U.S. Flag (2003)

In 2003, a senior on the Division III Manhattanville College women's basketball team caused "the webpage of the liberal arts college to [reach] 2 million hits [and receive] threats of violence" (Zirin, 2016). Sociology major student athlete Toni Smith had chosen to practice dissent by turning her back to the U.S. flag during the national anthem in her final season. Smith, who identifies as multiracial due to her mother's Jewish heritage and father's mixed ancestry of Black, White, and Cherokee, told sports journalist and author Dave Zirin that she felt activated to dissent as she was "learning more about the prison industrial complex and the wars against Native Americans . . . [and] this flag represents the slaughter of our ancestors" (Zirin, 2016). In a statement Smith released back in 2003, she also made reference to the potential U.S. entrance into war in Iraq as another reason for her silent protest.

The various reactions from those who didn't know Smith personally was expected; some spectators supported Smith, while others made sure to jeer her every time she touched the ball in basketball games. What was, perhaps, unexpected in the case of Toni Smith was the way her college's administration handled the situation and sought to protect her rights to free speech and expression:

> The Manhattanville president, Richard A. Berman, said he supported Smith's right to express her opinion because it was done in a quiet and dignified way. "It is not about the flag to us," Berman said. "We support our troops, but I think it is healthy to have kids on college campuses expressing their views. That's where the energy comes from." (Pennington, 2003, 1)

With the ability of Manhattanville administration to see past those who made Smith's protest "about the flag" and focus on her right to express her views in "a quiet and dignified way," Smith was able to continue her silent protest throughout her senior season. Smith was supported by her teammates on the court, even if not by teammates individually off the court. Smith did not lose her place on the team or at Manhattanville College. In fact, Smith graduated on schedule and has worked for the New York Civil Liberties Union (NYCLU)—a not-for-profit organization with a mission to defend and promote the fundamental principles and values espoused in the New York State and U.S. Constitutions along with the Bill of Rights—for roughly the last decade.

"Los Suns" in the NBA Playoffs (May 2010)

In early May of 2010, the state of Arizona was frequently the focus of national attention. A new law had passed in Arizona that required police to intensify their pursuit of illegal immigrants. Robert Sarver, a white, male native of Arizona and owner of the NBA Phoenix Suns, didn't agree with the law. During the 2010 NBA playoffs, in part to celebrate Cinco de Mayo and also in protest of the new immigration policy, he asked the Phoenix Suns to don Los Suns jerseys. In an interview with a senior editor from *The Atlantic*, Sarver explained his view:

> [P]arts of [the law] would encourage racial profiling, and people who were Arizona residents—and U.S. citizens—could be treated differently than me, based on the color of their skin. I also thought it would have a negative impact on Arizona's image. I did worry a little bit about angering fans who supported the law, but my dad taught me at a young age that you need to vote with your heart, not your wallet. And there are times when you need to stand up for what you think is right, regardless of the financial ramifications. (Sarver, 2010)

Opposition and outrage to Sarver's request of his team was not overwhelming. In terms of comments, Sarver estimates them to be "about half in support and half against" (Sarver, 2010) his team's public stance. And on the NBA's official website, Commissioner David Stern released a statement giving approval for what the Suns were doing. Publicly, Sarver gained some strong positive publicity. Whoopi Goldberg wore her Los Suns fan jersey on *The View*, and President Barack Obama gave "Los Suns" a shout-out in his address at the Cinco de Mayo celebration hosted in the Rose Garden. Despite any outrage that was expressed, Sarver was never fined money, never forced to apologize for his stance, nor seemingly blackballed from maintaining ownership of the franchise. Robert Sarver is still the owner of the Phoenix Suns.

"Kneeling for a [Indirect] Cause" (August 2016–Present)

Back in August of 2016 then NFL San Francisco 49ers team quarterback Colin Kaepernick first took a knee during the playing of the national anthem and never stopped until he lost his job in the NFL (see chapter 4: "Profiles" for more detail about Kaepernick). Before he went unsigned with any NFL team and became further removed from public consumption, Kaepernick's kneeling protest made an impression on other athletes who weren't necessarily being directly affected by the injustices in the United States that Kaepernick dissented over. First, U.S. Women's National Team star Megan Rapinoe became "the first high-profile white or female athlete to follow Colin Kaepernick's example in 2016 by taking a knee during the anthem" (Bieler, 2019b).

Rapinoe took a knee before three games in September 2016 and immediately was lambasted for her stance. In fact, Rapinoe and her family members have taken more criticism for her protest for the anthem than for Rapinoe's coming out as a lesbian back in 2012. In October 2016, Megan Rapinoe explained her decision to kneel in as essay she wrote for *The Player's Tribune*:

> I haven't experienced over-policing, racial profiling, police brutality or the sight of a family member's body lying dead in the street. But I cannot stand idly by while there are people in this country who have had to deal with that kind of heartache. There is no perfect way to protest. I know that nothing I do will take away the pain of those families. But I feel in my heart it is right to continue to kneel during the national anthem, and I will do whatever I can to be part of the solution. I can understand if you

think that I'm disrespecting the flag by kneeling, but it is because of my utmost respect for the flag and the promise it represents that I have chosen to demonstrate in this way. When I take a knee, I am facing the flag with my full body, staring straight into the heart of our country's ultimate symbol of freedom—because I believe it is my responsibility, just as it is yours, to ensure that freedom is afforded to *everyone* in this country. (Rapinoe, 2016)

In this essay, Rapinoe does three significant things. First, Rapinoe establishes herself as an ally and not an alleged victim of an oppressive system. She makes it clear for everyone that she hasn't experienced those heartaches, but that she is willing to "do whatever…to be a part of the solution." Secondly, Rapinoe tries to find common ground with those who oppose her choice to kneel when she says she "can understand if [they] think [she's] disrespecting the flag" and then goes on to share the way she views the flag and what it represents. And finally, Rapinoe also issues a call to action from readers to actually do something to create change.

As the years have passed since first kneeling in 2016, Rapinoe has sustained the anthem protest into present day. Along the way, Rapinoe has continued to garner support and remain resilient in the face of harsh criticism because she understands that is what being a true ally means:

Whenever you're trying to be an ally, and it's super easy and comfortable for you, you're not an ally. . . . This is what it's going to take for things to change, norms to change, conventions to change, to try to break down white supremacy and break down racial bias. It's going to take it being hard. For everyone. (Bieler, 2019a)

For example, Rapinoe, rather than ending her protest, simply adapted it when the U.S. Soccer Federation responded to Rapinoe's kneeling in March 2017 with a mandated organizational policy "that players 'stand respectfully' during the anthem be-fore national team games" (Bieler, 2019b). Rather than vio-late the policy and damage her career and powerful platform for protest, Rapinoe simply shifted what her anthem protest looks like. For example, in the Summer 2019 Women's World Cup Championship run, everyone except Rapinoe on the U.S. women's team held their hands over their hearts and sang along when the anthem played. Rapinoe stands with her hands at her side and never mouths a word. She has even said she'll "prob-ably never put [her] hand over [her] heart . . . [or] sing the national anthem again" (Weisholtz, 2019).

About a month after the U.S. Women's National Team de-feated the Netherlands for the FIFA World Cup Championship, another high-profile White athlete protested during the playing of the national anthem. This time, it was a twenty-six-year-old male fencer named Race Imboden. After earning a gold medal among his teammates on the United States men's foil team on August 9, 2019, in the Pan-American Games held in Lima, Peru, Imboden asked his teammates if they'd be okay with his kneeling during the medal ceremony. With no objections from his teammates, Imboden knelt as the American flag was raised and the national anthem played. Another athlete at the Pan-American Games also protested, choosing to raise her fist during the national anthem after accepting her gold medal in the women's hammer throw competition. Her name is Gwen Berry, but the media did not focus their attention on Berry, perhaps because she is Black and the media has had plenty of Black athlete protestations to report on, unlike protests by White male athletes like Imboden. In interviews and social media platforms, Imboden explained why he chose to kneel, citing "racism, gun control, mistreatment of immigrants, and a president who spread hate [being] at the top of a long list" (Taylor, 2019).

Similar to Rapinoe, Imboden faced public criticism and sup-port for his protest, as well as consequences brought down by a sports organization. Within two weeks after their protests at the Pan-American Games, both Race Imboden and Gwen Berry received letters from the U.S. Olympic and Paralympic Committee (USOPC) that informed them they'd spend the next twelve months on probation for their actions. In a statement from Mark Jones, a USOPC spokesman, it was stated:

> Every athlete competing at the 2019 Pan-American Games commits to terms of eligibility, including to refrain from demonstrations that are political in nature... In this case, Race didn't adhere to the commitment he made to the organizing committee and the USOPC. We respect his rights to express his viewpoints, but we are disappointed that he chose not to honor his commitment. (Taylor, 2019)

The USOPC essentially states that they "respect [Imboden's] rights" to freedom of expression, but that his rights to make statements related to politics aren't welcomed to be expressed at the Pan-American Games. Therefore, Imoboden—and Gwen Berry—are vulnerable to punishment for breaking a promise.

However, the USOPC decided to also be proactive in the letter sent to Berry and Imboden. USOPC CEO Sarah Hirshland wrote the letter notifying both athletes of their probation, while also putting them and other athletes "on notice" about more severe consequences that would occur if future protesting occurred at competitions. Hirshland emphasized the importance of her pointing out that "going forward, issuing a reprimand to other athletes in a similar instance is insufficient... [and] we must more clearly define for Team USA athletes what a breach of these rules will mean in the future...we are committed to more explicitly defining what the consequences will be for members of Team USA who protest at future Games" (Brito, 2019). This warning to Imboden, Berry, and other U.S. athletes who will all be training towards the upcoming Olympics set for Tokyo may prove difficult to heed. The summer Olympic Games are coming just months before what is sure to be an extremely contentious presidential election, but it's clear that the USOPC—similar to some other professional U.S. sporting organizations—intends to create "definitive consequences" for anyone who mixes sports and politics leading up to and during Tokyo competition.

Discussing the Solutions: Race, Sport, and Politics

In the abbreviated snapshot of controversies and problems offered above that have occurred with relation to race, sport, and politics, it does become clear what the default response from critics of athlete protests is: politics has no place in sports or the athletic agenda. In the cases of Muhammad Ali, Tommy Smith, John Carlos, Mahmoud Abdul-Rauf, Kaepernick, Rapinoe, Imboden and Berry, and even the Black track and field athletes from the Knights of Columbus meet mentioned in the Madison Square Garden controversy, athletes involved in political protestation were given tangible and significant punishments for their actions. These punishments varied from jail time, expulsion from the Olympics, forced suspensions and disqualifications, monetary fines, and the loss of potential endorsements. And, of course, for Hodges, Kaepernick, and Abdul-Rauf in particular, protestation allegedly cost them all their careers in professional sports. And yet, politicians, athletes, and sporting bodies continue to give and receive mixed messaging as to the presumed separation of sports and politics.

For example, if one looks to the most recent case of kneeling with fencer Race Imboden and track and field athlete Gwen Berry, it initially appears that the USOPC is simply holding both athletes to the clear rules about mixing sports and political opinion. However, in late September 2019, the USOPC announced its 2019 class of U.S. Olympic and Paralympic Hall of Fame inductees and there were two surprising names included: Tommie Smith and John Carlos. If one is confused by this decision, it makes sense to feel that way. After all, over fifty years ago, the USOPC banished the two track and field athletes from the 1968 Mexico City Olympics, suspended them from the U.S. team, and left them "alone" to face public scorn—which included death threats—and financial struggles. In fact, "the USOC sent out a statement to reporters expressing its 'profound regrets . . . for the discourtesy displayed by two members of its team'" (Maese, 2019). Now, in 2019, Smith and Carlos have been inducted into the USOP Hall of Fame "because of their 'character, conduct and off-field contributions,' as well as their athletic achievements" (Armour, 2019). If over time, the USOPC is going to label athletes who participate in political protest during sports competitions as being people of positive "character," then why have athletes sign waivers and contracts to disregard that very character? The disregard of athletes' humanity seems to be the flaw in the solutions related to fines, disqualification, suspension, or worse.

It can also be gleaned, from some of the controversies presented, that the support, protection, or punishment for those who combine political protest with sports depends greatly on the race and power of the person protesting and/or the political stance of the institution deciding the ultimate solution for the protestor. This nuance in treatment could be seen with the Boston Celtics boycott, the anthem controversy at Madison Square Garden, Toni Smith and her college, and Phoenix Suns owner Andrew Sarver. The Black players on the Celtics were supported in their decision to boycott by their white coach, Red Auerbach, who could effectively serve as a protective barrier against significant repercussions for his players' decision to not take the court. Toni Smith was able to both keep her place on the basketball team and enrollment in Manhattanville College because of the school's political stance toward freedom of speech; without support from the top-down, she likely would not have been able to continue with her protest without significant consequences. And the controversy around "Los Suns" and its owner, Andrew Sarver, strongly demonstrates how race and power factor into the type of solution that is offered to handle political protests in sport.

In the November issue of *The Atlantic*, Sarver spoke to the widely held belief that politics and sports should not be intermingled. He states:

> I think it's naïve to say that sports and politics don't mix. I mean, how do stadiums and arenas get built? They get built through politics and political connections. Almost all professional sports owners are active in politics to support candidates and causes, but it's usually based on a financial agenda. To me, this law was more of a human-rights issue—and just an issue of fairness—than it was political. (Sarver, 2010)

The issues that so many of the athletes mentioned previously have everything to do with "human-rights and fairness," too, yet those athletes were not in positions of sporting industry power and privilege like Andrew Sarver. Therefore, those athletes were either vulnerable to or very much suffered punishment for their peaceful protests. As of right now, it seems that various sporting bodies at the national *and* international levels need to figure out how to rationalize the punishment of athletes for protesting human-rights issues such as racism, poverty, and police brutality, while simultaneously doing very little to discourage the mixture of sports and politics that is based on financial agendas of politicians and sports industry leadership.

The double standard of mixing sports and politics being off limits to some while being willfully ignored for others is definitely changing, though. The induction of Tommie Smith and John Carlos into the USOP Hall of Fame is certainly a sign of this change, as is the fact that athletes Rapinoe, Imboden, and Berry have not been forcibly removed from their sporting teams and organizations in the ways that Carlos, Smith, Abdul-Rauf, Ali, Hodges, and Kaepernick were. A significant reason for this change seems to be social media and the ability of protestors "to respond in real time to their critics, often capturing the high ground right away" (Platt, 2018). So although the solutions for controversies surrounding race, sport, and politics are still very imperfect—and at times blatantly hypocritical and confusing—at least it is the athlete who appears to be on their way to less harmful consequence for their protest.

Race and the Sports Industry

The U.S. sports industry here should be understood as the individuals, organizations and corporations that financially profit from sports. Individuals in the sports industry are team coaches, managers, and owners. Organizations include professional and amateur sports teams, leagues, and competition organizers (e.g., the NCAA, the NFL, and U.S. Open Tennis Championships). And corporations should be understood as including retail, media, and marketing corporations whose sole focus is confined to the sports industry (e.g., Nike and ESPN). In terms of contextualizing the history of race and the sports industry, it's important to know that a number of individuals of color had opportunities to coach, manage, and even own sports teams. For example, African American, Andrew "Rube" Foster (1879–1930) founded the National Negro League in baseball and served as player, manager, and owner. And renowned football coach Eddie Robinson Sr. served in that capacity at Grambling State University—a historically Black college and university (HBCU)—for a total of fifty-six years. However, "[i]t was after the 1960s that the first black man was hired as a manager of a major league baseball team or became a television network commentator for NBA basketball games" (Wiggins and Miller, 2005, 317). A couple of decades later, in the 1980s and 1990s, would be the first time Black Americans could claim partial ownership in any big-time sporting franchises. In 2012, Pakistani American Shahid Khan made history by becoming the first Asian owner of color and first majority owner of color of an NFL franchise. As of 2017, there have only been three Latinx and no Native American or Asian head coaches in the NFL (Burton et al., 2019). It is only since 2011 that people of color have become *majority* owners of big-time sports franchises.

These snippets of sports history pertaining to the sports industry along racial lines give context to the enduring reality that the majority of the U.S. sports industry is managed, owned, and operated by White Americans. White Americans in power over the livelihood of athlete bodies of color has tended to result in the uninterrupted maintenance of racism broadly, unless the athletes have been willing to join forces or the Whites in power have looked to build partnerships and work towards addressing the concerns of athletes of color.

Benching Leonard Bates (1940) and Lucien V. Alexis Jr. (1941)

At the intercollegiate level, African Americans have been participating since the late nineteenth century, on predominately White college teams. These Black athletes at times suffered dehumanizing and offensive treatment, which sometimes occurred when their "northern institutions acquiesced to southern racial practices by agreeing to keep black players out of games against the colleges and universities of the white South" (Wiggins and Miller, 2005, 193). Black collegiate athletes Leonard Bates and Lucien V. Alexis Jr. both experienced this "racial benching" in 1940 and 1941, respectively. Bates played football for New York University (NYU), and Alexis Jr. played lacrosse for Harvard University. The benching of both players was not received well by segments of the student population, and each of these athletic contests resulted in institutional controversy, student protest, and divergent institutional solutions to try and prevent further unrest.

In the fall of 1940, the NYU "Violets" football team was scheduled to play an away match against the University of Missouri on November 2. NYU students learned that their Northern institution was honoring the "gentleman's agreement"—that is, the "Jim Crow tradition in collegiate sports against having an interracial game if one of the parties involved objected" (Spivey, 1988)—and decided to take a stand against the school's administration. By mid-October, thousands of students began picketing the NYU administration building with signs the read things like "Ban Gentleman's Agreement," "Bates Must Play," and "End Jim Crowism at NYU. A few days later, students who formed the All-University Committee on "Bates Must Play," passed four resolutions:

> [T]hat Len Bates be released from his gentleman's agreement and be allowed to make his own decision as to whether he will or will not play, that New York University never again enter upon any contract with Jim Crow schools; that the University administration make a statement clarifying its views on this issue; and that if the administration fails to comply with the aforementioned resolutions, there be a boycott of all the home games for the remainder of the season. (Spivey, 1988, 285)

Rather than working with the newly formed All-University Committee, the NYU administration actually used Leonard Bates's own words as their defense. At a press conference held just three days before the game was scheduled to take place in Missouri, George Sheiebler, NYU's director of publicity for the athletic department, produced a letter that had been written by Bates to the president of the Negro Cultural Society at NYU. The letter acknowledged that Bates understood that he would be unable to compete in arranged contests between NYU and Missouri when he first entered the school. He went on in the letter, expressing that he didn't wish to play in the game *at that time* because his major personal focus was in gaining a college education second to football.

Bates was not happy that the NYU administration had placed his words out of their original context and publicly used them to escape institutional accountability for a continued racist practice within college sports. Despite the efforts of the "Bates Must Play" movement and Bates's proven contribution to the team, the NYU squad kept to the agreement and left him behind when it traveled southward to take on Missouri (Spivey, 1988, 298). Bates was the starting halfback on the team, and without him, NYU suffered greatly in the game, ultimately losing to Missouri 33–0. The embarrassing loss only escalated the amplified the calls of the All-University Committee on Bates Must Play, and the protest began to evolve into one of direct confrontation. Students formed a new Council for Student Equality, whose aim was to fight discrimination and challenge inaction of NYU on issues related to race. In the face of growing protestation and calls for change, the university's administration continued to reject the notion that the institution was racist and often offered the defense that the university was acting in a way that protected its Negro players from a Southern environment that would be inhospitable to Blacks. The Council for Student Equality rejected these explanations and started to circulate a petition in the first week of March, 1941, calling for the university's Board of Athletic Control to end its policy of Negro discrimination. NYU's administrative response went like this:

> The administration moved to stop the petition. When the council failed to heed the administration's warnings to desist, its leadership was charged with violating University rules and regulations and brought before Dean McConn . . . the dean suspended Naomi Bloom, Jean Bornstein, Mervyn Jones, Robert Schoenfeld, Argyle Stoute, Anita Kreiger, and Evelyn Maisel. (Spivey, 1988, 300)

Many students, academics, and national organizations expressed outrage at the university's decision to suspend these seven students. Many calls for a reversal of the decision were made, but ultimately, the suspension of the seven NYU students was upheld and lasted three months.

The NYU administration made no effort to stop honoring the gentleman's agreement and it played the University of Missouri again—although this time in the north at Yankee Stadium—in the 1941 season. Bates would have been able to participate in the northern held contest, but he was injured and did not suit up. With the U.S. involvement in World War II, the football program began to diminish, and it was removed completely as a varsity sport in 1952. In a 1988 interview with Bates, almost fifty years after the NYU controversy, he stood firm and emphatic about his desire to play in the away game at Missouri:

I wanted to play. I remember the bogus way the athletic department tried to put my letter. They made it sound like I did not want to play. I very much wanted to play Missouri. I wanted to play! (Spivey, 1988, 293–94)

Ultimately, Bates was used and abused by New York University athletic department and administration to avoid accountability at the institutional level of upholding racism and White supremacist athletic infrastructures in the United States. As for the seven students who were suspended for three months in 1941? In March of 2001, New York University honored the seven students for their commitment to social justice.

Also in 1941, and roughly four hours north, on the campus of Harvard University in Cambridge, Massachusetts, a similar student-administration upheaval took place surrounding race and sport. On April 5, 1941, the Harvard University men's lacrosse team was scheduled to play an away match, during what was spring recess for the rest of the University, against the Naval Academy in Annapolis, Maryland. The Naval Academy had no players of color on its team, but Harvard University had one: Lucien Alexis, Jr., an African American. While Harvard University had been admitting and graduating African American scholars and scholar-athletes since the late nineteenth century, the U.S. Naval Academy would not see its first African American *graduate* until 1949.

It's important to note here that the controversy around Lucien Alexis Jr. showcases how the "gentleman's agreement" between Northern and Southern colleges and universities, had everything to do with race and preserving Jim Crow structural racism in athletics. Lucien Alexis Jr. had arrived on Harvard's campus with an incredible southern and academic pedigree—prep school at Phillips Exeter Academy and the son of a Harvard class of 1918 alum who was serving as a principal of a New Orleans high school. Alexis Jr.'s pedigree would not exempt him from what was to unfold in the spring of his junior year as a midfield player on the Harvard lacrosse team:

> Upon the team's arrival at the Naval Academy they ate in the dining room, but as soon as it was discovered that Alexis was on the team the coach, Richard Snibbe, former St. John's College of Annapolis All-American lacrosse player and the manager, Robert B. Seidman, a senior, were called in by Commander Davis, director of athletics, and were told that it would be impossible to play Alexis against the Navy. One reason being fear of race riots in the town—an assertion dropped when informed of Alexis playing at College Park [a game versus University of Maryland] . . . finally they were taken to see Admiral Wilson, the superintendent of the Naval Academy . . . The Admiral gave the coach and manager three choices: (1) to bench Alexis for the game and Navy would bench a player of similar ability; (2) to take the game from Navy on forfeit; (3) to permit the Admiral to phone the authorities of Harvard and settle the issue. The last of the three was chosen and then ensued a series of agitated telephone calls and telegrams and finally the Harvard director of athletics, William J. Bingham was reached at Brattleboro, Vermont. (Wiggins and Miller, 2005, 194–95)

Initially, Mr. Bingham stood firm against Admiral Wilson on the grounds that Harvard was the guest of the Naval Academy and therefore expected decent treatment toward every member of the team. The admiral first expressed the historical significance of such an idea—citing the ninety-six years that Navy had not competed against a team with a Negro—and then blamed Harvard for not informing the Naval Academy that Harvard had a Negro on the team beforehand. The admiral also made a point to recuse himself of any prejudiced because he was a northerner himself; that his stance was merely about following Navy policy. Later that evening, a wire from Mr. Bingham came for coach Snibbe that said Alexis would not play or even dress for the game versus Navy. What took place between the time of the admiral's conversation with Bingham and the wire telling Alexis not to play, no one seems to know; however, Alexis took the evening train, twenty-four hours ahead of the team, and returned to Boston (Wiggins and Miller, 2005, 195). The result of the Harvard-Navy lacrosse game the next day? Navy 12, Harvard 0.

Upon the return of Harvard students from the spring recess, the university newspaper, *The Harvard Crimson*, took to accusing the administration of prostration to the system of Jim Crowism. As students read about the incident in the newspaper, prominent student leaders gathered to craft a petition asking for clarification on Harvard's policy towards race and its place in athletics. The petition stated the following:

> We believe that almost unanimously the undergraduate body is of the opinion that racial consideration should not be allowed to determine the fit or unfitness of a student to compete on an athletic team. In view of this belief, we, the students of Harvard University, wish to disapprove heartily of the course of action taken by the college authorities when under pressure from the United States Naval Academy, they agreed to bar a student because of racial consideration from participating in an athletic contest. By

yielding to the Naval Academy's demands, Harvard has taken an indefensible position in the eyes of a democratic nation. In the belief that the University's action was the result of an over-hasty decision rather than a sanction of Jim Crowism we request from the Harvard authorities a clarification of the University's athletic policy with regard to colored athletes. We believe that Mr. Bingham will make it clear that in the future Harvard will not tolerate athletic relationships with institutions which discriminate on the basis of race or creed, and that such discrimination has never had, and never had, and never will have, any place in Harvard. (Wiggins and Miller, 2005, 195–96)

The petition was circulated throughout campus, reaching students and teachers alike, and then was presented to Mr. Bingham on a Wednesday morning. There were student protests, condemnation by the Harvard Teacher's Union, inquiries made by rights groups and prominent newspapers. Even congressmen weighed in and asked for explanations about what had happened in Annapolis.

Ultimately, the pressure on Harvard's administration from students, faculty, and others soon led to a public statement being released by the university's athletic association. The statement condemned further acts of discrimination, that everyone entitled to compete would be able to do so, and that the school would no longer compete against other institutions that violated Harvard's standards of fair play. Harvard's response to its protestors and full community reached well beyond its ivied walls. For example, "When the lacrosse team arrived by bus for a game at the US Military Academy at West Point, New York, black cadets were waiting to greet Alexis, to offer their support, and to demonstrate that their academy was a cut above their Southern cousin [and] that fall, Harvard played football against Navy, fielding a black player, Ray Guild" (Gup, 2004). While it's incredibly doubtful that scholars and alums of Harvard in the 1940s would say that the elite university suddenly became the epitome of racial equality after this incident, the institution's response to the way they handled the treatment of Lucien Alexis mattered greatly and paved the way for a truly just experience for Black student athletes at Harvard.

Curt Flood's Antitrust Suit vs. MLB (1969)

The 1969 lawsuit that Major League Baseball (MLB) player Curt Flood initiated against administration of the MLB is regarded as one of the most significant pieces of baseball history and sports litigation in the United States. Although a deeper dive into Curt Flood's life and legacy can be found in chapter 4, "Profiles," of this book, the focus now shall be on the actual legal case and the way MLB responded to Flood's claims. Flood had been playing for the St. Louis Cardinals club since 1958 and had built himself an arguable reputation as the best centerfielder in all of baseball. Thus, it came as quite a shock to Flood when, in 1969, he was informed by the Cardinals vice president that he'd been traded to Philadelphia.

At this time, there was no such thing as a baseball player with a million-dollar contract. In fact, the highest paid player in 1969 made less than $140,000 a year. Flood was making a little over $90,000 at the time and decided to do something extreme: he refused to go to Philadelphia. Flood wrote to the MLB commissioner Bowie Kuhn and let Kuhn know that he didn't like feeling as though he were "a piece of property to be bought and sold irrespective of [Flood's] wishes" (Rhoden, 2006, 232). However, from a legal standpoint, Curt Flood and all other professional baseball players *were* essentially owned by his team due to the reserve clause in MLB:

> The reserve clause allowed teams to hold on to players as long as they wanted but forbade the players from testing the market on their terms. . . . The owners were given license to do this by the federal government. The reserve clause prevented players from moving to another team unless they were traded or sold. Flood challenged

the fairness of a system that kept players in perpetual servitude to their teams at the owners' pleasure. (Rhoden,
2006, 232)

Given the athlete activism of the late 1960s and general political climate around racism and race relations, it's understandable that Flood's own race consciousness had been heightened.
Flood saw the connection between the reserve system in MLB
and a sort of neoslavery, with MLB teams acting as different
plantations full of "slaves" of all different races.

Yet, what Flood was fighting went beyond racial lines. This is
likely why the executive board of the Players Association voted
unanimously to support Flood in his battle with Major League
Baseball and agreed to back him financially. However, the executive director of the player's association also "warned Flood
from the start . . . that if he went forward with the suit, his life
in baseball was over; he would not be elected to the Hall of
Fame, he would never manage or be given any significant management position in baseball" (Rhoden, 2006, 234). Most of
Flood's athletic peers were terrified of what he was attempting
to do and therefore, very few showed support of him. In fact,
only retired players Jackie Robinson and Hank Greenberg took
to the courtroom stand to testify on behalf of Flood's cause. The
reserve clause was the centerpiece of Flood's case and his lawyers "argued that this represented collusion, violated antitrust
legislation, and that it also violated the Thirteenth Amendment
as a form of involuntary servitude" (Crepeau, 2007, 184). Both
Robinson and Greenberg were effective witnesses for Flood in
speaking out against the reserve clause.

Unfortunately for Curt Flood—and really all of the MLB
players at the time—MLB as an organization had historical
legal cases on their side. The lawyers representing MLB relied
on the rulings in two prior cases: *Federal Baseball Club v. National League* (1922) and *Toolson v. New York Yankees* (1953).
In *Federal Baseball,* the owner of the Baltimore Federal League
team charged conspiracy to destroy his business and violation

of antitrust law. The Supreme Court unanimously decided against the owner of the Baltimore Federal League, noting that:

> [B]aseball exhibitions were a form of business, but they were purely state affairs and therefore did not constitute interstate commerce. Although the players moved between states the game itself, when played, was held in one state. Therefore, federal antitrust law did not apply to baseball. Baseball is also not commerce . . . because it is personal effort not related to production. (Crepeau, 2007, 184)

It would be this ruling in *Federal Baseball* that established what was referred to as antitrust exemption in baseball. The Supreme Court again dealt with the reserve clause in 1953 with the *Toolson* case, which involved a minor league player who had been demoted but was refusing to accept this demotion to Class A baseball from Triple A. Toolson's lawyers argued that the coming of radio, television, and air travel, along with the expansion of the minor leagues, clearly represented new conditions that placed baseball within the realm of interstate commerce (Crepeau, 2007). In the Toolson case, the Supreme Court relied upon the precedent of *Federal Baseball* (1922).

In the Supreme Court case *Flood v. Kuhn* (1972), Flood's lawyers attempted to argue that *Toolson* and *Federal Baseball* were irrelevant and dated. His lawyers also argued that Flood should be able to seek redress under state antitrust law if the court, indeed, agreed that baseball was not interstate commerce. The lawyers representing MLB argued that the Supreme Court should not dismiss the relevance of the past cases that baseball had come to rely on for thirty years and "that the players had agreed to the reserve clause in contract negotiations, and therefore under labor law were not allowed to bring an antitrust suit" (Crepeau, 2007, 186). Ultimately, the Supreme Court upheld the antitrust exemption in baseball with a 5–3 majority decision.

Curt Flood's loss to MLB did affect him personally and professionally in profoundly negative ways, but his case helped to galvanize fellow baseball players to continue to act on the reserve clause, and raised consciousness about the clause itself among the press and public. Meanwhile, the MLB team owners naively felt that the *Flood v. Kuhn* decision was a victory over their players, failing to see how Curt Flood and his case against them had effectively exposed them to future fights from more players. Just a few short years later, the reserve system in baseball came to an end. In December 1975, what Curt Flood had started in baseball was finished when baseball arbitrator Peter Seitz ruled in favor of pitchers Andy Messersmith and Dave McNally; both were granted free agency (Bryant, 2018). McNally, a white player from Montreal, and Messersmith, a white player from Los Angeles, successfully brought a grievance against the MLB owners. In a 1996 interview with sportswriter William Rhoden, Curt Flood expressed his sentiments about the success of McNally and Messersmith compared to his own loss:

> Flood said that he was happy for the victory, but that he felt the decisions had a tinge of racism. "It disappointed me that I didn't win," Flood said, "but I had to feel that somewhere in the equation, America was showing its racism again. They were just merely waiting for someone else to win that case. (Rhoden, 2006)

It's not at all provable that Flood's losing outcome had anything to do with racism. However, Flood's life after his battle with MLB was very accurately predicted by the executive director of the Players Association back in 1969. Flood was never welcomed back to the game of professional baseball. He struggled with employment, alcoholism, and continuing to reside in the United States. Flood died at the young age of fifty-nine due to health issues and, as of the 2020 induction class, has yet to be inducted into the Baseball Hall of Fame.

Syracuse 8 (1969)

Although referred to as the "Syracuse 8" by media outlets, there were actually nine Syracuse University football players who chose to boycott the 1970 football season. Quite simply, these young Black men were tired of putting up with the racial injustice experienced on their team and on their campus, as it only compounded the racial injustices already present in being Black in the United States. The nine Black players were attending Syracuse in the U.S. racial and political climate following the assassinations of Bobby Kennedy, Malcolm X, and Martin Luther King Jr. And in choosing to attend Syracuse University, these Black athletes were following in the legacies of Jim Brown, Ernie Davis, and Floyd Little. The names of the nine Syracuse 8 players are: Abdullah Alif Muhammad (then known as Al Newton), Dana Harrell, Gregory Allen, Ronald Womack, Clarence "Bucky" McGill, John Lobon, Richard Bulls, Duane Walker and John Godbolt. All but John Godbolt went on to earn their degree from Syracuse University.

The frustrations for these nine football players started from the moments they arrived on campus. The rules seemed to be different for the Black athletes than the white athletes and there were no Black football coaches for the players to turn to for guidance. The Black players often met late at night at a restaurant called Ben's Kitchen because it was a spot owned and operated by Black people. It was at Ben's Kitchen that they discussed their plans to boycott and drafted the petition with four demands they asked the Syracuse University administration for (1) better medical treatment; (2) better access to academics for all athletes; (3) fairness; and (4) diversify the coaching staff.

The demands of the Syracuse 8 were all grounded in their personal experiences at Syracuse during 1968 and 1969. Running-back Greg Allen recalled a conversation he had with one of his white coaches when that coach was driving him to campus for the first time:

> We get in the car and we begin, you know, the small talk.
> You know, "Greg, Gee, I'm glad you're here," he recalls.
> "We want you to have a good time while you're at Syra-
> cuse. We want you to get a good education. We want you
> to grow. We want you to have a great career as a football
> player. But the one thing we're gonna ask you to do is
> not date any white girls while you're here." It was a little
> bit of a shock for me, because I knew that I had traveled
> north of the Mason-Dixon Line, not below it. (Given and
> Springer, 2017)

Conversations like that certainly never happened with white
athletes attending Syracuse. In addition, divergent academic
expectations and policies were placed on the Black football
players. Allen was told he couldn't be a biology major because
his labs would interfere with practice, yet he noticed that the
white players were not told this same directive. Alif Muhammad was discouraged from being an engineer, even though he
had earned a near perfect SAT math score. Alif Muhammad
recalls feeling "kind of, insulted . . . they wanted me to take
general reading classes and general education classes. And it
was like, 'Wait a minute—no, no, no, no, no, no. I didn't come
here for that'" (Given and Springer, 2017).

In addition to the social and academic parameters they
were prescribed by the athletics department, the Syracuse 8
wanted to see institutional change around medical treatment
for all athletes and dismantling the use of the old "quota system" from the 1950s and 1960s. At the time, the Syracuse
University football team doctor was trained as a gynecologist,
which meant he wasn't the ideal candidate to be handling
the injuries and concerns of male college athletes. And despite Syracuse's reputation of being one of the more progressive Northern schools in its integration of athletic teams, the
university continued to operate under an unfair racial quota
system in athletics—that is, a system of "unofficial rules about
how many black players could be on the field at the same

time. Even at home games" (Given and Springer, 2017). Alif Muhammad recalls, "We wanted an equitable and transparent system for determining when black players played. . . . One week you'd be the second strong fullback and then it'd be time to travel to an away game and all of a sudden you'd be the third string defensive end, and left off the team bus" (Game, 2015). Ultimately, the four demands the Syracuse 8 sought seemed reasonable, considering the majority of those demands would better the experience of *all* athletes, not just the Black athletes.

However, the true controversy between the Syracuse 8 and Syracuse University athletic administration seemed to erupt when the nine Black players approached head coach Ben Schwartswalder regarding hiring a Black assistant coach. John Lobon recalls that when he and his Black teammates continued to press their head coach about finding a Black assistant, Schwartswalder said, "I looked for one on the way home and I looked for one on the way back from coaching and I didn't find any" (Game, 2015). The flippant tone in which Schwartswalder responded to his Black players after they'd given time for the administration to really address their concerns told them everything they needed to know. The players began their boycott in the Spring of 1970. It would also be the demand to diversify the coaching staff of the school that turned the activism of the Syracuse 8 into an issue not of improvement for all athletes but rather an issue of White versus Black in the public eye.

When the press heard about the boycott of Syracuse's Black football players, the players themselves lost control of the narrative of their cause. Only the demand about Syracuse attaining a Black assistant coach was focused upon in the media, with the three other demands being overlooked or completely dismissed:

[T]he papers labeled the Syracuse 8 as "black dissidents" or "black militants" or sometimes just "the blacks." "We

were never asked any questions, or the media never contacted us to get any of our opinions," Greg [Allen] says.
"No one was really interested in our perspective." (Given
and Springer, 2017)

Without Black players being given an opportunity to explain
their perspectives, Syracuse University responded to the publicity of the protestation by its Black football players by suspending them from the team. White teammates offered their
Black teammates no support and even threatened to boycott
themselves if the Syracuse 8 were allowed back on the team.
Fans threatened to boycott games, and the letters from irate
Syracuse alums overwhelmed the chancellor's office, threatening terminated donations and calls for the scholarships of the
nine Black players to be rescinded. Summer soon arrived, and
the nine Black players returned to their respective homes for
the summer, not knowing what outcomes would result from
their protestation.

Over that summer of 1970, the chancellor's office required
head coach Schwartzwalder to find a Black assistant coach. Of
course, the majority of the Black coaches who were contacted
turned down the opportunity to walk into a racially divisive
work environment under a head coach who didn't really want
them there in the first place. When the Syracuse 8 returned to
campus in the fall of 1970, "a black assistant coach had been
hired, but Alif Muhammad says 'He was not on the program
listed as a coach. I remember going to a meeting, and the
coaches were meeting with a blackboard with X's and O's, and
he's sitting in the back of the room with his head down on the
desk like he was sleeping . . . I felt deeply, deeply hurt'" (Given
and Springer, 2017). With a continued lack of willingness by
the coaching staff to meet the needs of its Black players, the
Syracuse 8 decided to continue with their boycott, sitting out
the entire season in 1970.

However, in a definitive move of monumental importance, the Syracuse University chancellor, along with a group

of faculty members, sought to have the Syracuse 8 maintain their scholarship status. This decision to quash any desires from coaching staff, White teammates, alums, or boosters to demolish the ability for the nine Black students to remain at Syracuse set a tone within the realm of college athletics—or at least at Syracuse University—that these were *students* before athletes. This decision by Syracuse University administration allowed the Syracuse 8 to make a valuable shift in their focus on campus. In 2006, thirty-six years after their boycotted season, Syracuse 8 member Clarence "Bucky" McGill reflected on the school's decision to allow the players to keep their scholarships when interviewed after the Syracuse 8 received the Chancellor's Medal of Courage:

> When the athletic doors were shut to us at 18, 19, 20 years old, we made an adjustment. And that adjustment was education, and it was based on what Syracuse taught us. It was all those mentors, instructors, colleagues, friends and confidantes, both black and white, who we relied on. (Game, 2015)

Of the nine Black players who protested, eight of them graduated from Syracuse; John Godbolt left the university.

The eight Black men who did earn degrees from Syracuse University, some of whom would go on to return to the team for future early 1970s seasons, did sacrifice and suffer athletically for their stance. Any chance of playing at the NFL level disappeared for the Syracuse 8, despite many of them having the talent to do so. In addition, Syracuse University denied the Syracuse 8 the honor of four-year letterman jackets and didn't apologize for the way they were treated while student-athletes at the institution. The letterman jackets and apology came thirty-six years later, and the Syracuse 8 all appreciated and acknowledged that "very few universities would have the courage and integrity to circle back, this many years later, and say 'You guys got it right'" (Game, 2015).

Questioning the NCAA's Eligibility Standards: Propositions 48, 42, and 16 (1986, 1989, 1995)

For many in the United States who do not identify themselves as being athletically gifted, the process of what happens when a talented high school athlete is recruited to play a sport in college—particularly at the Division I level—goes something like this: Athlete excels on high school or organized youth travel team. Athlete gets noticed by college scouts who begin to recruit athlete rigorously. Athlete gets their pick of any of the schools that want them to play their sport in college. Athlete automatically gets into the school for free.

While it's incredibly understandable why the process of receiving a college athletic scholarship *appears* that way to the public, the real process is far more complicated and has continued to remain controversial due to the requirements set up for young student-athletes by the National Collegiate Athletic Association (NCAA) Eligibility Center (formerly known as the NCAA Clearing House). Neither "A" in NCAA stands for "academics," but the NCAA has always set academic requirements for high school student-athletes to meet in order to be eligible to receive any form of athletic scholarship—full or partial—from an NCAA Division I or II institution. However, due to the racial history of the United States, both the sectors of education and sport have been affected in a way that has caused inequities in access to quality education for many people of color and inequities in the types of sports youth have chosen to/have access to participate in. As the United States moved out of the civil rights era of the 1950s and 1960s and through the various protests movements that made up the 1970s, the 1980s and 1990s saw a number of talented student-athletes earn scholarships to NCAA Division I and II institutions under newly enriched eligibility requirements. The 1980s and 1990s also saw a number of talented student-athletes struggle, and often fail, to meet the sometimes controversial academic qualifying standards of the NCAA for athletic scholarship.

In 1986, the NCAA instituted Proposition 48, effectively establishing eligibility requirements for high school student-athletes to meet upon signing a National Letter of Intent with the collegiate institution they intended to matriculate. Proposition 48 requires incoming freshman have at least a 2.0 grade-point average and a minimum score of 700 on the Scholastic Aptitude Test (SAT) or 15 on the American College Test (ACT) to be eligible to play. So-called partial qualifiers, those who satisfy only one of the requirements, could receive a scholarship but, like a nonqualifier, could not play or practice during the freshman year and would sacrifice one year of eligibility (Associated Press, 1989). Many opponents of Proposition 48 surfaced within the Black community because they felt it intentionally disenfranchised Black athletes. However, at the time, others within the Black community, such as sports scholar Harry Edwards suggested that:

[T]he rule was really more about class bias than it was race bias or a desire of HWIHE [Historically White Institutions of Higher Education] to intentionally deny Black access. He essentially argued the bigger issue was an American educational system (PreL-12 through higher education) that set standards too low, and a failure on the part of this system and actors within it to properly prepare Black and other students for productive lives as citizens in American society and throughout the world. (Hawkins et al., 2017, 16)

As racism, race, and class in America are inextricably linked to one another historically, both groups of opposition are unsurprising. However, it is Harry Edwards who has the most rational argument, as it would be unfair to assume the NCAA seeks to "intentionally deny Black access" to higher education and continued athletic success. Indeed, proponents of Proposition 48 feel that the NCAA should be ensuring that young people who can prove they are "student-athletes" and not "athlete-students" are gaining entry into institutions of higher education with financial support. Unfortunately, the NCAA didn't do itself any favors to quiet its challengers of its eligibility decisions when, just a few years later, it introduced Proposition 42.

Proposition 42, which was originally voted down in January 1989 at an NCAA convention, was reconsidered the very next day and passed with a slim margin, 163–154. Proposition 42, essentially took Proposition 48 to the next level of academic eligibility difficulties. Proposition 42 eliminates any partial qualifiers, meaning that those student-athletes who may have qualified to receive a scholarship under Proposition 48 for having made the 2.0 GPA or SAT/ACT score, are no longer eligible to receive any athletic funding from the university that is recruiting the athlete. Between 1986 and 1989, "the N.C.A.A. estimated at 1,800 prospective student-athletes" (Associated Press, 1989) had been partial scholarship qualifiers. This means that under Proposition 42, those same 1,800 athletes could have only relied on financial aid from the government or private sources.

With the slim margin of majority support for Proposition 42, there arose a prominent—and very public—diversity of opinion shared by university presidents, trustees, athletic directors, and coaches. One prolific coach in particular, John Thompson Jr., made national headlines when he walked off the court before a game against Boston College in the winter of 1989. In 1989, John Thompson Jr. was undeniably one of the best Division I college coaches in the United States. He had transformed a losing Georgetown University men's basketball program from his start in 1972, to a team that would make NCAA's "Final Four" round ten years later and win a national title in 1984. When Thompson Jr. did or said something, people in the college athletics world paid attention:

> Thompson and others who oppose the rule believe that it could shut out athletes from disadvantaged backgrounds.

Others fear that the rule could result in players flocking to two-year colleges and reviving the proliferation of sweet-heart deals between junior colleges and major institutions in which certain players are earmarked for certain colleges. (Associated Press, 1989)

A majority of these "athletes from disadvantaged backgrounds" happen to racially identify as African American. And when one considers that Proposition 42 makes a student athlete's scholarship eligibility completely dependent on earning a high enough score on the SAT—which studies have shown is a test with "factual racial disparity in exam scores" (Shropshire, 1996, 112), Thompson Jr.'s court walk-off "to bring attention to the issue in hopes of getting [NCAA members] to take another look at what they've done, and if they feel it unjust, change the rule" (Berkowitz, 1989) is urgent and deserving of public amplification.

Those in charge felt the same of Thompson Jr.'s and others' stance toward Proposition 42, as a year later, at the eighty-fourth annual NCAA convention in Dallas, Texas, the controversial Proposition 42 was discussed again among three alternative proposals. Essentially, the membership of the 1990 convention needed to decide whether they'd let Proposition 42 kick in for the 1990–1991 academic year, modify it, or rescind it altogether:

> What the 1990 convention in Dallas, Texas, did yield was a compromise. On the one hand, athletes not making the grade and achieving the ACT or SAT minimum scores would be eligible for financial aid based on need. However, those marginal students not making the grade would still be barred from athletic programs as freshmen and still would lose one year of playing eligibility. (Cole, 1995)

This compromise seemed to ease the dissent of most and the newly compromised Proposition 42 went into effect in August

1990. The NCAA even took to reviewing whether the SAT was an appropriate measure to use in its initial eligibility rules in 1993 and 1994.

The NCAA membership voted to continue utilizing the SAT and ACT in initial eligibility standards in 1995 and also began to introduce changes associated with a new piece of eligibility policy in the early 1990s: proposition 16. In his 1996 work, *In Black and White: Race and Sports in America*, Kenneth Shropshire explained the racial disparities of the standardized test in student-athlete NCAA scholarship eligibility:

> No matter what one hears about how many points a student gets for signing his or her name on the SAT, the average African-American student is only about 30 points above the minimum cur off for financial aid, while the average white is 230 points above. Further, assuming an average student has a grade point average of 2.0, he or she would have to score nearly 200 points above average on the SAT to qualify. One has to consider that only the rare student is going to excel in a composite of the arts, academics, and athletics. . . . A test score should not be the single determining factor for financial aid or, in a more indirect way, for an opportunity for a college education. (Shropshire, 1996, 115)

In certain ways, Proposition 16, which effectively superseded Proposition 48, shifted some of the focus away from the SAT and ACT amid concerns of their inherent racial biases—biases backed with factual evidence like that presented by Shropshire in *Black and White*.

Proposition 16 was actually adopted by the NCAA in 1992 but did not take effect until 1996. Proposition 16 introduced an increase of two in core course requirements, increased the required years of high school English from three to four, and instituted a sliding scale method called the "initial-eligibility index" to manage the SAT/ACT and GPA requirements. In the Fall 2000 issue of the *Catholic University Law Review*, author Lee J. Rosen explains the nuances of the Proposition 16 initial-eligibility index:

> The "initial-eligibility index" allowed student-athletes to establish eligibility with a 2.0 GPA in thirteen core courses, provided they also obtained SAT scores of 1010 (or combined ACT score of 86). The other end of the scale allowed a student-athlete to receive an SAT score of 820 (or 68 ACT), provided he maintained a GPA of at least 2.5. The new standards also changed the meaning of "partial qualifier" to include student-athletes whose total SAT scores fell between 720 and 810 with corresponding GPAs. (Rosen, 2000)

This sliding scale model helped to shift the focus off the SAT/ACT inherent racial bias issues because a student-athlete was able to effectively achieve a higher GPA to offset the importance of the standardized test score. In other words, the higher the GPA, the lower one needs to score on the SAT/ACT. Proposition 16 is what is currently still utilized by the NCAA in determining student-athlete scholarship eligibility. Of course, that still means that the inherent racial biases within the standardized testing in the United States have yet to actually be rectified or eliminated overall in the determination of an athlete of color's ability to receive an NCAA Division I or II scholarship.

Venus and Serena Williams Boycott Indian Wells (2001–2016)

The tennis tournament commonly known as "Indian Wells" is one of the mandatory events elite female players in the Women's Tennis Association's tour membership attend each year. The actual name of the tournament is the BNP Paribas Open, which takes place at the Indian Wells Tennis Garden in the desert near Palm Springs, California. Should a player not play one of these events, she risks suspension—unless she opts to engage in promotional activities in support of the tournament she has skipped (Drucker, 2009). After a controversial experience at Indian Wells in 2001, African American tennis superstars Venus and Serena Williams boycotted this mandatory tournament for fifteen years and fourteen years, respectively. Considering the fact that at the time of the 2001 Indian Wells tournament, Venus was a twenty-year-old and Serena nineteen, it makes their boycott incredibly significant in its length and begs a deeper exploration into why two of the world's best tennis players would skip a specific tournament for the majority of their professional careers.

The 2001 controversy at Indian Wells started when Venus and Serena were scheduled to face each other in the semifinal match of the tournament. Venus pulled out of the match due to a tendonitis injury and the announcement about her withdrawal wasn't announced to the packed stadium and likely thousands of viewers tuned in to ESPN until roughly ten minutes before the match was scheduled to begin. The fans in the stadium ardently boo the news and rumors emerge about how Venus and Serena's father, Richard, allegedly plans which daughter wins the match beforehand when they face off. Things get much worse two days later when Serena faces off against Kim Clijsters in the tournament final:

[T]he crowd unleashes its frustration on Serena and her family by booing the teenagers as she walks on to the court, cheering her every unforced error—a crowd etiquette no-no outside of team competitions such as Davis Cup, Federation Cup or World Team Tennis—and emphatically backing the foreign opponent over the home finalist. In response, Richard raises a clenched fist, evoking John Carlos and Tommie Smith's iconic 1968 Olympics Black Power salute. (Jones, 2015)

After rallying from a first set loss, Serena ended up winning her second Indian Wells title. As Serena attempted to celebrate her win while waving to the crowd, a mixture of applause and boos could be heard as she prepared to accept her trophy and $330,000 winner's check. As media interviews were conducted after Serena's victory—with Serena, Venus, and Richard Williams—allegations of racist comments came to light, and people within and outside of the tennis world began to take sides. To this day, either one believes that the Williamses encountered racism at Indian Wells and understands their boycott of the event, or one believes the family fabricated a story and childishly refused to participate in a mandatory tennis match because they could afford to do so financially and due to professional ranking.

Since roughly a week after Serena's 2001 Indian Wells victory, Richard Williams and Venus Williams have maintained that racist comments were launched at them while they made their way to their seats to watch Serena's final match against Clijsters. Comments reported from Richard Williams were that "when Venus and [he] were walking down the stairs to our seats, people kept calling [him] 'n-----.' One said, 'I wish it was '75, we'd skin you alive'" (Drucker, 2009). Although none of the fans at the stadium reported hearing the racist comments that Richard and Venus Williams reported, Charlie Pasarell, the tournament chairman at Indian Wells, said he "was cringing when all that stuff was going on. It was unfair for the crowd to do that" (Drucker, 2009). At first, people speculated on the validity of the Williamses claims and felt that perhaps they were "playing the race card," rather than accepting the fact that fans were disappointed in the late notice of the semifinal cancellation. As the years continued to pass with the Williams sisters refusing to attend Indian Wells, however, the negative sentiments shifted toward those of the sisters being "unfair to fans by boycotting the event" (Jones, 2015).

Fortunately, many people in the world of tennis did support the sisters' boycott of Indian Wells and are aware of the historical racism and classism within the sport. The significance of the Williamses boycott comes in the longevity and that the sisters refused to yield to the requirements of the Women's Tennis Association. In fact, "former Women's Tennis Association CEO Larry Scott said in 2008 that he wouldn't penalize the Williamses for skipping the event because he refused to put them in a situation 'that is going to be awkward'" (Jones, 2015). The only "awkwardness" felt in that situation would not be from the Williamses but rather from the WTA in financially penalizing two of the top tennis players in the world for an incident that "weighed on [Serena's] mind for years [and caused her to look to] Nelson Mandela's words and actions of forgiveness as motivation for her decision to return" (Jones, 2015). Indian Wells simply needed the Williams sisters more than they needed Indian Wells.

Since 2009, Indian Wells had been suffering enough financial struggles to cause a change in ownership. Billionaire Larry Ellison bought the tennis event and the entire venue, and reached out to the Williams sisters about returning. Eventually, in 2015, Serena chose to return to Indian Wells, but did so on her own terms. Serena used the Indian Wells tournament "as a way to highlight mass incarceration: every donation made [went] to the Equal Justice Initiative, a criminal justice group in Montgomery, Alabama" (Jones, 2015); she even hosted a competition leading up to the tournament where a lucky fan would be able to attend the tournament, meet Serena, and watch her practice. By mining a positive angle from her return, Serena has become a rare modern-day superstar athlete willing to highlight the immorality of mass incarcerations, wrongful convictions and unstable policing still prevalent in America (Jones, 2015). Serena was warmly welcomed back at Indian Wells and won the tournament in her return to the venue fourteen years later. Venus Williams, after seeing the warm reception her sister received, decided to end her boycott of Indian Wells one year later.

An NBA Owner's Racism Caught on Tape (2014)

In April 2014, then NBA Clippers owner, Donald Sterling, was heard via leaked audio tape making racist remarks in a conversation with his half-Black, half-Latina girlfriend. The racist remarks were not directed at the girlfriend, but rather at the Black men—namely Black male athletes—she had been posting pictures of herself alongside of on Instagram. The incident led to a week of national discussions in the U.S. media about sports and race, along with visual protestation from the Clippers players and a lot of public outcry against Donald Sterling's comments. At the time, Donald Sterling's net worth was an "estimated $1.9 billion—making him, according to Forbes, the 972nd richest person in the world" (Yglesias, 2015). So what happened when one of the wealthiest White men in the world, who also happens to own a predominantly Black-identifying NBA team, gets outed in his racism toward Black male athletes? The short answer: unprecedented institutional response to a race and sports-related controversy.

Donald Sterling, the man, had been able to dodge previous "significant" repercussions for his racist personal actions and behaviors due to his financial power before April 2014. Sterling faced lawsuits in 2004, 2006, and 2009 all related to discrimination. In the 2004 and 2006 lawsuits, Sterling paid millions of dollars to settle the suits. The 2009 lawsuit involved Hall of Fame basketball player Elgin Baylor. At the time of the lawsuit, Elgin Baylor had been recently terminated as general manager of the Clippers organization and Baylor felt strongly that his termination had been made on the basis of race and age. Baylor alleged that for years before his 2008 resignation, Sterling had frozen his salary at $350,000 per year for racial reasons...[and] that Sterling had a "pervasive and ongoing racist attitude" while negotiating with African American players, once telling Baylor that he wanted a team made up of "poor black boys from the South and a white head coach" (Yglesias, 2015). Eventually, Elgin Baylor dropped the allegations related to race in the lawsuit, and in 2011, a jury ruled in favor of Sterling.

Roughly three years later, on April 24, 2014, the celebrity and entertainment news network, *TMZ*, released the recording of a conversation with his bi-racial girlfriend that reportedly took place on April 9, 2014. The following racist comments were said by Sterling in the audio recording:

> "It bothers me a lot that you want to broadcast that you're associating with black people. Do you have to?"
> "I'm just saying, in your lousy f— Instagrams, you don't have to have yourself with, walking with black people."
> "You can sleep with [black men]. You can bring them in, you can do whatever you want.
> The little I ask you is not to promote it on that . . . and not to bring them to my games."
> "Don't put him [Magic Johnson] on an Instagram for the world to have to see so they have to call me. And don't bring him to my games." (Spears, 2019)

If the racism in Sterling's comments isn't obvious at first glance, consider that this is the owner of a professional sports team whose employees—players, coaches and staff—are predominantly Black, and he's asking another person to disassociate with Black *people* as *people* publicly. Sterling has given permission for "sleeping [read: sex] with" Black men in private, but not "to broadcast . . . associating with black people" in a public way via social media or in person at the very basketball games he makes major profits off from Black male athletes. The comments that Donald Sterling made in the audio recording make it clear that there's a difference in the way he views and values Black male athletes: valuable athletes to profit from, worthless people to be associated with.

What made matters even more publicly controversial for Sterling was the timing of the audio release. The Los Angeles Clippers were in the middle of pursuing an NBA title as the number-three seed in the 2014 Western Conference playoffs. The Clippers were facing the Golden State Warriors in the first round and had earned a 2–1 lead in the series before the news of Sterling's comments were released. The reality of the situation was not shared with African American coach of the Clippers, Doc Rivers. In an interview for *The Undefeated* five years after the Sterling controversy, Rivers reflected on how the news was communicated to him: "I was misled in that whole thing . . . I was told there was a story coming out and it wasn't a big deal beforehand. I had a chance two days before to look at it. But they told me it wasn't a big deal" (Spears, 2019).

Understandably, Rivers and the majority of the Clippers players were infuriated by Sterling's comments. Other members of the team were annoyed, yet unsurprised at the overt racism of Sterling despite his being the team owner. For example, former NBA player Matt Barnes recalls, "As far as the racial comments, I've heard much worse and have had worse done to me, so it wasn't that big of a deal. I thought he wasn't the only owner that felt that way. He was just the only one dumb enough to get caught saying it" (Spears, 2019). Despite varied reactions, the team agreed on two things: they'd trust unified communication and messaging to go through Doc Rivers; and whatever action (or inaction) they decided to take would also be unified.

The Clippers team decided they wouldn't boycott the game, but that they did want to protest in some other visual way. As the team took the court in Game 4 on April 27 at Golden State's arena, they appeared with their shirts inside out and proceeded to warm up in seemingly generic red shirts. When it was time to start the game, the Clippers removed their shooting shirts and dumped them near center court. The Clippers' blue jerseys said "Los Angeles" on the front, and the players wore black socks and arm bands in protest of Donald Sterling (Spears, 2019). The Clippers lost to Golden State in Game 4 and tensions continued to build up to the fifth game on April 29. The NBA Players Association, whose president also happened to be the star player of the Clippers (Chris Paul), along with other current and former NBA players, and even then-president of the United States Barack Obama publicly expressed support for the Clippers players and condemnation for its team owner. Promptly, the call to punish Donald Sterling and hold him accountable for his words was being made emphatically to NBA Commissioner Adam Silver.

Well before game time on April 29, Adam Silver, in his very first year in the role of commissioner, handed a lifetime ban to Los Angeles Clippers owner Donald Sterling. Mr. Sterling was also fined $2.5 million—the largest amount that league bylaws would allow but a small percentage of his estimated $1.9 billion fortune (Branch, 2014). An unprecedented form of punishment forced onto Sterling by the NBA organization, however, came a month later when the NBA owners gave the needed vote to force Sterling to sell the team. The NBA organization's response was harsh and seemed to be exactly what Sterling's critics hoped for. With rumors of both the Clippers and the Warriors players refusing to play game five earlier in the day, Adam Silver's announcement kept the NBA playoffs to its regularly scheduled program. Additionally, the move to vote Sterling out of NBA ownership made significant history among a U.S. professional sports industry with previous racial incidents that did not result in loss of ownership:

> George Steinbrenner, the Yankees' principal owner, was given a lifetime ban from the day-to-day operations of his team in 1990 for conspiring with a gambler in an effort to defame Dave Winfield, a [African American] Yankees player. But Mr. Steinbrenner was not forced to relinquish his ownership of the team, and he was reinstated three years later. In 1993, Major League Baseball suspended the Cincinnati Reds owner Marge Schott from the day-to-day operation of the team for one year and fined her $25,000 for using racial slurs towards employees and making anti-Semitic remarks. (Branch, 2014)

The swiftness of the response and problem solving from the NBA Commissioners and owners has established a new level of expectation in terms of punishment for any professional sports team owner caught in similar discriminatory controversy. Former Microsoft chief executive Steve Ballmer won a bidding war for ownership on May 29, 2014. Of the 2014–2015 Clippers team, only coach Doc Rivers still remains a part of the organization (there have been retirements and trades) and he'll be the first to confirm the improved quality of the Clippers organization and his professional relationship with Ballmer.

University of Missouri Football Team Boycotts Football (2015)

Like many predominantly white college institutions that also have big time NCAA football programs, the racial demographics of the University of Missouri football team in 2015–2016 differed greatly from the university as a whole. Missouri's campus in 2015–2016 was 77 percent White and 7 percent Black; 69 percent of the school's scholarship football players were Black compared to 48 percent of the team as a whole (SI Staff, 2016). And again, like many predominantly White college institutions that also have big time NCAA football programs, the University of Missouri had racial issues unrelated to the playing fields and courts. That fall, a number of incidents were reported including "repeated racial slurs, and an alleged swastika of feces was smeared on a building, but none of the campus incidents targeted football players directly" (SI Staff, 2016). One graduate student named Jonathan Butler caught the attention of some of the Black football players when he began a hunger strike in the first week of November 2015. Once the football team got involved, the campus controversy became national news.

A campus group called Concerned Student 1950 formed to raise awareness about race on the predominantly white Missouri campus. Butler, a member of the Concerned Student 1950 group, vowed to maintain his hunger strike until

University of Missouri system president Tim Wolfe resigned. Concerned students felt administrative response to their concerns was apathetic at best, and Butler decided to use the form of nonviolent protest to push the issues they were concerned with. Concerned Student 1950 put forth a list of demands asking for a number of initiatives related to racial awareness and inclusion that they hoped the university would adopt (SI Staff, 2016). Four days after Butler's hunger strike began, several football players prompted a team meeting. Some of the players knew Butler and other members of the Concerned Student 1950 faction; during the team meeting, more than thirty players announced they would boycott all football activities until Butler ate:

> The Legion of Black Collegians, which administers campus groups that primarily serve black students, posted a photograph to Twitter on Saturday night of more than 30 football players linked in arms with a graduate student who is staging a hunger strike. "The athletes of color on the University of Missouri football team truly believe 'injustice anywhere is a threat to justice everywhere,'" a message accompanying the photo said, quoting a line from the Rev. Dr. Martin Luther King Jr. (Southall and Tracy, 2015)

By the next day, the protesting players were publicly supported by their coaching staff and many of their white teammates.

The involvement of the football team in the protest drastically affected the timing of the administrative response. Suddenly, meetings were being scheduled and public statements were being released. The involvement of the football team had the potential to cost the university in reputation and finances. With an upcoming game scheduled for Saturday, November 14 against Brigham Young University that, if forfeited, would result in Missouri being "required to pay $1 million to B.Y.U." (Southall and Tracy, 2015). Missouri administration had to expedite a response and solution:

> Within hours of the announcement of the boycott, public opinion was divided on the players' actions; for every message of support for using their platform to spur change, there was another criticizing the men for acting beyond the scope of their (unpaid) jobs. . . . That Monday, not hours after the team's boycott began, Wolfe resigned, ending Butler's hunger strike. (SI Staff, 2016)

It's unsubstantiated whether the potential financial athletic impact played a factor in Wolfe's resignation announcement. Wolfe himself cites a desire to avoid any violence that could have erupted on campus as the fuel for his choice to resign. Yet, the athletic reputation of Missouri football locally and publicly, was not suddenly "back to normal" with Wolfe's resignation.

While Missouri football players received much praise for taking a stand and did receive support from coaching staff, teammates, and even public officials, the players also saw a backlash. Some people wanted the protesting players' scholarships to be revoked, and there's reason to speculate whether internal university administrators really agreed on head coach Gary Pinkel's decision to support his players' protest involvement. In an interview with *Sports Illustrated* staff a year after the protest, former Missouri team safety Ian Simon reflected on the backlash Pinkel received:

> "It was so hard," Simon says of watching fans turn on Pinkel. "I honestly kind of felt like I let coach Pinkel down because of all the negative feedback he was getting. Talk about [taking Missouri] from the bottom to the top. This man took us to SEC championship games. This man has done so much for this university and this state, and to see people turn on him because he was supporting his players, it really hurt me." (SI Staff, 2016)

In the same *Sports Illustrated* article, former president Wolfe amplifies Simon's sentiments, and goes on to implicate—on record—the University of Missouri board of curators of forcing Pinkel's fate. Pinkel planned to coach the rest of the season before announcing his retirement . . . "then the board leaked that he had cancer," Wolfe said (SI Staff, 2016). Instead of announcing his own diagnosis to his players after the season, suddenly Gary Pinkel was announcing his retirement and diagnosis with lymphoma to everyone twenty-four hours before the kickoff against B.Y.U. Pinkel finished out the season and was later replaced by former Missouri linebacker and defensive coordinator, Barry Odum, finishing the season with an overall record of 5–7.

The controversy at the University of Missouri had shown what successful protest looks like today for athletes, as well as caused an important conversation about race and college athletics. The football players of the Missouri 2015–2016 season stood united in a cause and remained resolute to see it through. The players ceased their boycott, as promised, once Butler ended his hunger strike and went back to focusing on football. The boycott validated the notion that "universities can't count on their most prominent and powerful students to hide behind their helmets, and athletes now have a precedent for how to spur change as well as an idea of the risks they run in doing so" (Staff, 2016). If any students were nervous about their level of power against a university or even the NCAA, the University of Missouri football team has shown that there's power in unification for a cause.

Nike Supporting Colin Kaepernick and Black Lives Matter (2018)

To honor the thirtieth anniversary of their "Just Do It" campaign, the athletic brand Nike aligned itself with a controversial athlete of color. In 2018, Nike revealed Colin Kaepernick, the polarizing former National Football League (NFL) quarterback, as the face of the "Just Do It" marketing campaign. As a result of their alignment with Kaepernick, Nike has received praise and contempt from their buyers. The quote associated with the thirtieth anniversary "Just Do It" marketing campaign and Kaepernick's image is: "Believe in something, even if it means sacrificing everything." This particular controversy related to race and the sports industry is important because Nike is an athletic brand and company that makes deals with athletes *and* sports organizations; it's unclear whether their hearts are at the center of their decision to align with Kaepernick or just potential profit.

Within the past few decades, Nike has, at times, backed controversial athletes of color and made efforts in taking a stand for the initiatives and causes of people of color. Masters at marketing, and with a brand purpose clearly stating their intentions with regards to equality, this latest rebellious and irreverent move is more of the same from Nike, and beyond the message they're projecting, a clever positioning move, especially given their target demographic (Coulman, 2018). This "target demographic" Nike markets to is young people and always has been. It's youth that keep Nike, as a global brand, relevant, and the majority of American youth are identifying with the liberal and antioppression agenda that Colin Kaepernick continues to push while seemingly blackballed from the NFL. Nearly two-thirds of individuals who wear Nike in the United States are under thirty-five years old, and are much more racially diverse than the baby boomer population, said Matt Powell, a sports industry analyst at the NPD Group (Draper et al., 2018). The timing of the partnership between Nike and Kaepernick—which was announced with a tweet by Kaepernick himself—immediately sent young, liberal audiences cheering Nike for its validation of Kaepernick and those suffering from racialized marginalization and oppression. In less than three days after the launch, "the brand benefitted from over 2.7 million mentions online" (Coulman, 2018), although not all of the mentions were positive.

The timing of the "Just Do It" thirtieth anniversary campaign launch partnership also caught the NFL and many industry veterans off guard. Nike waited over a year to decide to use Kaepernick in any of its marketing campaigns despite his being under contract with the brand since 2011. With all of the controversy around Kaepernick, the majority of the sports industry likely assumed Nike was prudently ignoring him altogether. Yet, it could be argued that Nike was simply calculating the timing of the campaign so the company could benefit most financially with minimal backlash:

> The new partnership comes months after Nike extended its agreement with the N.F.L. to provide on-field uniforms for all 32 of the league's teams. On Monday, when asked if Nike had informed the N.F.L. about the campaign beforehand, a Nike spokeswoman said that "Colin is not currently employed by an N.F. L. team and has no contractual obligation to the N.F.L." (Draper et al., 2018)

With Kaepernick no longer being employed by the NFL, Nike did not have any legal obligation to inform the NFL of its plan to feature Kaepernick as the face of its "Just Do It" anniversary campaign. However, Nike put the NFL in a legal position to honor its agreement with the global brand to have every professional football team don a uniform with the iconic Nike "swoosh" on it. Any confrontation with Nike about the new campaign from the NFL would actually have amplified Kaepernick's lawsuit allegations that the NFL owners conspired to blackball him from the league. Thus, the league's response was to avoid addressing the campaign directly. Instead, the NFL released a statement that said, "The social justice issues that Colin and other professional athletes have raised deserve our attention and action" (Draper et al., 2018).

The NFL would have to let the public dissent come from the politically conservative, that still equate Colin Kaepernick with disrespect for police and military, and an overall lack of patriotism. Much like rapid responses of support for the Nike brand, there also came rapid backlash. On Twitter, more than 100,000 posts in the first 24 hours included the hashtag #BoycottNike

(Draper et al., 2018). In addition to tweets, some Americans took to social media, posting videos and photos of burning and cut up Nike apparel. U.S. President Donald Trump once again took to disparaging Colin Kaepernick—as he did back in 2016 when Kaepernick began kneeling—and Nike's decision to make Kaepernick the central face of its "Just Do It" campaign.

Aside from vocal backlash and the symbolic destruction of some Nike apparel, the *financial* backlash towards Nike was minimal in comparison to the financial gains Nike has received from its Kaepernick ad campaign. On the day after the marketing campaign release, shares of Nike "were down $2.60, or more than 3 percent" (Draper et al., 2018), but over the weeks that followed, Nike saved millions in marketing and made billions in profit:

> According to CBS, Nike's stock [had seen] a 5 percent increase since Labor Day—the day it revealed that Kaepernick, the former quarterback for the San Francisco 49ers, was the star of company's 30th-anniversary "Just Do It" campaign . . . the $6 billion increase in overall value that Nike has experienced since Labor Day clearly overshadows [#boycottNike] efforts. (Abad-Santos, 2018)

Colin Kaepernick has also financially benefited from the Nike campaign, with his deal reportedly being worth millions and "his message carried globally, taking a stand for all the people impacted by racial oppression his initial sacrifice now stands for, and most essentially, the mindsets it helps shift" (Coulman, 2018). Nike has certainly delivered in its support of an athlete of color through providing financial gain and amplified messaging, but what remains problematic is their solution to also continue to do business with the professional sports organization that Kaepernick feels blackballed by. Nike is successfully profiting financially and morally through "playing both sides" of the Kaepernick controversy. Kaepernick is a retailer's force—his jerseys are still one of the most popular among customers, even though he hasn't played in the NFL for over three years—and the NFL is contractually linked to the Nike brand through 2028. Nike is very comfortable, regardless of their motive for the thirtieth anniversary "Just Do It" campaign.

Jay-Z Partners with the NFL (2019)

In the years that have passed since Colin Kaepernick began kneeling in August 2016, a number of his supporters remain celebrities: actors, musicians, politicians, and fellow athletes. Support of Kaepernick by a number of musicians has been quite powerful, as certain musicians have very publicly turned down paid gigs at NFL events like the Super Bowl. One musician in particular that showed strong support for Kaepernick and his cause is Shawn Carter, known in the hip-hop and popular culture realms of society as Jay-Z. When Jay-Z performed on "Saturday Night Live" in 2017, he wore a customized version of Kaepernick's 49ers jersey (Belson, 2019). He also joined fellow Black music artists Rihanna and Cardi B. in declining to perform at the Super Bowl and boldly rapped in his June 2018 hit song "Apeshit," "I said no to the Super Bowl/you need me, I don't need you."

Thus, it came as a true surprise a little over a year later on August 13, 2019, when it was announced that the NFL had entered a partnership with Roc Nation, the entertainment company created and led by Jay-Z. According to the NFL's announcement, Roc Nation will "advise on selecting artist for major NFL performances like the Super Bowl . . . [and] play an important role in the NFL's recently launched 'Inspire Change' initiative" (Lockhart, 2019). The "Inspire Change" initiative—a collaboration between the NFL Players Coalition and the league—focuses on criminal justice reform, education and economic advancement, and police and community relations. The positive potential of the partnership for nationwide communities with NFL teams is immediately recognized by some. Jay-Z has supported numerous social justice causes that seek to address police brutality, racial profiling, and the punitive probation system. Jay-Z is responsible for the executive production of two documentary miniseries about deceased young Black males, Kalief Browder and Trayvon Martin, and is a co-founding member of the REFORM Alliance, an organization that seeks to limit the number of people serving unfair parole and probation sentences, Thus, some are confident that perhaps "Jay-Z is playing the long game . . . seeking an ownership stake of an NFL team as evidence that the deal will somehow lead to something bigger" (Lockhart, 2019) and more valuable for all Black people in and out of the sporting world.

However, it has been Jay-Z's public change-of-tune about Colin Kaepernick and kneeling, as well as what appears to be a lack of sound research on the inner-workings of the NFL, that has some feeling Jay-Z's partnership is a duplicitous method to simply financially capitalize off Kaepernick's protest. During a January 2018 CNN interview, Jay-Z referred to Kaepernick as an "iconic figure" and compared him to prolific boxer and activist, Muhammad Ali. Then, in an August 2019 interview a day after the NFL and Roc Nation partnership was announced, Jay-Z completely shifted his view, sparking criticism from many:

> "I think we have moved past kneeling," Jay-Z said when asked a hypothetical question about whether he would kneel during the anthem if he were an athlete. "I think it's time to go into actionable items." That ignited criticism from the African-American community, and from Kaepernick's allies in the N.F.L., including his former teammate Eric Reid, who has also knelt through the anthem. (Belson, 2019)

Jay-Z also made reference to his choice being related to a belief that he—and all Black people—have to decide to either help millions of people *or* get stalled on Colin Kaepernick still being unemployed with the NFL. Eric Reid made a point to post on Twitter responding to the notion of choice and posted: "These [actions to help millions or continuing to support Kaepernick] aren't mutually exclusive. They can both happen at the same time! It looks like your goal was to make millions and millions of dollars by assisting the NFL in burying Colin's career" (Bieler, 2019b). Reid's claim that Jay-Z's goal "was to make millions and millions" doesn't seem particularly off base, as the rapper is a billionaire who openly and often raps about money and his growing entrepreneurial endeavors.

Of course, the NFL plays a significant role in this controversial partnership as well. *Should* the NFL as an organization be deeply committed to social and racial justice? Absolutely; its professional athlete employees overwhelmingly identify, racially, as Black. Yet, the NFL's leadership has consistently continued to make choices that exude racism and silencing social justice causes:

[T]he fact that several NFL owners are prominent donors and supporters of President Donald Trump—who has repeatedly attacked Kaepernick and other kneeling NFL players, framing their protest against injustice as unpatriotic—has led to arguments that the league cares more about pleasing the president and his supporters than the predominantly black group of players who sought to highlight injustice. (Lockhart, 2019)

In addition to some NFL owners being "prominent donors and supporters" of a President who openly "attacked" the NFL's protesting players, the NFL has a need to bolster their reputation after settling the two lawsuits from Kaepernick and Reid in February 2019. The fact that the NFL settled an undisclosed amount of dollars in two legal settlements that alleged their owners had "colluded to keep [Kaepernick] off the field" (Lockhart, 2019) doesn't exactly project innocence against Kaepernick and Reid's claims against the league. A partnership with one of the most—if not the most—revered Black rapper and entrepreneur alive, however, most certainly establishes a strong barrier against continued claims that the NFL isn't act-ing in support of social justice issues that affect its players and large segment of its fan base.

In the months that have passed since the NFL announced the partnership with Roc Nation, it's unclear which organi-zation is benefitting the most from the partnership. In many ways, Jay-Z and Roc Nation has become a diversion against the fact that Kaepernick still remains unemployed. For example, when it was reported that Jay-Z and NFL officials had spo-ken to Kaepernick before the Roc Nation deal and that claim was "denied by the ex-quarterback's girlfriend, radio personal-ity Nessa Diab" (Bieler, 2019b), criticism was mostly hurled at Jay-Z. Then, less than a month later, when Roc Nation and the NFL announced a joint $400,000 donation split between two Chicago nonprofit organizations, a concerned citizen did further research into one of the nonprofit organizations and unearthed troubling imagery and information:

> A Twitter user named Resist Programming quickly un-earthed numerous controversial tweets from the ac-count [of Crushers Club], including two 2016 posts that showed photos of the group's founder, a white woman named Sally Hazelgrove, cutting the locs of two different boys involved in the organization. (Lockhart, 2019)

The Crushers Club runs boxing, leadership and music pro-grams to support one of Chicago's most disadvantaged neigh-borhoods. The uncovered images and posts from Hazelgrove, which also included a tweet in support of Donald Trump, led to increased criticism of the NFL and Roc Nation. With the continued scrutiny, the perception about and respect granted to the NFL and Jay-Z seem to be reliant on the fate of Colin Kaepernick.

In mid-November 2019, Colin Kaepernick attended a pri-vate workout with several NFL teams in attendance. Alleg-edly, "Roger Goodell and Jay-Z both wanted Kaepernick to at least get a chance to try out for a team" (Belson, 2019), but it's unclear whether that claim is genuine or not. For Goodell and the NFL, the tryout for Kaepernick helps to show that there's a chance Kaepernick could return to the NFL and quell continued backlash toward the NFL. By helping Kaepernick get a tryout with the NFL, Jay-Z is hoping to help resolve the contentious issues surrounding the quarterback's absence from the league, according to a person with knowledge of the entertainer's thinking (Belson, 2019). As of December 2019, there has been no report of Kaepernick being contacted by any NFL team that saw him. For now, the controversy surrounding Kaepernick's protest and the partnership between Roc Nation and the NFL has encountered a mostly failed solution.

Discussing the Solutions: Race and the Sports Industry

In the abbreviated snapshot of controversies and problems offered above that have occurred with relation to Race and the Sports Industry, it becomes apparent that money, power, and reputation are incredibly important when it comes to race and the sports industry. Whether at the college, professional, or wider industry level, some combination of money, power, and reputation plays a role in the pace of positive progress in the experience of athletes of color in the sports industry. This claim is best understood through Derrick Bell's interest-convergence principle:

> [I]nterest-convergence principle posits that White elites will tolerate and support the advancement of racial minority interests, but particularly when doing so promotes their own self-interests, and renders substantial and disproportionate outcomes in their favor (e.g., financial gain and positive image). (Hawkins et al., 2017)

When the interest-convergence principle is combined with race and sports industry, one can see how the whites in power within various realms of the sporting industry—university administration, coaches, and the NCAA; professional sports organizations like MLB and the NFL; and sports companies like Nike—have made choices to "support the advancement of racial minority interests" most willingly when "doing so promotes their own self-interests."

At the college level, in the cases of NYU's Leonard Bates and Harvard's Lucien Alexis Jr., there were nuances between student reaction/accusations that caused a difference in the way each institution responded publicly to sustain their reputations and self-interests. With Leonard Bates, protesting students outright accused the school of racism and the school administration responded defensively to those claims, metaphorically "throwing Bates under the bus" and suspending several students who refused to willingly back down against the powerful institution with their claims of racism. Alternatively, the protesting students at Harvard crafted a petition that was clever in its wording, expressing "the belief that the University's action was the result of an over-hasty decision rather than a sanction of Jim Crowism," which gave the powerful institution the benefit of the doubt about racism rather than overtly accusing it of racism.

In the collegiate-level cases of the Syracuse 8 and the most recent protest by the University of Missouri football players, administration made choices to support the advancement of its Black athletes based on reputation or money and not necessarily on moral ethics regarding race. With Syracuse's history as being one of the pioneering universities in integrating its football team (e.g., players Ernie Davis and Jim Brown), it was strategically intelligent for university officials to decide to allow all nine of the protesting Black players on the team to keep their scholarships and enrollment in the institution. A decision to kick the players out of the university completely would tarnish Syracuse's reputation and likely bring more public attention to its race relations and athletics department practices. Similarly, if the University of Missouri had decided to punish its football team, it would only reinforce what the initial hunger strike had been all about: a significant population of the student body feeling as though the University of Missouri doesn't handle racial incidents well.

One can also see how the dissolution of the unofficial quota system once accepted among colleges regarding how many Black players could be on the field or court has helped shift the power dynamic toward a more balanced one between athletes of color and administrators. The protesting Syracuse players were small in number and not "significant" enough in playing time to truly disrupt the team's ability to continue the season; there was no reason for their White teammates to step up and support them—even if that support were to stem from the desire to win or avoid forfeit of football games. Without a unified stance from the team as a whole, the fear of a powerful, usually majority or completely white administration, can keep players in silence.

New York Times sportswriter, William Rhoden, wrote about why Black players in the NFL are afraid to speak out about racial issues, stating, "In an industry without guaranteed contracts, where one misspoken word can result in removal without explanation, players think long and hard before saying something management may construe as impudent" (Wiggins and Miller, 2005). While Rhoden is talking about a professional sports league, a similar argument can be made about the NCAA, where scholarships and playing time can be easily taken away when people in power feel players are not being compliant with expectations set by coaches, athletic departments and university administrators. The lonesome fight of Curt Flood is also an example of a case where, had more MLB players—regardless of skin color—been unafraid of speaking out against the reserve clause, an amazing athlete of color could have continued to have an outstanding athletic career *and* pushed the sports industry toward a more balanced power structure. The University of Missouri football players, in their unified stance, shifted the power structure to one in which the athletes controlled what would happen monetarily.

The unified stance of a majority Black Missouri football team and the controversy around Venus and Serena Williams at Indian Wells tennis tournament, exemplify how unity and superstar status can also work to shift power in sport from whites to athletes of color. The sheer number of Black football players on the University of Missouri team meant an ultimatum for school administrators: pay one million dollars to BYU or give Jonathan Butler at least some of what he wants so that he eats again and the football team can continue to bring *in* millions of dollars to the university. While the Williams sisters were also unified in their protest of Indian Wells, it's their athletic superstardom that proved just as, if not more, powerful against the majority white tennis world. If Venus and Serena did not take control of their own narrative and remain true to their politics in the controversy, they would have likely been used. David Zirin discusses the predicament of famous athletes of color in the film *Race, Power, and American Sports*:

> DAVE ZIRIN: [P]eople who are famous, if you don't take control of your own politics and your own identity, you're going to be used. You're going to be used to further whatever the aims and needs are of what I call the "Athletic Industrial Complex"—this multibillion dollar global industry. (Young et al., 2013)

Serena Williams, specifically, ensured that it would be her own "aims and needs" that would be met in ending her protest of the Indian Wells tournament and returning to the competition. And with their strength, the Williams sisters were able to put the WTA in a position of reputational damage if they actually forced the sisters to pay a fine after an alleged racial incident occurred at a WTA event.

With the most recent controversies involving Nike and Colin Kaepernick, along with the complicating partnership between

Jay-Z's Roc Nation and the NFL, one can see what some of the needs of Zirin's description of the Athletic Industrial Complex are when solving controversies: money and staying relevant. Consumers of athletic brands like Nike are put in a tough spot if they cannot separate sport from politics. Anyone who is truly dissenting against Nike shouldn't ever put on any apparel that the company has made for the NFL—this includes their apparel line dedicated to military veterans, too. Nike is a very visible sign of the profitability in the sports industry's hypocrisy of crafting of rules and regulations that attempt to keep personal politics out of sport while also "forcing" athletes to participate in political endeavors (e.g., visiting the White House after a professional championship; playing the national anthem; and team community service endeavors aligned with local politicians). Nike is a company that has been able to profit off race and sport regardless of sides of the issue. Meanwhile, the NFL has put itself in a position where it's at risk of losing valuable future fans and investors in its product of American professional football for its alleged racism. Therefore, its solution to partner with Roc Nation is one with enough social capital to keep hope alive for young fans that the NFL does seek to do better by its athletes of color and support social justice issues affecting marginalized populations. However, the fact that one of the wide receivers that Kaepernick asked to catch for him during the lone workout he's had for the league has been signed to the NFL's Washington, D.C., squad's practice team again amplifies Kaepernick's claims of being blackballed from the NFL. Americans should expect to see Kaepernick's supporters to remain resolve in their criticism of the NFL and Jay-Z until Kaepernick gets another shot to end his professional football career on his own terms.

The fact that so many professional athletes' closest advisers are not people of color means that they're often never around people of color modeling leadership, "a situation that undermines their own ability to become leaders, rather than pampered, passive followers" (Rhoden, 2006, 193). The controversy surrounding Donald Sterling exemplifies how perverse racist white people in leadership positions in professional sports can be when left unchecked systemically. Fortunately, the NBA as an organization was willing to administer its harshest punishment possible to Donald Sterling for his racist remarks. Any other solution offered in the Donald Sterling case would likely have resulted in further protestation, certainly the league losing millions of dollars, and damaging the NBA's reputation. The relationship between race and the sports industry is one that will ultimately continue to be fraught unless more attention is paid to putting people of color in leadership positions in the various sectors of the sports industry. Solutions should arise to controversies related to race and racism based on achieving equity in the sports industry, rather than on institutions and organizations maintaining reputation, power, and profit.

Race, Sports, and Representation

The lack of representation of people of color in leadership positions within the sports industry is an issue that ultimately affects the development of problems and controversies related to race, sports, and representation. The problems and controversies related to different racial groups involved in sport that have occurred in the last decade or so often relate to situations where the Whites in power within the sports industry do not view athletes of color as being connected to the racial groups these athletes identify with. When racialized incidents happen in U.S. society that do not have anything to do with sport, the expectation is for athletes of color to remain silent because the incident doesn't have to do with sport. On the other hand, citizens of color look to these athletes of color to be a public voice of support for the issues that plague people of color in the United States. Some of these controversies deal with social movements, and others are about ensuring that light is shed on the lack of understanding around various racial identities and histories in the United States.

Black Lives Matter and Protesting the Killings of Unarmed Black People (2012–2016)

In 2013, the social justice movement Black Lives Matter was born out of the acquittal of a man named George Zimmerman. Zimmerman had been on trial for killing an unarmed Black teenager named Trayvon Martin in 2012. The events leading up to Zimmerman shooting Martin had everything to do with race and racism. As the country began to divide over the incident as the investigation ensued, celebrities—including athletes—began to speak out on the killing of Trayvon Martin. Martin was killed on February 26 in Sanford, Florida, and had been wearing a hooded sweatshirt that night. Martin's hooded sweatshirt was used by some media outlets as a defense against claims of racism on Zimmerman's part, as though anyone in a hooded sweatshirt should be viewed as dangerous. The NBA's Miami Heat took particular offense to this narrative and took action via social media:

> Led by [LeBron] James and Dwayne Wade, several members of the Miami Heat posed together for a photo in hooded sweatshirts. . . . Their heads were bowed. Their faces were hidden. (Hill, 2012)

The hashtag that accompanied James's Twitter photo was "We are Trayvon Martin," a clear response to the biased remarks Zimmerman had made during a call with a 911 operator the night he shot Martin. Zimmerman, just by simply looking at Martin, decided that Martin "looks like he's up to no good, or he's on drugs or something" (Hill, 2012). Does looking like someone "up to no good" automatically look like a Black male in a hoodie?

So many Black athletes, especially men, began speaking out on social media, and the NBA Players Association released a statement demanding Zimmerman's arrest. NFL players Ray Lewis, Jamaal Charles, and Justin Tuck and NBA players Carmelo Anthony, D. J. Augustin and Amare Stoudemire all publicly expressed their views. The investigation and eventual ruling on July 13, 2013, that George Zimmerman was not guilty for Martin's death took over a year. In an article written one day after the verdict for *The Nation*, sports journalist Dave Zirin noticed and analyzed something in his observation of athlete response to the Zimmerman verdict:

> [I]nterestingly, even though there are a lot of right-wing athletes, I couldn't find evidence of the horrific gloating seen in the darkest recesses of social media, not to mention Zimmerman's defense attorney following the verdict. That speaks, in my mind, to the fact that even the most right-wing, white-survivalist, gun-loving player shares a more integrated existence in the locker room than many do in their daily lives. Once you see someone as a human being and not as an avatar of a predator, it's damn hard to accept the word of this jury that they are disposable. (Zirin, 2013)

Zirin alludes to the time that elapsed between Trayvon's death and Zimmerman's verdict potentially having created an environment for White and Black teammates to have conversations of understanding. Conversations where even "right-wing athletes" could see that Trayvon Martin was just as much "a human being and not an avatar of a predator" as their Black teammates. There were also no calls for or sanctions placed on any of the players who spoke out; after all, the players weren't refusing to continue with their jobs on the fields and courts.

No one, however, could have predicted the deaths of more unarmed Black people would come in what felt like days apart between July 2014 and September 2016. The difference between the losses of Black lives during this time period and Trayvon Martin, though, is that the persons ending the lives of these Black people were police officers. The killings of unarmed Black people that caught the most national attention were the ones where citizens who witnessed events recorded what occurred on cell phones. Michael Brown. Tamir Rice. John Crawford. Walter Scott. Freddie Grey. Alton Sterling. Philando Castile. These are only some of the names that passed through national news headlines and sparked more athlete activism connected to racial representation and the growing Black Lives Matter Movement.

The first athlete activist of the U.S. Black Lives Matter movement was a young Black Division III basketball player at Knox College named Ariyana Smith. On November 29, 2014, Smith chose to protest the killing of Michael Brown right before an away game in Clayton, Missouri against Fontbonne University. A little less than four months earlier, eighteen-year-old Michael Brown was shot to death by twenty-eight-year-old white police officer Darren Wilson in the city of Ferguson, Missouri. Just five days before Smith's protest, news broke that the St. Louis County grand jury had decided not to indict Darren Wilson. Protests erupted in Ferguson and other U.S. cities in response to the failure to indict decision. About a week and a half before the game scheduled against Fontbonne, Smith and her teammates were informed by the Knox athletic director that "your safety is all of our concern, and we're looking to see if we're going to reschedule the Fontbonne game at Knox, or whether we'll play at a neutral site so, we'll get back to you all" (Zirin, 2014). It was after that brief meeting that Smith actually looked up the distance between the cities of Clayton and Ferguson, Missouri: twenty minutes. Smith waited for the part where the athletic director would follow up with the team as stated, but that further conversation never happened. After being inspired by a friend who didn't stand during the playing of the national anthem at the game before Fontbonne, and with still no word from the Knox athletic department, Smith arrived on the court of Fontbonne University in Clayton, Missouri, and did something:

> I raised my hand in the air, knelt at the flag and on the last line of the national anthem I collapsed to the ground, and I lay there for four and a half minutes. While I lay there

the trainer came over and tried to shake me and tried to get me to stand up. They were asking me if I was OK. My coach walked over and all she said to me was, "Ariyana, you need to move. The ref won't start the game until you move." After four and a half minutes, I stood and raised the black power salute. I held that for thirty seconds and continued to walk out of the gym with my fist still raised. (Zirin, 2014)

Smith chose four and half minutes to represent the four and a half hours that Michael Brown's body lay on the street before it was removed by authorities. While Smith's actions were silent, the gestures she utilized were symbolic, powerful, and forced everyone to pay attention whether they wanted to or not. The attention Smith received post-protest was mixed, and the punishment she received from Knox College was harsh.

Smith's coaches and teammates wouldn't really look at her after the game. She was called into a meeting with the Knox athletic director at 7:45 a.m. on the Monday after her game and told she was indefinitely suspended from athletic participation and would be contacted three days later. On her way to inform her teammates of the decision, Smith's head coach, Emily Cline, approached Smith and told her to leave immediately or she'd call security. Cline had Smith escorted out of the building. It was then that Smith's teammates began to step up in support of her:

[At the next game] they linked hands, raised them in the air, and they had my initials and my jersey number written on their wristbands. I mean, I think in all of this I was hoping that the attention wouldn't necessarily be on me. I'm just glad to see the larger collective action. I was hoping to spark larger collective action. (Zirin, 2014)

The action of Smith herself and the collective action of her teammates after her suspension caught the attention of the media.

Smith was ultimately reinstated on the team, and her suspension was rescinded—a decision Smith feels was only made due to the media. Smith elected not to return to the team at Knox because "it's just not a space to have to endure treatment from racists and people who have demonstrated that they don't care to learn about who you are and what struggles you face in life" (Zirin, 2014). Interestingly, Knox College was founded in 1837 in West Central Illinois by anti-slavery advocates from upstate New York and has been titled a "Freedom Station" by the National Underground Railroad Freedom Center.

One day after Ariyana Smith's protest at Fontbonne University, another act of protestation related to the killing of Michael Brown occurred, but this one was at the professional athlete level. On Sunday, November 30, 2014, the NFL's St. Louis Rams had a home game against the Oakland Raiders. As teams were being announced, "five members of the St. Louis Rams ran onto the field before their home game against the Oakland Raiders with their hands raised, a response to the killing of Brown, who was unarmed when he was shot" (Belson, 2014). At the league level, the choice of the players was supported, and the five Rams players were not disciplined by the NFL or their own team. The gesture was not well received, however, by the St. Louis Police Officers Association. The association called the players' actions "tasteless, offensive and inflammatory," and demanded that they be disciplined and the team and the NFL apologize (Belson, 2014). The St. Louis Rams' chief operating officer let the St. Louis County police chief know that he was regretful of any offense the officers may have taken, but didn't apologize for the actions themselves. The police officers association decided to interpret the Rams' "regret" as an apology and the nation moved on to the next news story.

The next news story related to killings of unarmed Black people and athlete protest came just a couple of weeks later on Sunday, December 14, 2014, in Cleveland, Ohio. NFL wide receiver, Andrew Hawkins, took the field for the Cleveland

Browns' matchup against the Cincinnati Bengals wearing a black shirt over his Browns uniform that read "Justice for Tamir Rice and John Crawford III" in white lettering. On August 5, 2014, John Crawford III was killed by police officers in a Beavercreek, Ohio, Walmart while holding a BB gun. In September 2014, it was announced that there would be no indictment charges against the officers, even though Crawford III was unarmed. Then, on November 26, 2014—three days before Ariyana Smith's protest—a video made national headlines. The video was of a twelve-year-old Black boy named Tamir Rice being shot to death by two police officers outside of the Cudell Recreation Center in Cleveland, Ohio, on November 22. Rice had been playing with a toy gun that did not have an orange cap on the end. The person who called 911 informed them multiple times that the gun was likely fake and that Rice was probably a juvenile; the police arrived on the scene, and one officer, Timothy Loehmann, immediately opened fire on Rice.

Similar to the conflict between the police association in St. Louis and the Rams, the president of the Cleveland Police Patrolmen's Association, Jeffrey Follmer, criticized Andrew Hawkins' decision to wear the shirt. Follmer stated, "It's pretty pathetic when athletes think they know the law. They should stick to what they do best on the field" (Cullinane, 2014). Follmer also called upon the Cleveland Browns organization to make a public apology, as it is Cleveland Police who protect and serve the stadium the team plays in.

The Cleveland Browns' vice president of communications tried to smooth things over with the police by stating how much respect the organization has for the Cleveland police. The Browns also made it clear that they were going to respect Hawkins'—and any other players'—"rights to project their support and bring awareness to issues that are important to them if done so in a responsible manner" (Cullinane, 2014). Hawkins took to responding individually to the comments made by president Follmer and Follmer's call for an apology, in a media statement the day after Hawkins' action. Some of what Hawkins shared in the statement was as follows:

> I was taught that justice is a right that every American should have. Also, justice should be the goal of every American. I think that's what makes this country. To me, justice means the innocent should be found innocent. It means that those who do wrong should get their due punishment. Ultimately, it means fair treatment. So a call for justice shouldn't offend or disrespect anybody. A call for justice shouldn't warrant an apology. To clarify, I utterly respect and appreciate every police officer that protects and serves all of us with honesty, integrity, and the right way. And I don't think those kind of officers should be offended by what I did. . . . I have family, close friends that are incredible police officers and I tell them all the time how they are much braver than me for it. So my wearing a T-shirt wasn't a stance against every police officer or every police department. My wearing the T-shirt was a stance against wrong individuals doing the wrong thing for the wrong reasons to innocent people . . . there are some not-so-good police officers that would assume the worst of me without knowing anything about me for reasons I can't control . . . they could potentially do me harm and most times without consequences. Those are the police officers that should be offended. . . . And the No. 1 reason for me wearing the T-shirt was the thought of what happened to Tamir Rice happening to my [son] scares the living hell out of me. And my heart was broken for the parents of Tamir and John Crawford knowing they had to live that nightmare of a reality. (Lopez, 2014)

Hawkins' statement gives some real perspective on the reality of being Black in America and navigating the police. Hawkins speaks against "wrong individuals doing the wrong thing for the wrong reasons to innocent people," and those wrong individuals are poorly trained police officers choosing to use lethal force because of what a Black suspect seems to represent in a police officers' psyche.

Black Americans are disproportionately likely to be stopped, arrested, and killed by police, according to the available, limited FBI data (Lopez, 2014). As more killings of unarmed Black people occurred, the strength and support for the Black Lives Matter Movement also increased. As the nation moved into the year 2015, the country saw new outrage as the names and stories of Freddie Gray (a twenty-five-year-old Black man who died of injuries while in police custody) and Walter Scott (a fifty-year-old Black man who was caught on camera being shot in the back to death by a police officer) passed through news headlines and social media hashtags. Then, in a seventy-two-hour span in July 2016, three more tragic events occurred involving police and the Black community that led to "one of the most united, persistent political statements in sports history" (Cauterucci, 2016). On July 5 in Baton Rouge, Louisiana, two White police officers shot Alton Sterling, a thirty-seven-year-old Black man, as they pinned him down. The very next day, in Falcon Heights, Minnesota, a thirty-two-year-old Black man named Philando Castile was pulled over and fatally shot by a St. Anthony, Minnesota police officer. Both shootings were highly controversial, as Alton Sterling's death was caught on a cellphone camera and Castile was shot in the car with his girlfriend and her young child in the backseat. Immediately after the shooting, Castile's girlfriend began livestreaming on social media about what happened, viewers literally watching him bleed out in real time. Then, on July 7, a Black, twenty-five-year-old military veteran named Micah Johnson ambushed and fired upon a group of Dallas police officers, seeking revenge for the latest killings of Black people—Castile and Sterling—killed by the police. Five police officers were killed, and nine others were injured.

Then, only July 9, 2016, members of the WNBA's Minnesota Lynx wore shirts to their game that said "Black Lives

Matter," "Change Starts with Us," "Justice and Accountability," the names of Alton Sterling and Philando Castile, and a picture of the Dallas police shield. The New York Liberty arrived at their game the next day wearing shirts that said "#BlackLives-Matter" and "#Dallas5." The WNBA's Indiana Fever and Phoenix Mercury did something similar in the following weeks. The WNBA as an organization did not support the change in athletic apparel, however. The WNBA issued fines to teams and individual players, but that didn't stop the momentum of the players' protestation:

> [T]he league fined the Fever, Liberty, and Mercury $5,000 each and fined each player on those teams $500 for wearing the black shirts. . . . Since the fines were announced, the players' protests have gathered steam and deeper consequence...The Liberty, Fever and Washington Mystics have all refused to answer reporters' post-game questions unless they relate to the Black Lives Matter movement or other social issues. (Cauterucci, 2016)

The WNBA hoped the fines would stop the protests, but the players on multiple WNBA teams used their collective power to pose an ultimatum to the WNBA: support the protesting players or endure continued media blackouts from the players. WNBA President Lisa Borders announced that the fines the league had imposed on the players and teams would be canceled and tweeted that the WNBA "appreciate our players expressing themselves on matters important to them" (Cauterucci, 2016). Despite WNBA players expressing their support of the Dallas police force, the police officers in Minneapolis were not supportive of the Lynx's actions. In fact, "four off-duty cops who were hired as arena security personnel left their posts" (Cauterucci, 2016) when the Lynx wore their shirts for the July 9 game. In time, the gestures of protest died down, and the WNBA organization and teams returned to their typical basketball-focused operation.

"Linsanity" and Beyond: Being Asian American in the NBA (2012–Present)

California native Jeremy Shu-How Lin signed with the NBA's New York Knicks on December 27, 2011. Initially, Lin played limited minutes for the Knicks, but in February 2012, Lin had an incredible run of play, helping to lead the Knicks to the 2012 NBA playoffs. The roughly one-month period where Lin was a part of the Knicks' starting lineup became known as the global phenomenon "Linsanity." Linsanity occurred partially because Lin had risen from a virtually unknown player from Harvard University to the breakout star of one of the most historically revered NBA franchises. The other major reason for Linsanity becoming a global phenomenon is Lin's racial identity; Lin is the first Taiwanese American player in NBA history. In the several years that have passed since Linsanity swept the globe, Lin has faded in his professional athletic successes, but he has grown more vocal in sharing his personal experiences as an Asian American athlete at various levels of play.

Lin speaks openly about racial bias in professional basketball, and his insights underscore stereotypes across the news media and among fans. Lin's presence in the NBA both challenged and affirmed the model minority myth and other stereotypes about Asian Americans. The model minority myth essentially posits that "through hard work and perseverance, Asian Americans supposedly show how any minority can overcome institutionalized inequality" (Leung, 2013). In some ways, this model minority myth works to uplift Asian Americans in certain realms of society (e.g., education, business, and family structure) while in other ways, it limits the richness of the Asian American experience:

> When research and portraits of Asian American are consistently framed this way, Asian Americans are almost always seen as superior to other minority groups in terms of educational achievement, economic stability, and social acceptance. . . . Popular culture has long portrayed Asian

American men as geniuses, overachievers, computer geeks, or nerds. They're shy and docile, humble and passive. If Asian American women are presented as exotic and hyper-sexualized, men are rendered effete, weak, and physically and sexually inferior. . . . Such representations leave Asian Americans to struggle against broad stereotypes that are as inaccurate as they are negative—especially in a culture that prizes traditional masculinity. (Leung, 2013, 54)

Though Jeremy Lin does fit the stereotype of the Asian American who has achieved educational achievement—or perhaps "overachievement" when one can see that the educational pedigree of the majority of NBA basketball players doesn't include an Ivy League institution—what Lin *destroys* of the Asian American male stereotype is of his alleged "weakness" and "physical inferiority." Lin is tough, aggressive, and tall.

Seeing Asians and Asian Americans playing basketball in the United States isn't some new phenomenon, but Lin is really the first professional basketball player to claim his Asian American heritage, directly confront the experience of social invisibility he experienced on his journey to stardom, *and* be acknowledged by his fans for uplifting Asian American identity. Similar to any athlete of color who has been one of the early "firsts" of their racial or ethnic group to achieve high athletic success in a sport, Lin experienced the pressure of representing the whole Asian race—not just Asian Americans or Taiwanese—and it was a journey to accept that burden. In a February 2019 interview with *The Undefeated* while playing for the Toronto Raptors (Lin's eighth team in nine seasons), Lin reflected on representing the Asian race:

At first it was something I ran from and really struggled with. Now I embrace it way more and am more equipped to handle it. I'm not perfect, but I kind of know who I want to be at this point in my career, so I keep trucking along and doing things the right way and stay above all the distractions. I've taken teammates to Taiwan and to China and they love it . . . they have a new appreciation for Asian culture, who I am, who we stand for. There's a deeper appreciation for it when you're on the ground and can see, feel and touch and don't rely on mainstream media to form their opinions. (Chow, 2019)

The Toronto Raptors would go on to win the NBA Championship in 2019, resulting in Jeremy Lin becoming the first Asian American to win an NBA title. Although Lin wasn't much of a contributor to the team arriving in the playoff finals or in the championship game itself, Lin still used his platform to uplift Asian and Asian American identity. Lin "arrived at the areas for every Raptors playoff game in apparel that celebrated Asian Pacific American Heritage Month" (Wong, 2019). His T-shirts said things like, "Phenomenally Asian" and "It's an Honor Just to Be Asian" and he wore clothes designed by Asian American designer, Phillip Lim.

Jeremy Lin is no longer in the NBA, but he still plays professional basketball overseas in the Chinese Basketball Association (CBA) for the Beijing Ducks organization. There's no telling if Lin will make another appearance in the NBA in the future—there is a chance, given how well he's playing in the CBA—but the impact Lin has made in representing and uplifting the presence of Asians and Asian Americans in the NBA is immeasurable. Lin is "an Asian-American who went undrafted in 2010, turned into a worldwide sensation in 2012 and became an N.B.A. champion in 2019" (Wong, 2019) and uplifted Asian racial and ethnic identities along his journey. As a representative of his race, Lin has grown comfortable in publicly confronting racial stereotypes and jokes, and he's "rooting for so many more Asians to come in [the NBA]" (Chow, 2019) to continue challenging everyone's viewpoints and perspectives about Asian people and their experiences. According to the Institute for Diversity and Ethics and Sport (TIDES) 2018 Racial and Gender Report Card, Asians constitute 0.6 percent of players in the league, 1.2 percent of assistant coaches, and 0.0 percent of head coaches (Lapchick, 2018). It will be interesting to see if those numbers have significantly increased a decade from now.

Racism and Contemporary Native American Athletes (2008–Present)

The controversy over the NFL's Washington, D.C., team name is one about racial representation of Native Americans. The problem is actually quite simplistic: the word "Redskins" is racist, so Native Americans don't want to see it on a jersey or have it be a source of profit when reproduced on team apparel. What's been controversial, however, is that the White owner of the Washington, D.C., NFL sports team, Dan Snyder, refuses to accept that his team's name is racist and therefore wouldn't change it freely. Although professional athletes of color tend to experience racism in the forms of upward mobility (e.g., coaching and ownership opportunities) rather than overt public acts of racism, "this stands in stark contrast to Native Americans who are confronted with racist names and mascots in many sports across the country" (Goodluck, 2019).

Dr. Richard Lapchick and his team at TIDES have reported a continued rise in racism within U.S. sports between 2014 and 2018, with Native American athletes and fans often being subjected to racist harassment. Yet, for Native Americans, the racism has been par for the course for its athletes since the early 2000s:

> From 2008 to 2018 there have been at least 52 reported incidents across the U.S. of racial harassment directed at Native American athletes, coaches and fans, according to data compiled from news articles, federal reports and court documents. . . . Reported incidents ranged from racist vandalism and tweets, to banners that read, "Hey Indians, get ready for a Trail of Tears Part 2," a reference to the 19th century death march endured by tribal

citizens who were illegally and forcibly relocated to Oklahoma by the U.S. government. Other instances include players being called names like "prairie nigger," "wagon burners" and "dirty Indians." Nearly all 52 reported incidents involved high school sports, but there were also four university game cases and even a fast food restaurant sign. . . . Nineteen incidents occurred at basketball games; 20 incidents were at football games. (Goodluck, 2019)

The fact that the majority of the reported incidents "involved high school sports" points to a problem of real miseducation—or complete absence of education—about Native American history and culture within American schools. The inclusion of Native American history in U.S. public school education, authored by Native Americans themselves, is a recent and still emerging practice. More than half of the states in the United States still recognize Columbus Day, even though it's known that Christopher Columbus supported the destruction of Native American civilization and its people. This ignorance and apathy toward the Native American experience has led many public schools to mishandle the educational and sporting experiences of Native American student-athletes.

Two of the most mishandled problems regarding Native Americans and sport are the school mascot and harassment of Native American athletes. The NFL's Washington "Redskins" was the most prominent controversial mascot, but is by no means the last offensive mascot utilized by sports teams throughout the United States. According to psychology studies, race-based mascots evoke associations with negative stereotypes and establish unwelcoming and even hostile school environments for Native students (Goodluck, 2019). These unwelcoming and hostile environments can result in lower self-esteem for Native American students while resulting in "white youth 'feel[ing] better about their own group'" when presented with a Native mascot, said researcher Stephanie Fryberg, professor of psychology and American Indian studies at the University of Washington" (Goodluck, 2019). And when these reported incidents of racial harassment related to Native Americans and sport occur, the responses have been remedial, disciplinary, or nonexistent:

> Of the 52 incidents, 26 resulted in remedial actions, including 15 apologies to the Native victims. At times, multiple responses were taken, including nine disciplinary actions—a team suspension, a few school investigations, an academic suspension, volunteer positions revoked at school, an athletic team meeting, a juvenile detention sentence and a disorderly conduct charge. But in the remaining 26 incidents, no remedial or disciplinary action was taken. (Goodluck, 2019)

This means that half of the reported racist incidents over a ten-year period resulted in no response taken by school administration to support the victimized Native Americans.

Discussing the Solutions: Race, Sports, and Representation

The United States has an overwhelming majority of white people making impactful decisions and comments that are laced with racism—whether conscious or unconscious—that affect people of color who work for them *and* the greater society that participates in the observation of these sports competitions and idolization (or animosity) of certain players. Thus, there has to be disruption at the player level from athletes of color and their White ally teammates because the majority of leaders in the sports industry are not people of color. And often, when institutions and organizations don't understand what's at stake for athletes of color when they face racism, they often mishandle the responses to controversies that arise. The cases of Ariyana Smith at Knox College, the WNBA's initial response to players' support of the Black Lives Matter movement, and the research gathered on Native American racialized incidents surrounding sport are examples of mishandled responses to controversy. There was no initial inquiry about how these athletes of color were doing personally in the face of the national headlines where people that looked like them were being murdered, again surfacing the disconnect that some people have about athletes of color and the fact that athletes of color are also *people* of color. The initial suspension of Smith at Knox and the WNBA's team and individual fines were a result of this disconnect. Moreover, the research presented on the Native American experience with race and sport points to a need for improved education on Native American history and culture in public education and educator preparation, as well as a larger network of support for these athletes that helps build self-esteem. There's no reason any sports team should have a mascot that represents an entire race of people in the United States, and there shouldn't be a double-standard when it comes to Native Americans. What might the response be to a banner that said "Get ready for a Holocaust part 2" instead of "Get ready for a Trail of Tears part 2?" It's doubtful a reference to the Holocaust would be seen as anything other than hate speech, so the accountability for the problem is with those who decide how Native Americans are being represented in history and in the present within American society and those who respond to these incidents of racist bullying and harassment.

On the more positive side of race, sports and representation, it's clear that the NFL and the NBA are doing a somewhat better job at supporting athletes of color who are calling for awareness of racial representation issues. The acts of protest from the NBA's Miami Heat and the NFL's St. Louis Rams and Cleveland Browns, as well as the professional basketball career of Jeremy Lin, are all about men of color—who happen to be wealthy and famous athletes—reminding the rest of the country and world that they relate to the stereotypes and perceptions that affect people that look like them:

> According to the Kaiser Family Foundation, homicide is the leading cause of death for black men ages 15 to 29. It doesn't matter whether you're wealthy and in a gated community or whether you have athletic ability, being a black man is a health risk. (Hill, 2012)

For Black male athletes, the way they are represented to the world is a life-or-death situation—an actual "health risk." And for Asian American Jeremy Lin, it's about shifting the public perception about the experience and abilities of Asian Americans in society generally and specifically as serious athletes.

Sports arenas, stadiums and fields are the perfect sites for ideological racial contestations; the locations where racialized stereotypes and misperceptions can be called out for all to see. For some, seeing an exceptional athlete speak out on behalf of a social movement or national news story is the only way that person will ever stop and really think about that social movement or national news story. It's easy not to notice—or even deny—racial underrepresentation and/or misrepresentation when one is always well represented racially. This is why more athletes need to speak up in relation to racial representation, regardless of their personal racial identity. The work is everyone's work, and not just that of people of color. The entirety of the sports industry has the means to support and represent the experiences of athletes of color in positive ways, but there has to be a will and understanding of the necessity to do so.

References

Abad-Santos, Alex. 2018. "Nike's Colin Kaepernick Ad Sparked a Boycott—And earned $6 billion for Nike." *Vox* (September 24).

Amdur, Neil. 1973. "Garden to Hear Anthem at Track Meet, After All." *The New York Times* (January 17): 1.

https://www.nytimes.com/1973/01/17/archives/garden
-to-hear-anthem-at-track-meet-after-all-garden-meet-to
-hear.html.

Armour, Nancy. 2019. "Opinion: 'We Were Wrong,' as
USOPC Finally Do Right by Tommie Smith, John Carlos."
USA Today (September 23).

Associated Press. 1989. "N.C.A.A. Presidents Urge Delay
on Proposition 42." *The New York Times* (January 20): 25,
Section A. https://www.nytimes.com/1989/01/20/sports
/ncaa-presidents-urge-delay-on-proposition-42.html.

Belson, Ken. 2014. "St. Louis Rams Players' Display Is
Condemned by Police Association." *The New York Times*
(December 2).

Belson, Ken. 2019. "Why Roger Goodell and Jay-Z Want
Colin Kaepernick to Get a Shot." *The New York Times*
(November 16).

Berkowitz, Steve. 1989. "Thompson Stages Protest, Walks
Out of Game." *The Washington Post* (January 15), A1.
http://www.washingtonpost.com/wp-srv/sports/gtown
/longterm/1999/thompson/archives/thomp011589.htm.

Bieler, Des. 2019a. "USWNT's Megan Rapinoe Says She's
a 'Walking Protest' of the Trump Administration." *The
Washington Post* (May 15).

Bieler, Des. 2019b. "Jay-Z Defends NFL Partnership as Eric
Reid Accuses Him of Helping Bury Kaepernick's Career."
The Washington Post (August 15).

Borsa, Joan. 1990. "Towards a Politics of Location:
Rethinking Marginality." *Canadian Woman Studies* II (1):
36–39.

Brackney, Peter. 2014. *Lost Lexington Kentucky*. Charleston,
SC: The History Press.

Branch, John. 2014. "N.B.A. Bars Clippers Owner Donald
Sterling for Life." *The New York Times* (April 30).

Brito, Christopher. 2019. "U.S. Athletes Punished for Protesting at Pan American Games." *CBS News* (August 21).

Bryant, Howard. 2018. *The Heritage: Black Athletes, A Divided America, and the Politics of Patriotism*. Boston, MA: Beacon Press.

Burton, Laura J., Gregory M. Kane, and John F. Borland. 2019. *Sport Leadership in the 21st Century*. 2nd ed. Burlington, MA: Jones & Barlett Learning.

Cauterucci, Christina. 2016. "The WNBA's BLack Lives Matter Protest Has Set a New Standard for Sports Activism." *Slate.com* (July 25).

Chow, Cary. 2019. "Jeremy Lin: 'There's Definitely Some Bittersweetness to My Career.'" *The Undefeated* (February 22).

Cole, Kevin R. 1995. "Proposition 48 and Proposition 42 in the NCAA: A Social Constructionist Case Study." Master of Arts, Department of Sociology, Western Michigan University.

Coulman, Lauren. 2018. "Who Benefits from Nike's Controversial Ad Campaign with Colin Kaepernick?" *Forbes.com* (September 5).

Crepeau, Richard. 2007. "The 'Flood' Case." *Journal of Sport History* 34 (2): 183–191.

Cullinane, Susannah. 2014. "Cleveland Police Slam NFL Player's Protest over Tamir Rice Death." *CNN.com* (December 15).

Draper, Kevin, Julie Creswell, and Sapna Maheshwari. 2018. "Nike Returns to Familiar Strategy with Kaepernick Ad Campaign." *The New York Times* (September 4).

Drucker, Joel. 2009. "What Happened at Indian Wells." *ESPN.com: Tennis* (March 11).

Eig, Jonathan. 2017. "The Cleveland Summit and Muhammad Ali." *The Undefeated*.

Eskenazi, Gerald. 1973. "Garden Track Meet Will Drop U.S. Anthem to Avoid Incidents." *The New York Times* (January 16): 1.

Game, The Voice of the. 2015. "The Syracuse 8." *The Players' Tribune* (October 22).

Given, Karen, and Shira Springer. 2017. "Before Kaepernick, The 'Syracuse 8' Were Blackballed by Pro Football." In *Only a Game*. Boston, MA: WBUR-Boston University.

Goodluck, Kalen. 2019. "Native American Athletes and Fans Face Ongoing Racism." *High Country News* (April 10).

Gup, Ted. 2004. "Southern Discomfort: With Quiet Grace, Two Black Men Change the Heart of Harvard in 1941." *The Boston Globe* (December 12).

Hawkins, Billy J., Akilah R. Carter-Francique, and Joseph N. Cooper, eds. 2017. *Critical Race Theory: Black Athletic Sporting Experiences in the United States*. 1st ed. New York: Palgrave Macmillan.

Hill, Jemele. 2012. "The Heat's Hoodies as Change Agent." *ESPN.com* (March 26).

Jones, Andrew Jerell. 2015. "What Everyone Is Getting Wrong about Serena Williams' Return to Indian Wells." *The Guardian* (March 12).

Lapchick, Richard E. 2018. "2018 Racial and Gender Report Card." In *The Institute for Diversity and Ethics and Sport: Making Waves of Change*, edited by Lee Bowman Brittany Barber, Meaghan Coleman, Yeehang Fan, Nate Harvey, Daniel Martin, Miranda Murphy, William Thomas II, and David Zimmerman. Orlando, FL: University of Central Florida.

Leung, Maxwell. 2013. "Jeremy Lin's Model Minority Problem." *Contexts* 12 (3): 52–56.

Lockhart, P. R. 2019. "The Controversy Surrounding Jay-Z's Partnership with the NFL, Explained." *Vox* (September 9).

Lopez, German. 2014. "Cleveland Browns' Andrew Hawkins Refuses to Apologize for 'Justice for Tamir Rice' Shirt." *Vox* (December 16).

Maese, Rick. 2019. "They Were Once Sent Home for Their Olympic Protest. Now They'll Get the USOPC's Highest Honor." *The Washington Post* (September 23).

McRae, Donald. 2017. "Craig Hodges: 'Jordan didn't speak out because he didn't know what to say.'" *The Guardian* (April 20).

Pennington, Bill. 2003. "College Basketball; Player's Protest over the Flag Divides Fans." *The New York Times* (February 26).

Platt, Larry. 2018. "Athlete Activism Is on the Rise, but So Is the Backlash." In *Global Sport Matters: An Arizona State University Media Enterprise*. Phoenix, AZ: Global Sport Matters.

Rapinoe, Megan. 2016. "Why I Am Kneeling." *The Players' Tribune* (October 6).

Rhoden, William C. 2006. *Forty Million Dollar Slaves: The Rise, Fall, and Redemption of the Black Athlete*. New York: Three Rivers Press.

Rosen, Lee J. 2000. "Proposition 16 and the NCAA Initial-Eligibility Standards: Putting the Student Back in Student-Athlete." *Catholic University Law Review* 50 (1): 175–217.

Sarver, Robert. 2010. "Robert Sarver." *The Atlantic* (November 2010).

Shropshire, Kenneth. 1996. *In Black and White: Race and Sports in America*. New York: New York University Press.

SI Staff. 2016. "One Year after Protest Rocked Missouri, the Effects on the Football Team and University Remain Tangible." *Sports Illustrated* (November 8).

Smith, Sam. 1991. "Hodges Makes Most of Visit with Bush." *Chicago Tribune* (October 7).

Southall, Ashley, and Marc Tracy. 2015. "Black Football Players Lend Heft to Protests at Missouri." *The New York Times* (November 9).

Spears, Marc J. 2019. "Inside the Clippers' Final Days with Donald Sterling as Owner." *The Undefeated* (April 24).

Spivey, Donald. 1988. "'End Jim Crow in Sports': The Protest at New York University, 1940–1941." *Journal of Sport History* 15 (3): 282–303.

Taylor, Derrick Bryson. 2019. "U.S. Fencer and Hammer Thrower Lead Silent Protests at Pan-American Games." *The New York Times* (August 11).

Washington, Jesse. 2016. "Still No Anthem, Still No Regrets for Mahmoud Abdul-Rauf." *The Undefeated* (September 1).

Weisholtz, Drew. 2019. "Megan Rapinoe Explains Why She's Not Participating in National Anthem." *NBC Today* (June 17).

Wiggins, Daivd K., and Patrick B. Miller. 2005. *The Unlevel Playing Field: A Documentary History of the African American Experience in Sport*. Champaign: University of Illinois Press.

Wong, Alex. 2019. "Jeremy Lin, 'Reppin' Asians with Everything I Have,' Is Bigger Than an N.B.A. Title." *The New York Times* (June 18).

Yglesias, Matthew. 2015. "Donald Sterling's Racist Outburst." *Vox* (May 13).

Young, Jason, Jeremy Earp, and Sut Jhally. 2013. *Race, Power and American Sports*. Northampton, MA: Media Education Foundation.

Zirin, Dave. 2005. *What's My Name, Fool?: Sports and Resistance in the United States*. Chicago: Haymarket Books.

Zirin, Dave. 2013. "'America's Justice System Is a Joke': Athletes Respond to Trayvon Martin Verdict." *The Nation* (July 14).

Zirin, Dave. 2014. "Interview with Ariyana Smith: The First Athlete Activist of #BlackLivesMatter." *The Nation* (December 19).

Zirin, Dave. 2016. "Thoughts on Colin Kaepernick from an Athlete Who Walked That Path." *The Nation* (August 29).

3 Perspectives

This chapter presents seven essays written by contributors from various states in the United States that discuss sporting experiences at the youth, collegiate and professional levels. Specific sports addressed in the essays are soccer, football, Korean martial arts, rowing, volleyball, and basketball. Some of the topics addressed in these perspective pieces address are: issues of race and access to sport; racial stereotypes and perceptions related to sport; viewing U.S. racism and sport through the international lens; and student-athlete experiences at predominantly White universities.

A Player in a New Game
Andre Alicea

August 1989

"They shootin'!" someone yells. Everyone scatters until we all meet up in front of my building. "Dre, I think that was your brother's crew." The drug game is a game that can cause someone's world to change in a manner of seconds. It's a violent reality that we are forced to live in, and my seventeen-year-old brother is a player in the game. Not knowing if he is OK or able to defend himself, I run upstairs and return with a gun. While looking for my brother, I see a police car approaching. I enter a phone booth

---

Simone Biles at the Rio Summer Olympics on August 7, 2016. Biles set a U.S. record for the most gold medals received in women's gymnastics at a single Olympics in Rio. In 2019, Biles became the most decorated gymnast in world championship history. (Zhukovsky/Dreamstime.com)

and pretend to make a call when the officers call me over. They throw me on the hood and search me but find nothing as the gun was hidden inside the phone booth. They eventually leave, and I retrieve the gun and run to the apartment. My brother opens the door, grabs me by the collar and slams me against the wall. "What the hell were you doing out there? Didn't I tell you never to get involved in this? You almost ruined everything! You have a ticket out of here, and you are just looking to throw it all away? Get to mom's house, and I don't want to see you back on these streets until the day you're leaving!"

I'm fourteen years old and in three days I start 9th grade at The Hotchkiss School, an elite private boarding school in Lakeville, Connecticut.

August 2019

I was raised in the Red Hook Houses, a low-income housing project in Brooklyn, New York. According to a 2014 survey report by the New York Department of City Planning:

> [M]ore than half the neighborhood's roughly 10,000 residents live in subsidized rentals at Red Hook Houses, with 32 total buildings on 39 acres. The report summarizes the community as ". . . largely Hispanic and Black/African American (43 percent and 36 percent respectively as of Census 2010), the population is characterized by lower educational attainment than the rest of the borough and New York City. Nearly 40 percent of residents are living in poverty, and unemployment is 21 percent, more than double [the] unemployment in Brooklyn and New York City. (New York City Department of City Planning, 2014)

In July 1988, Life Magazine called Red Hook the "Crack Capital of America." We were on the front line of the "War on Drugs" and we were losing. Unlike many of my peers, I was able to find a way to escape the neighborhood. The Albert G.

Oliver Program, a nonprofit in NYC, nominated me as a high achiever in Middle School. As a result of my work with them, I was the recipient of a full scholarship to attend high school at Hotchkiss.

When I arrived at Hotchkiss in 1989, I entered a world that I had no idea existed. Established in 1891, this institution was originally designed to prepare young, affluent White males for success at Ivy League universities. Schools like Hotchkiss are where the top 1 percent of our country send their children to be educated. I went from a school where the population was predominantly people of color to a school where everyone was rich and White.

This is where I got my first real lesson about the income disparity between the races in the United States. I could not understand how it could be normalized for a generation of Black and Brown kids to grow up poor in crime-infested neighborhoods and for White kids to casually talk about vacationing in Aspen or abroad. What frustrated me was that there was no peer I could talk to who would be able to relate to the feelings I was having. *How do I tell these wealthy White kids that I came from the "Crack Capital of America"? How can I tell them that a week before coming to campus, I was almost caught with a gun?* It was an isolating experience . . . until sports began.

Boarding schools become a lonely place for under-represented students. There were only two faculty members of color, and the curriculum was taught from a Westernized, imperialistic worldview. Many sources used in class were culturally biased and racially insensitive, and the teachers did not teach from different perspectives. I knew of other Black and Brown students at boarding schools who were sharing many of the difficulties that I had when it came to adjusting to life at these elite institutions. There was no focus on equity and inclusion, and because of this, many students chose to return home to finish school. Returning home was not an option for me. If I was going to survive and thrive at Hotchkiss, I would have to find a way to break down these barriers to success.

Sports became the tool for me to overcome those barriers at Hotchkiss. In the fall of 1989, I signed up for football. On the first day of practice, I was given a set of football equipment. I brought it up to the locker room, put it on the bench, and just stared at it. As a kid in Red Hook, we never played organized football because we couldn't afford the equipment or registration fees. As I stared at that equipment, a White classmate sat near me and started to put his equipment together. I shyly asked if I could see what he was doing, and he offered to show me how to put everything on. He asked if I ever played football before, and I told him this was my first time playing "real" football with equipment. This led to a conversation about sports we'd played in the past and life back home, but I didn't yet open up about the realities of life in Red Hook.

That first year of football set the tone for my four years of high school. My teammates began looking to me as a leader on the team. As my success on the field grew, my confidence in the classroom and in social circles also grew. I began to find a sense of self and meaning at Hotchkiss. As we began to trust each other on the field, we were able to trust each other with meaningful discussions in the locker room.

It was through this bond that a White kid from Kalispell, Montana, who never saw a person of color in real life, could have conversations with a kid from the projects of Brooklyn. Despite our differences, we discovered that we all struggled with issues of belonging and of lacking confidence. We learned that we all wanted to do well in school, please our parents, and have fun in high school. It didn't matter if we came from Brooklyn or Kalispell. We all had the same goals. It was in these moments that I started to feel less isolated, realizing that we are more alike than we are different. This became the framework that I gravitated to when I felt homesick or separated from the larger community. On those days when I felt that no one at Hotchkiss knew me, or knew what I was going through, being with my teammates allowed those problems to fade into the background. I would emerge with a renewed sense of belonging that would carry me into the next day.

Being a successful athlete at Hotchkiss was instrumental to my success later in life. In my senior year, I was voted team captain for my football, wrestling, and track teams. It was through these sporting experiences that I learned the importance of working with others to find common ground. I learned how to be a leader among peers, how to be a liaison between my teammates and our coaches, and how to be a mentor to youth. It is paramount that kids of color at predominantly White institutions find an outlet by which they can excel and build up their sense of self. For me, it was athletics. For others it may be visual or performing arts. Without the stability that athletics provided, I would not have found a sense of belonging and would have left Hotchkiss, destined to become another statistic to the war on drugs. While many of my childhood friends were victims to the drug game, I was able to become a player in a new game. Being an athlete at Hotchkiss changed the destiny of my life and ensured my children would not experience the same childhood that I did. The legacy that I started at Hotchkiss continued as my daughter graduated in 2018, and my son graduated in 2020.

References

New York City Department of City Planning. 2014. "Existing Conditions and Brownfields Analysis: Red Hook, Brooklyn." Final—September 2014. https://www1.nyc.gov/assets/oer/downloads/pdf/red-hook-brooklyn.pdf.

Andre Alicea is a 1993 graduate of the Hotchkiss School and a 1997 graduate of the University of Pennsylvania. He lives in King of Prussia, Pennsylvania, with his wife and three children, where he serves on the board of directors of Men to Men Mentoring Inc.

Black Quarterbacks: A Troubling Reflection of America
Daniel R. Davis

"Daddy, when can I play football?" I asked at eight years old. My father replied, "I think next year you'll be old enough to play flyweight at Booker [a local community center named after Booker T. Washington], right, Paulette (my mother)?" I immediately felt a mixture of excitement and frustration about having to wait another year. Football was my love, passion, and obsession. I would write the statistics down off the back of my football cards and memorize them. I was creating fantasy football teams long before it became "a thing." I was told that I cried when the Chicago Bears didn't make the Super Bowl in the 1986–87 season, losing in the NFC playoffs. I remember thinking, *They lost because they wore the black jerseys* [yes, I thought their blue jerseys were black]; *they should have worn the* white *ones* [in hindsight perhaps a belief more disturbingly telling than I give credit]. Football was my everything, and like many children, I knew what I wanted to be when I grew up—a football player.

But what kind of football player? As I think back, I recall countless sessions of "catch" in the front yard with my father, which consisted of me trying my best to emulate his perfect spiral passes. I remember being in awe of my brother, ten years my senior, and his friends throwing the football so high that it appeared to be on track to hit the sun. And one of my favorite players back in 1992 was Randall Cunningham, an All-Pro quarterback for the Philadelphia Eagles and arguably the best player in football in the early 1990s (Harrison, 2017). Yet, despite all of that, I never considered trying out for *quarterback* when my time came to officially play "pee-wee" football. Why?

It's popular belief that the quarterback position is the most difficult position in all of sports. The NFL quarterback is the leader of the team. He is responsible for reading defenses, starting every offensive play, changing play calls, clock management, and, of course, throwing the football accurately. This position is for *thinkers* and athletes with a certain level of *intellect*. Stereotypically, African Americans, particularly African American athletes, are not heralded for their intellectual abilities. Often, Black athletes are considered physical specimens with "natural ability" to perform on playing fields. Sadly, this reflects the long-held and patently false belief that African Americans in general are intellectually inferior beings compared to their White counterparts. This reality is so blatantly, yet informally, enforced that award-winning Black college quarterbacks are often reassigned to new positions (often cornerback) upon entering the NFL. Perhaps this is at least partially why, despite the NFL being 70 percent Black, only 19 percent of quarterbacks are African American (Sonnad, 2018). Conversely, the cornerback position, which primarily requires a fast athlete to follow and chase a receiver to prevent him from catching a pass (not known as a cerebral position), is astoundingly 99.4 percent Black (Reid and McManus, 2017).

Hall of Fame quarterback Warren Moon, the only African American quarterback inducted into the Hall of Fame, knows firsthand the dense energy surrounding the idea and reality of being a Black professional quarterback. Moon noted, "In football, the 'thinking' positions down the middle—quarterback, center, [inside] linebacker—were the ones that *we* weren't allowed to play. He also stated, "Despite the fact that there were a lot of African-Americans playing in the National Football League in the '50s, '60s and '70s, there was a stereotype that *we* weren't capable of succeeding at certain positions. If you played those positions in college and you got drafted, you knew you were probably going to get moved in the NFL. Supposedly, *we* weren't smart enough or had the leadership qualities or whatever it took" (Reid and McManus, 2017). These sentiments were echoed by Black NFL Hall of Famer and Super Bowl winning head coach Tony Dungy, who mentioned that "we've kind of stereotyped our young kids into different thought patterns.

And most of it is based on perception. . . . There was a time when we didn't have black quarterbacks. The thought of, for black kids, 'OK, I'm going to play quarterback and I'm going to the NFL,' it wasn't there" (Reid and McManus, 2017). All of this makes the controversial "take a knee" protest in response to police brutality and unequal treatment of African Americans in general, spearheaded by Black former NFL quarterback Colin Kaepernick, even more fascinating. Here you have a Black NFL quarterback with the audacity and brains to lead a professional football team and finally achieve his dream *and* boldly use his platform to fight against the very racism and injustice that made his dream so far-fetched.

Once I turned nine years old, I excitedly signed up to play flyweight football for the Booker T. Washington community center football team. I can't help but wonder if my father unintentionally encouraged me to play wide receiver (a noncerebral position requiring speed and agility) because of some subconscious belief that I'd have a better chance at success in this position stemming from U.S. society's stereotypical and racist belief systems. I remember deciding between running back and wide receiver. These were the only positions I considered. I also remember my father telling me about his first football experience as a young boy in the early 1960s. Upon arrival at the first team practice as a preteen, his White coach said, "All right, you (Black kid), "you" (another Black kid), "and you" (the final Black kid) "get in this line" (the running back line), "and if you want to play quarterback, get in this line" (he said to the remaining White kids) and so on to fill the remaining positions.

Admittedly, major college football programs are increasingly recruiting and utilizing Black quarterbacks. Also, NFL teams are slowly, yet increasingly, adding Black quarterbacks to their rosters. I can only hope that in the coming generations, little Black boys will be completely empowered with the belief that they can be the leader, face, and brain of a team while playing the sport they love, and racist preconceived notions will be abandoned for the sport I once loved so much.

References

Harrison, Elliott. 2017. "Revisiting Notable MVP Races: When did voters get it wrong?" *NFL.com* (June 28). http://www.nfl.com/news/story/0ap3000000817724/article/revisiting-notable-nfl-mvp-races-when-did-voters-get-it-wrong.

Reid, Jason, and Jane McManus. 2017. "The NFL's Racial Divide: Teams Don't Consciously Build Rosters Based on Race, It Just Ends Up That Way." *The Undefeated.* https://theundefeated.com/features/the-nfls-racial-divide/.

Sonnad, Nikhil. 2018. "The NFL's Racial Divide in One Chart." *Quartz* (May 24). https://qz.com/1287915/the-nfls-racial-makeup-explains-much-of-its-national-anthem-problems/.

Daniel R. Davis is a professor, public speaker, author, and urban historian. His primary research interests are twentieth-century African American history, African American education, hip-hop/urban culture, and the enslavement era. He holds a PhD in African American and African Studies, specializing in history.

Race in Sport: From Bahamian Unity to American Discord
Andrew Cole Maura

Born and raised in the Bahamas, I have had a very distinctive athletic journey. A country with a population of only about 400,000, of whom roughly 275,000 live on the island of New Providence, many assume that our sports are not competitive. But what the country lacks in numbers playing sports, we make up for with raw physical talent and drive. With a history of Bahamian athletes recruited by U.S. colleges, many kids are eager to follow this path from a young age. Naturally, this common goal nurtured competition, and my game as both a soccer and tennis player developed quickly. However, as with all competitive sport participants, interactions were not solely limited to the fields and courts. I began to make strong outside friendships that I still have to this day with Black, White, and mixed-race Bahamians.

I have come to understand that it was the team hardships and even punishments—like "Indian runs" until sundown or no water during practice on a scorching Caribbean summer day—that have made my friendships through sport reliable and concrete. Having persisted through so many demanding challenges, my teammates and I grew extremely close. Whether it be hitting at the National Tennis Center or practicing on a local club team, I became close to kids who did not attend my small school. In the Bahamas, I did not play tennis with "a bunch of Black kids"; I played with my friends—my brothers. After moving to the United States to attend boarding school in New England, I was taken aback when my attempts to make new natural friendships through sport seemed to be now be heavily influenced by race.

Being White in the Bahamas, which is about 90 percent Black, I grew up feeling that race was detached from sport. My teammates and I were so devoted to the game that race was deemed a distraction to success.

Being the only White kid in the starting eleven as the whistle blew or the minority in the tennis team never even crossed my mind. Who cared what color my skin was? The goal was to win. That's all that mattered. And then, *it got real . . .* different.

As a fifteen-year-old living in a completely new country, my culture shock quickly extended beyond food and academics to skin color. "There are a lot of Black guys on your soccer team," or "No wonder you guys are winning; you have a bunch of Africans!" were common phrases from opponents throughout New England that blared in my ears. When I found the time to try and process these types of comments, so many questions popped into my head that I just could not seem to answer. Why do people seem to view others of a different skin color in a completely different manner? Why are so many stereotypes attached to people based on their appearance? Why do people seem to value skin color over athletic ability, character, and personality?

I vividly remember a conversation I had with a few African American and African teammates after an opposing White player had told me on the field, "You are only winning because you have so many Africans on your team." Initially, I was a bit tentative to share this encounter with my teammates at the dinner table. I had never been exposed to racial stereotyping on the field. I had no clue how my teammates would react, and I did not want to sour the mood after a big win. Nevertheless, I felt that this experience should be addressed . . . and I was completely surprised by the response. My African and African American teammates were so amused about the inaccuracy of the kid claiming that everyone Black was African that our table roared with laughter, startling the whole dining hall. "I forgot that every Black person was born in Africa!" one of my African American teammates sarcastically responded. Our game reflection quickly transformed into a humorous mockery of closed-minded and unfounded stereotypes. Yet, later that night, as I spent some time by myself reflecting on what had happened, I became very frustrated. My teammates and friends brushed what I had told them aside because they have been subject to stereotypes *so* often.

Over the last four years, I've become closest to my African American and African teammates. I have witnessed and become frustrated, alongside those teammates, when White peers living among me within the small boarding school community often assumed that Black athletes here are simply concerned with athletic success, rather than students who are serious about their education. By identifying Black individuals who play on a varsity team as simply "recruits," one becomes quick to neglect or even dismiss their other attributes that are so significant to the betterment of our community. Why is it that when acknowledging a Black athlete as another basketball, football, or soccer recruit, their involvement and positive influence in other organizations such as Caribbean Club, choir, or the Political Union are thrown out the window? Why isn't my belonging at a strong academic school being questioned like that of Black students? Why did I now seem to have a higher status than those who are Black? Is it because I am White? But we are all biologically the same. So why are so many Americans intent on discriminating between race?

After four years of living in the United States, I have come to understand that American culture emphasizes labels. Individuals in the United States, who seem to be attracted socially to historical familiarity and comfort, have largely surrounded themselves with people of similar backgrounds and, therefore, similar skin color. While there are exceptions, this lack of intentional genuine and immersive exposure to the lives of people of other races breeds a cycle of ignorance. Sports provide the perfect opportunity to build trust and deep friendship with teammates who come from diverse races and experiences. It is my hope that Americans begin to increasingly look at character and ability rather than skin color, not only in sports but also in everyday life. Yet, as I recognize the extent to which racial stereotyping is so ingrained in American culture, I realize that athletes of minority ethnicity and race will continue to experience prejudice and discrimination.

Andrew Cole Maura is a tennis and soccer player who has represented his country, the Bahamas, internationally. Having graduated from the Hotchkiss School, he currently attends the College of Literature, Science, and the Arts at the University of Michigan.

They Say Confidence Is Key: A Sports Memoir
Tayler Simons

I realize I have a love-hate relationship with sports. I love the sudden rush I feel when my favorite football team is down one touchdown, and I can barely hear my thoughts above my family's cheers and screams. On the other hand, I've grown to truly dislike sports, and even with all the fun and joy it may bring, sports have become a reflection of what Black culture is supposed to represent. For instance, visualize a tall, Black young man with broad shoulders and huge hands. Without asking what this young man's hobbies or goals are, society has already decided where his destiny should lie. In life I have learned that the media has left out a lot of the layers the Black community (as well as other ethnic groups) have within them. With these types of views, one might think I didn't play sports as a child. However, for years I was a student athlete who, although I worked very hard at both, was more of the former than the latter.

From the very start, my involvement in sports disrupted the strong confidence I proudly embody. Volleyball, in particular, was fun and exciting for me. Yet, while I became "decent" at volleyball, the sport just never gave me the feeling I was searching for. Quite often I was told by my peers that I had the "typical athletic build," which I guess, looking back, was code for the little girl with muscular arms and legs. I felt an indistinct pressure to showcase my undefined star athleticism. What I didn't know as a child was that being perceived as an athlete was not a novelty for members in my community: most Black kids are told similar things daily.

Growing up I was always active. Like most kids, I enjoyed playing outside, and unlike most girls, I had no problem getting dirty. As a child, I was on the bigger side for my age group, so I usually played with boys, who took the phrase "no mercy" to heart. I never played for any awards or prizes, merely for the love of competition. This love for the competition did not start on the field or on the tetherball court, where I was a renowned champion. Rather, my love for the competition started in the classroom, and my main competitor was someone I am still very close with: myself.

Since my first day of school, I was always striving to excel in my classes. I was a perfectionist and my own worst enemy. I was the student who would ask the teacher why I got an A- instead of an A+. Looking back, I could see why my teachers

may have thought I was obnoxious, even if I was merely looking for ways to improve. I yearned for knowledge, and the
feeling of knowing how to solve math problems or read thick
chapter books was exciting to me. I competed with myself daily
and made sure I was never too comfortable with my education.
And even though I had an internal drive to do well in school,
I also had a constant external motivation to make my mother
proud. Though my mother never pressured me to do well, she
always said, "I know my number one will make it happen."
Even with my success in school, my competitive spirit yearned
to tap into my athletic ability. In spite of all the sports I played
while in middle school, volleyball would become one of my
biggest challenges for the next five years.

At first, I thought playing volleyball would be similar to the
activities I played as a child. As a growing teenager, I was no longer physically considered "chunky" or "big"; I was now a strong,
powerful young woman. I figured my strength, learning ability,
and tough demeanor were sufficient qualities to have for competitive sporting success. When I moved on to playing volleyball in
high school, I discovered I did not hold the same natural ability
or mental confidence as I had in the classroom. Even with extra
workouts and studying volleyball YouTube videos, I still improved
at a slower rate than my teammates, causing my confidence to
become almost nonexistent. Instead of lifting myself up, I con-
stantly put myself down. I compared myself to other players who
played my position, asking myself, "How come my swing wasn't
as fast as hers? Why didn't I follow through with my hits as she
did?" Similar to my academics, I competed with myself internally.
Yet unlike my academics, sports were not my natural forte. I may
have won a few awards, but my confidence was slim to none in
the sporting department. I guess I was more disappointed that I
wasn't the natural everyone expected me to be, and even with constant practice, it took years for me to feel like I had actual skills.

Presently, I tend to pride myself for marching to the beat of
my own drum, always taking my own path. However, after reflecting on it, I realize I badly wanted to be a star athlete because

it was, one, a challenge, and two, the thing I was "supposed" to be good at. Everyone else's expectations had become my new external motivation. Nevertheless, I tried to make myself feel like I was in control by choosing a sport that was not typical for Black girls. For most of my life—and currently—people ask if I play or played basketball. This has always brought up the internal question: *Why do you think I play basketball—because I'm Black?* Although most people might suggest this line of thought is an overreaction, I learned in college that my internal skepticism may be an accurate assumption.

As a first-generation college student, I am blessed to have a free education. This is not due to a family inheritance but rather because I turned my love of school and education into what I call free money—or in colloquial terms, academic scholarships.

While attending a predominantly White institution, I have come across those who assume my time is college is funded by an athletic scholarship. Imagine sitting in front of an intelligent, intellectual professor, picking their brains on how to find research opportunities on campus. You want to make a good impression, so you spew out information about your classes, goals, and passions. Within the list of questions this professor asks, the one that sticks out to you is, "Are you on a sports scholarship?" Though this is a fair question to ask any college student, it stings just a tad more when you are Black and not an athlete. This widely accepted assumption of me being a debt-free college student only if I'm playing sports is tiring. It is even more unpleasant when the type of sport is narrowed down to just a few. For instance, when I played club volleyball, White parents were often surprised to see a Black girl play against their daughters, let alone have the money to be on a club team.

As a member of one of the only mixed-race teams within my volleyball conference, my team usually played athletes who were not of the same ethnicity as ourselves. Although I did not care about who I was playing against, I think the parents and supporters of the opposing teams would have enjoyed a more "even-toned" playing field. Being a fourteen-year-old girl and

listening to people make loud comments on how we—the ethnic girls—should not have beaten their children is truly memorable. After games like these, we as a team always reflected
on it with laughter but also with mostly unspoken exhaustion
from having to win a match for outsiders to understand our
right on the court. I can personally say my Blackness was never
challenged by what people may have thought about me during
my sports career or even long after. Both volleyball and my
academics played a major role in my development as a young
adult. Volleyball—and sports in general—taught me I do not
always have to be the best. It is okay to fail as long as I figure
out ways to improve and learn from my failure. School showed
me it's okay to not meet the expectations others have for you.
As long as I am doing what makes myself and my family proud,
I have no purpose for the path society may have laid out for
me. I will never stop enjoying Sunday night football or even
the basketball playoffs. However, for those who like to place
people in a box when they possess more than four walls, don't
stifle someone's potential due to personal ignorance. Their key
to confidence may lie in a variety of places.

*Tayler Simons is a recent graduate from Northern Arizona Uni-
versity (NAU), who earned a degree in biomedical sciences and
minors in chemistry and ethnic studies. In college, Tayler was a
primary lab assistant in a cardiovascular regulation lab, while also
being the first African American president of Alpha Lambda Delta
National Honor Society at NAU. As a resident assistant at NAU,
she worked closely with incoming freshman; and now, as a medical
scribe, she prepares for her entry into medical school.*

The Problems with the Lack of
Accessibility of Sports
Michaela Boyle

In my White, middle-class home, I was surrounded by sports.
Both my parents were coaches and educators who believed in

the importance of the lessons that sports teach. In my house we were not allowed to watch a lot of television, except for sports. The winter was my favorite season because that meant basketball was on almost every night. My dad played Division I basketball, walking on and earning a scholarship. As the son of immigrant parents, he understood from his college years the importance of sport and its ability to connect people across cultures, generations, and races.

The reality that basketball was on the television almost every night meant that I watched *a lot* of basketball. I learned about the nuances of the game and eventually was drawn to favorite teams and coaches. As I grew as a student of the game, I started to notice the language that was used by many broadcasters who covered each game. There were subtle comments they'd make that identified an issue of race in sports generally, but particularly basketball. A White point guard is often referred to as "smart" and "a strong leader" if he is particularly vocal, whereas a Black player with nearly identical attributes is often referred to as "extremely athletic" as opposed to smart. Even as an adolescent, I came to recognize these not-so-subtle generalizations. Neither description is negative in terms of what an athlete wants to possess, but I was led to believe the comments came out differently simply because of the skin complexion of the player. These comments begin to influence not only the identity of the athlete on the screen but also the thousands watching all over the country—and the world—was they identify with the athletes being described in this manner.

I unsurprisingly played basketball in high school on a team that won a host of accolades, including two independent school state championships. Many of my teammates went on to play college basketball at the Division I and II levels, and we were all so invested in the sport and the success of each season. On these teams I was usually one of two or three other women who identified racially as White. This racial ratio did not come close to the diversity of the small private school I attended. I am not an expert on why this was the case in a sport such as basketball and not . . . lacrosse, for example. Neither do I know the sociological reasoning behind it, but I am grateful to have had the opportunity to learn from my teammates about the different life experiences we had simply because of our skin color. I was challenged to be a friend and ally to my teammates in situations that I was never presented with prior to being part of these teams.

Currently, I am a Division I women's rower at Holy Cross, a school like most small liberal arts institutions, where most of the student body primarily racially identifies as White. My rowing team is 100 percent White, and most of the girls we compete against are also visibly White. This is something most lifelong rowers might not notice, but having come from a sport as diverse as basketball, this reality has actually been unsettling for me. Again, I am unsure of the reason behind this racial composition disparity on certain sports teams, but my hypothesis is that there are two basic reasons: accessibility of the sport and prior family exposure.

Rowing is expensive; the boats cost more than $10,000. Then, there has to be a sufficient body of water to practice and compete in. This body of water ideally needs to have a dock and a boathouse to make legitimate competitive rowing possible. The cost of all of this makes the sport expensive to join, immediately barring economically disadvantaged people from even being able to *try* the sport. In contrast, basketball courts and hoops can be found at almost any school or park, and all that is needed is a basketball, which on average costs $15–$20 for one of quality. It is true that team shoes and AAU and other club teams can become expensive, but no matter what, most people in the United States have access to a court and a ball where they can practice as long as they want without paying anything.

The other conclusion I have come up with is that most kids play sports their parents sign them up for and usually, parents sign their children up for sports that they played growing up. After all, I imagine it's natural for parents to want to be able to understand the sport their child(ren) participate in. Parents want to be able to give advice and support, which means they need a basic understanding of the sport their kid has signed up to play. Basketball has been popular among the masses, regardless of race, for generations. This means that basketball will likely continue to grow among different demographics, racial or otherwise. Rowing, however, was made famous by White men who often attended Ivy League colleges. Many non–Ivy League colleges are just beginning to grow their women's programs and the youth pipeline into rowing remains stunted in expansion because of the astronomical cost.

It is naive to deny the claim that race influences so many aspects of people's lives in the United States. Although sports can be an escape from a lot of social tensions and political strain, it is not exempt from the reality of race and racism in this country. From my experience as a White woman in two drastically different sports, I have learned that sport can teach so many lessons not only about physical and mental prowess but also about humanity and what it means to be a teammate and ally on and off the court—or the water. It's important to speak out when something isn't right and even more important to continually question *why* things are the way they are. This perspective essay is a part of my speaking out, and I hope it leads other White athletes to question their past and present sporting journeys through the lens of race and class.

Michaela Boyle is a History major at College of the Holy Cross, where she is also a member of the women's rowing team. Before joining the Division I rowing program at Holy Cross, Boyle spent her high school years at a small, independent day school in Connecticut and played varsity basketball, soccer, and lacrosse. In her sophomore year at Holy Cross, Boyle was named a collegiate rowing association scholar athlete. She is scheduled to graduate as a member of the College of the Holy Cross Class of 2021.

Black and Blue: Making the Most of the College Athlete Experience at a Division I PWI
Isaiah Alicea

I'll be the first to admit that I had an awesome four years as a college athlete. I had the pleasure of playing Division I football as a walk-on defensive back for the Villanova University Wildcats. Villanova athletes get a ton of respect on campus—especially the basketball team, who are treated like rock stars. Most of the Black population of students are athletes, so it isn't uncommon to see a Black person donned in athletic gear. However, the perks and shiny gear don't solve the problems that a Black student-athlete attending a predominantly White institution (PWI) may face. Many times, solving those problems takes protest and action.

Black students struggle to have a voice in the larger, predominantly White student body and Black athletes fight against the expectation that they'll never be seen as more than an "athlete." There are many times when this dual struggle was incredibly isolating from the rest of the student body because scholarship status, athletic prestige, and popularity were contingent on how well most of us performed on our athletic fields and courts in front of White audiences. In addition, we were socially separated from the lives of other Black students at Villanova. At a school where there is already an extremely low number of Black people, that small size was divided socially by athletic status. At Villanova, those Blacks who play sports get more respect and attention from the Whites on campus than the Black and Brown students who don't play varsity sports. This causes a strain and an ego trip for some Black athletes, as many think that they are "better" than our nonathletic brothers and sisters.

Time is also an issue for athletes at predominantly White institutions. Black athletes hardly have time to join outside clubs where they can meet other Black and Brown people or be as active in that club as they want to be. Black athletes generally develop cliques with other Black athletes because that's who they generally spend most of their days with. As hard as it was playing collegiate football, I couldn't imagine how hard it may have been for a nonathlete Black student at a PWI like Villanova. No matter how low things may have seemed, I knew that I at least had Black teammates that also shared my general experience going through the exact same thing as me, so I never truly felt alone in college. So how did I use that athlete-privilege for good?

While studying Sociology, I was fortunate enough to have a professor who taught me how to find my voice and use my power as a student-athlete at a school like Villanova. I studied social movements and the formation of race and sports in American history. In the era of Colin Kaepernick and NFL players kneeling during the national anthem, I decided to use my voice and my platform to put my beliefs into action. I, along with other Black football players, knelt during the national anthem of an away football game at Towson University just north of Baltimore, Maryland. We were booed by the fans surrounding us and even by the opposing Black football players, who frantically motioned for us to stand up. It was very unsettling and polarizing. We did not feel comfortable in that stadium or in that moment.

Although our coach was amenable to us expressing ourselves and pulling "that stunt," it was decided—perhaps by the athletic administration—that the team had to stay in the locker room for the remainder of the season during the playing of the national anthem. We were emboldened to stand up for the right thing and to support Colin Kaepernick's movement at the risk of our own statuses. Kaepernick's ideas were bigger than any one of us individually, and his fearlessness inspired us to carry that same spirit boldly. The track team soon got word of this, and its Black members pulled a similar act. When Villanova's athletic administrators heard about this expanded protestation, it became worried and decided to step in differently.

After all, colleges and universities have a brand and a reputation to protect. The NCAA, who generates billions of dollars annually off the guise of "amateurism," can't risk activism impeding their cash flow and having athletes kneel during anthems. To prevent the Villanova basketball team (who would win the NCAA National Championship that same year) from potentially also kneeling and upsetting the school's relationships with the TV networks, sponsors, and booster club(s), Villanova University and the athletic department created a forum where all student-athletes could meet and talk about issues that mattered to them in a safe space: *UNITAS*.

Since its inception in 2018, the *UNITAS* initiative creates circles for student-athletes who are passionate about different issues—including race and relations, international student affairs, LGBTQ+ athletes, women athletes, mental health, and more. The forum is open to all Villanova varsity athletes, coaches, and administrators. We would meet once a semester over pizza in the newly built Athletes' Lounge. During our forums, we talked openly and freely about divisive issues and problems in our small and large communities. Whatever new situations happened in the news or media regarding college sports, we discussed at our forums and used our collective platforms to seek positive change. We'd brainstorm possible solutions and create action plans accordingly—just like in our sports.

In the forum concentrated on race and sports, we talked about Colin Kaepernick's influence in our generation, the "13th Amendment" as a lawful defense for not paying college athletes, the arrival of Trump's presidency during our time in college, Zion Williamson's knee injury during the UNC game and his potential risk of losing millions of dollars, the idea and concept of "shut up and dribble," and many, many more topics. The meetings generated a lot of excitement and we tried to turn words into action by planning and coordinating events with the help and support of the Athletic Department.

I will be returning to Villanova in the fall of 2019 for graduate school, so in the coming year, we plan to organize a BBQ with cultural clubs on campus to promote social cohesion among athletes and other marginalized groups. We plan to work with Villanova's Black Cultural Society (BCS) and the African Caribbean Villanovans (ACV) to create positive relationships between Black and Brown student athletes and nonstudent athletes on campus. This will hopefully address some much-needed concerns regarding unity for Black and Brown Villanovans. At the end of the day, we want to at least ensure that we're all together, happy, and healthy.

The *UNITAS* initiative also recently put together pregame warm-up shirts that all Villanova athletes will wear at some point in the future. These black T-shirts are designed to promote unity within our athletics department. The T-shirts are a step in the right direction of bringing greater visibility to this new initiative and how it supports the Black athlete. I believe that I helped to start something positive for the next generation of minority athletes at Villanova, even if it starts with kneeling, T-shirts, and conversations over pizza.

Can you imagine if the men's basketball team had kneeled throughout the season and then subsequently won their second championship in three years? All kinds of explosions would've probably gone off. What was started by the university to appease the Black athletes and dissuade the basketball team specifically from actively protesting backfired somewhat. The Black athletes helped turn the siloed athlete initiative into a schoolwide effort to foster and support a safe space for Black athletes to organize and put their thoughts and frustrations into meaningful action plans for change.

I encourage all Black and Brown athletes at predominantly White institutions to work with each other so that we can leave our institutions better than when we arrived. If we do that, before we know it, we're helping to create the blueprints for meaningful change beyond wins, losses, and personal bests. It's crucial for student-athletes to get involved in important social movements and to recognize the voice and power that we each carry. Look at what the Mizzou Football team accomplished in 2015; they put pressure on the school's president to resign by threatening to sit out of NCAA games and practices. Black and Brown athletes shouldn't be afraid to use their voices and platforms to speak up against injustices they see in their own spaces. If they can also garner the support of their trusted teammates, coaches and administration, then that team truly is unstoppable.

Isaiah Alicea graduated with a degree in Sociology and Criminology from Villanova in the spring of 2019, where he played on the Villanova football team as a walk-on cornerback for four seasons. He returned to campus in the fall of 2019 as a graduate student pursuing his master's degree in public administration on a full academic scholarship. Isaiah's academic interests are in law enforcement, with specific focuses on how to address police and community relations, public policy, local government, and music.

Conversations (or Not) about Race in Martial Arts
Margaret Stansbery

The world of martial arts is steeped in tradition and history. There are rules about how we do things—a lot of rules. They are referred to as "protocol." I love the history and tradition of protocol, but more than anything, protocol makes it really clear how I am supposed to dress or act in any martial arts setting. For someone who is shy, like me, it can be comforting to have things spelled out for me explicitly. Protocol also explains whom you can talk to and how, and that makes it difficult to talk about problematic situations.

An interesting thing about martial arts (at least the one I practice) is that we don't compete as a team, but everything we do reflects on our team. Instructors are told that their students' actions are a mirror of them as instructors. Many martial arts originate from collectivist cultures, which believe a person's actions reflect upon their whole family, so it is unsurprising that collectivist belief has been carried on through the martial arts.

When I walk into a competition, the first thing I do (after bowing) is tell the judges my name and who my instructor is. In case they forget, my studio name is emblazoned on the back of my uniform. I basically wear my instructor's name on my back.

My actions reflect not only on my instructor but also on my studio as a whole. You think differently about what you do when you feel your actions bring honor or shame to those people you spend your most intense waking hours with. These are the people I sweat with, bleed with, who pick me up off the ground, and with whom I navigate moments of extreme disappointment and intense pride. In other words, my studio is my family. Do I want my actions to embarrass my family? No way.

In recent years, tournaments have been an exercise in conflict for me. I love tournaments, and I do pretty well. More important to me than how I score, however, is that I represent my studio in a way that makes me proud. I'm respectful, demonstrate good sportsmanship, and volunteer whenever and wherever I can. But the opening ceremonies are a problem.

Opening ceremonies begin with the national anthem. We are lined up by rank (imagine a military parade), and then we are ordered to "Attention." You don't go against an ordered action. Avoiding Opening Ceremonies is not an option, because my absence would be noticed.

I have become more and more uncomfortable standing for the national anthem. Ever since Colin Kaepernick took a knee during the anthem, in protest of the widespread systemic racial injustice in the United States, I've been in conflict about it. It is simply out of integrity with my personal beliefs for me to continue to stand. But I would embarrass my studio by kneeling. Integrity has always been one of the most valuable things I have, and I'm not used to questioning my integrity. Yet, this conflict between the individual and collectivist aspects of myself is a totally unfamiliar territory. So, I stand, because to kneel would directly defy orders and what I think my instructors believe. But I listen to that last line of the National Anthem—"the land of the free, and the home of the brave"—and I think, *This land is not free, and if I were brave, I would not be standing here.*

I've looked around at tournaments—I mean, as much as you can look around when standing at attention. No one kneels. Not once have I seen anything other than people stopping, standing, and turning to the flags. It honestly surprised me for a long time. But then, I can't bring myself to kneel when I know it would dishonor my studio, so why would anyone else be able to do anything different? Why am I waiting for someone else to defy orders first?

I've tried, carefully, to talk to other people about this conflict. I usually get no response. I know a lot of people in my association on a personal level and have joined with many of them in social justice–related protest marches. But it really seems like I am the only one thinking about this issue. The only response I've ever gotten is, "You're White—that's not your fight to fight."

And yet, I have noticed an interesting shift at tournaments over the last few years. We used to start all tournaments with the same canned, tinny-sounding recording of the National Anthem. A few years ago, however, they switched away from that recording. Now we *always* have a live person or group of people performing. We are overall a fairly White organization, but the groups performing the National Anthem are often people of color from within the association.

In the absence of any conversation about this, I've come up with my own reasoning about why this changed. This switch happened *after* Colin Kaepernick and kneeling became a national topic of conversation. It's harder to kneel in front of live performers, who might be insulted by it. And with this protest being about systemic racial injustice in this country, it just feels weird to kneel when the singers are people of color. It's clear this kneeling conversation is too big for the association to take on. And so, they do what they can to make it more uncomfortable to kneel, or maybe make it more palatable to stand. The only person I have ever brought this theory to thinks I give the association way too much credit. But if this is a contrived method to prevent kneeling within my sport, it's indeed a clever one.

I do have hope that our association will one day be able to enter into some difficult conversations about race issues within the organization. What I've been talking about is just a tiny sliver of the race-related things I notice. On the progressive end, we have done some really great things in other areas of diversity. We have an incredible group of women among our highest ranks, in a largely male-dominated sport, and have made the art accessible to individuals with physical and mental disabilities. There are definitely plenty more areas for growth, but I firmly believe we have amazing, caring individuals leading the organization. Maybe one day I will stumble on some others within the organization interested in helping to lead changes in racial awareness as well.

Margaret Stansbery is an educator and martial artist, practicing a Korean martial art. She is not a black belt yet, but she's getting close. She's been intentionally vague about the art she practices because she would really like to be a black belt soon, and that means not rocking the boat . . . yet!

This chapter profiles important people in the field of race and sports. While most of the profiles presented are of athletes, there are also profiles of non-athletes and sporting organizations that have made significant impacts related to race and sports. This chapter is organized by the self-identified racial identities of profiled individuals and then by organizations.

Biracial/Multiracial

Colin Kaepernick (1987–)

A nineteen-year-old White woman named Heidi Russo gave birth to Colin Kaepernick in Milwaukee, Wisconsin, on November 3, 1987. Colin Kaepernick's Black birth father was not in the picture when he found out Russo was pregnant. During her pregnancy, Russo decided that adoption was the best idea and decided to give her son to Rick and Teresa Kaepernick after meeting them and hearing their story. Rick and Teresa, a White couple from Fond du Lac, Wisconsin, had two children already but had lost two others shortly after their births due to heart defects. Rick and Teresa knew they had chosen to place a biracial son in their all-White family. It has been both the circumstances that Colin

A graffiti drawing on a brick wall in Atlanta, Georgia of bi-racial athlete Colin Kaepernick kneeling. The former NFL quarterback began kneeling during the national anthem in August 2016, in protest of police brutality and social injustices. Kaepernick's career in the NFL ended at the end of the 2016 season, arguably due to his protesting, sparking national debate and outcry. (David Carey/Dreamstime.com)

Kaepernick had no control over—like his adoption into a White family—and the personal choices he has made to learn more about his own roots that led to Kaepernick first kneeling during the national anthem as the quarterback of the National Football League (NFL)'s San Francisco 49ers in August 2016.

At the age of four, Kaepernick moved from Wisconsin to Turlock, California because his father took a job as operations manager of a cheese company based there. In Turlock, "the population of about 73,000 is overwhelmingly white and increasingly Latino. In Turlock, fewer than 2 percent of residents identify as African-American, according to the census" (Branch, 2017). As a young boy, Kaepernick became accustomed to people assuming he wasn't actually a member of his own family. Often, Kaepernick would use humor as a response when asked if he were adopted during his childhood. As he grew taller and older, Kaepernick recalls mounting frustration at how he was treated on family trips:

> We used to go on these summer driving vacations and stay at motels . . . every year, in the lobby of every motel, the same thing always happened. . . . It didn't matter how close I stood to my family, somebody would walk up to me, a real nervous manager, and say: "Excuse me. Is there something I can help you with?"(Branch, 2017).

Fortunately, Colin Kaepernick's best support system growing up was his family, and he thrived as a young athlete in the sports of baseball and football. Colin's older brother, Kyle, created DVDs of Colin's best high school highlights and sent them to college coaches around the country. The University of Nevada in Reno became the next important stop in his athletic development and in Kaepernick's growing interest in racial identity and social politics.

Athletically, Kaepernick excelled on the football team, starting for most of his four seasons, and became the first NCAA quarterback to throw for more than 10,000 yards and rush for more than 4,000 yards. As a Black quarterback, Kaepernick faced some of the historical misperceptions and judgements about his intellectual ability to lead a team in a position known for a reliance not just on athleticism but also on quick decision making and field analysis. A former offensive lineman and teammate for Nevada, John Bender, said in a 2017 interview about Kaepernick that "finding an identity was big for [Colin], because in some aspects in life, he would get the racist treatment from white people because he was a black quarterback. And some people gave him the racist treatment because he was raised by a white family. So where does he fit in in all this?" (Branch, 2017). Off the field, Kaepernick began to take action into exploring racial identity; in his junior year at Nevada, he successfully joined the historically and predominantly Black fraternity Kappa Alpha Psi. Most Division I college athletes are far too busy to join a sorority or fraternity while also balancing academics and athletics, but Kaepernick found balance in joining the fraternity despite all "the commitment required: the time, the rituals, the community service, the all-night study sessions of the fraternity's history and liturgy" (Branch, 2017).

Kaepernick graduated from the University of Nevada with a degree in business management and was then selected by the San Francisco 49ers in the second round of the NFL draft in 2011. Kaepernick came into national success as a quarterback after being called up by former coach Jim Harbaugh to take the role as starting quarterback for the team in the 2012–2013 NFL season. Suddenly, his jersey was being sported across the Bay Area and he even posed nude for the annual *ESPN Magazine*'s Body Issue. During his rising stardom, Kaepernick was fully aware of the impact that he has on fans for all types of reasons that transcend the football field. In a 2013 interview with *Sports Illustrated* writer, Peter King, Kaepernick said:

> I want to have a positive influence as much as I can. I've had people write me because of my tattoos. I've had people write me because of adoption. I've had people write me because they're biracial. I've had people write me because their kids have heart defects—my mom had two

boys who died of heart defects, which ultimately brought about my adoption. So, to me, the more people you can touch, the more people you can influence in a positive way or inspire, the better. (Branch, 2017)

With the positive also comes some negative, however, and Kaepernick wasn't immune to being affected by negative attention, either. At times, Kaepernick was judged by others for his tattoos and criticized by some journalists when he expressed no interest in building a relationship with his birth mother when she emerged during the rise of his fame. Over the next couple of NFL seasons, the 49ers didn't perform as well, and Kaepernick lost his starting job under one new coach in 2015 and remained out of the starting spot under another new 49ers coach in 2016.

In early 2016, there were some signs via social media that Kaepernick was continuing his personal journey in educating himself about African American history and culture. His Instagram and Twitter posts became less about football and more about acknowledging African Americans who resonated with him, like the late activist Malcolm X and rapper Tupac Shakur. Kaepernick had also returned to the classroom in the summer of 2016, auditing the summer course of University of California Berkeley doctoral candidate Ameer Hasan Loggins. The course focused on Black representation in popular culture and Loggins shared a reading list with Kaepernick that included seminal Black Studies scholars like bell hooks, Frantz Fanon, Carter G. Woodson, and Patricia Hill Collins. Then, in July 2016, Kaepernick's social media posts became more passionate after the murders of unarmed Black men Alton Sterling and Philando Castile by White police officers less than twenty-four hours apart from one another. Kaepernick was unfiltered in his anger toward the handling of police brutality in the country. Knowing that he wanted to take action that would be symbolic and lasting, without taking the attention away from the issue at hand, Kaepernick consulted with two other important people before deciding what to do: Dr. Harry Edwards and Nate Boyer.

Colin Kaepernick wanted to make sure he had no conflict with veterans or the military in the action he would take to make a statement about police brutality, so he spoke with Nate Boyer. Nate Boyer is a former long-snapper for the Seattle Seahawks and before that was a Green Beret. Boyer suggested quietly taking a knee during the national anthem (Bryant, 2018, 5). Kaepernick consulted with revered sociologist and activist Dr. Harry Edwards as well. Dr. Edwards organized the 1968 Olympic protest that concluded with John Carlos and Tommie Smith with their black-gloved fists on the medal podium in Mexico City. Colin Kaepernick decided to start his protest at the start of the preseason; it wasn't until the third preseason game on August 26, 2016, that reporters started to notice. When asked about his kneeling gesture during the anthem, Kaepernick said, "I am not going to stand up to show pride in a flag for a country that oppresses black people and people of color. . . . There are bodies in the street and people getting paid leave and getting away with murder" (Bryant, 2018, 6). He also clarified that he had not asked anyone for permission from the team or from sponsors. Kaepernick said, "I am not looking for approval. I have to stand up for people that are oppressed. If they take away my endorsements from me, I know that I stood up for what is right" (Branch, 2017). Much like the careers of Black athlete activists before him, Colin Kaepernick's future NFL career outlook went from bright, to unknown, to nonexistent for standing up against racial oppression and police brutality.

Response to Kaepernick's kneeling has ranged from support to the burning of Nike apparel—Kaepernick is the face of a new ad campaign for the thirtieth anniversary of Nike's "Just Do It" slogan—and support or opposition wasn't based on race. Some opponents of Kaepernick's kneeling during the anthem found it insincere for a millionaire who was raised comfortably in a White family to speak out on the oppression of Black people. Others simply thought Kaepernick was seeking some attention after a decline in the quality of his NFL quarterback career.

And most said the kneeling during the anthem was antimilitary, despite Kaepernick stating that was not his intent on the very first day he was interviewed on it:

> The message being sent by . . . a white player or coach with no stake in the issues that motivated Kaepernick yet were asked their opinion anyway, was shut up and play, and it was a message that largely resonated with the ticket buyers and the talk-radio honkers, who did not make up the demographic for whom police brutality was actually a personal issue. It was a charade of platitudes to democracy, the old lines of "You can speak out, but there are other ways to protest" . . . shorthand for the white mainstream still making the rules, of telling the players what they could do and when they could do it, which naturally defeated the entire purpose of protest. Protest didn't ask permission. (Bryant, 2018, 12)

Kaepernick had no intention of listening to the "shut up and play" crowd, and he wasn't the only professional athlete who felt that way.

By the fourth preseason game, Kaepernick was taking a knee on the sideline joined by teammate Eric Reid and Seattle Seahawks player Jeremy Lane sat for the anthem before a different NFL match-up on the same day. White U.S. professional soccer player Megan Rapinoe showed solidarity by kneeling during the anthem of a professional women's soccer match in the Netherlands, and other NFL players began to kneel as NFL regular season play began. National Basketball Association (NBA) players Carmelo Anthony, Lebron James, and Chris Paul all voiced support for Kaepernick as well. Many veterans came to the support of Kaepernick as well. In an open letter to the NFL that was signed by more than two dozen veterans of the Iraq and Afghanistan Wars, these veterans wrote: "Far from disrespecting our troops, there is no finer form of appreciation for our sacrifice than for Americans to enthusiastically exercise their freedom of speech. . . . Far too often, people are dying at the hands of law enforcement personnel in the streets, our jails, and their homes. Indictments are rare and convictions are essentially nonexistent" (Bryant, 2018, 17). Despite those sentiments expressed by some veterans, Kaepernick's kneeling protests against police brutality and racial oppression continue to be interpreted as "anthem protests" that are steeped in politics.

After the 49ers finished a terrible 2–14 for the season, the coach and general manager were fired and replaced. Kaepernick's contract with the 49ers was due to pay him millions once he made the team, but with the turnover in coaching and leadership, Kaepernick knew making the team was not a sure thing. So Colin Kaepernick opted out as a free agent on March 1, 2017, and has been out of the NFL ever since. The question of whether Kaepernick has been intentionally kept out of the NFL is an ongoing debate and legal case in the making. In late August 2018, "Kaepernick won a legal victory in his grievance against the NFL, in which he alleges the owners have conspired to keep him off the field because of his protests, when an arbitrator denied the league's request to throw out the case" (Graham, 2018). The burden for Kaepernick will be in proving collusion by the league's "32 non-Black league owners" (Branch, 2017).

In the years since Colin Kaepernick has played in an NFL game, Kaepernick has hardly been silenced. He initiated the "Know Your Rights Camp," a free campaign for youth to raise awareness on self-empowerment, higher education, and how to properly interact with law enforcement in various situations. During these camps:

> [C]hildren received free breakfasts and T-shirts listing 10 rights: The right to be free, healthy, brilliant, safe, loved, courageous, alive, trusted and educated, plus "the right to know your rights" . . . seminars and sessions on black history, including segregation and Jim Crow laws . . . lessons on healthy eating and household finances . . . advice on

speaking and dressing for respect, and for how to calmly handle interactions with the police. (Branch, 2017)

Kaepernick also successfully fulfilled a one-million-dollar pledge he made, donating $100,000 every month to up to four charities since October 2016. Most of the recipients of the donations were small organizations that were relatively unknown and assist Americans for all different reasons: supporting single mothers in Georgia; clean-energy advocacy; immigration rights in Los Angeles; Black veterans; healthy food through urban gardening; and reproductive rights, to just name a few. And with Kaepernick's endorsement by Nike in 2018, "some people posted videos of themselves burning Nike products on social media, but huge numbers of Americans are with Kaepernick. Look no further than the ovation he received . . . at Arthur Ashe Stadium when he was shown on the JumboTron raising his fist as Serena and Venus Williams faced off at the US Open" (Graham, 2018).

The NFL kneeling continued into the 2018–2019 NFL season despite Kaepernick's absence. The League, showing just how much it still has to come to understand protest and supporting its players, came up with a proposed anthem policy that was quickly restrained by the NFL Players Association in July 2018. According to sportswriter Howard Bryant, "what Kaepernick revealed was that sports was no less divided along racial lines than the rest of the country, even if its workforce comprised a black majority. The only difference was, the players were black millionaires" (2018, 13). Players continue to protest during the national anthem, continuing the movement that Colin Kaepernick started. It will be significant to see how/ if the anthem policy may change in the NFL and what happens with Kaepernick's legal grievance against the NFL. Most importantly, everyone should pay attention to what Colin Kaepernick does next because he's clear about his identity as an African American man descending from Africa with a mission to remain persistent in the end of racial injustice and racialized forms of police brutality.

Hines Ward (1976–)

Hines Ward is a South Korean and African American former NFL Steelers football player and advocate for children's literacy and social acceptance of mixed-race children in South Korea. Ward also served as the head of football development for the Alliance of American Football, a new, eight-team professional football league that debuted in February 2019. Unfortunately, the first season was cut short, and the Alliance of American Football filed for bankruptcy in April 2019. Ward's South Korean mother, Young He Ward, gave birth to Hines in 1976. Ward's parents were not a couple meant to last, and they divorced not long after moving from Seoul to the United States when Hines was a year old. After spending his early years with his African American soldier father, Hines moved to his mother's home in Atlanta when he was in the second grade.

For Ward, sports became a space where he didn't have to worry about the color of his skin. In an interview with *New York Times* writer, John Branch, Ward told him:

> It was hard for me to find my identity. . . . The black kids didn't want to hang out with me because I had a Korean mom. The white kids didn't want to hang out with me because I was black. The Korean kids didn't want to hang out with me because I was black. It was hard to find friends growing up. And then once I got involved in sports, color didn't matter. (Branch, 2009)

Ward found a sense of belonging and inclusion in sports and excelled in football and baseball. Eventually, Ward chose to stick with football, attending the University of Georgia on a football scholarship. Ward's collegiate career saw him earn All-SEC honors and finish as the team's second all-time receiver. The Pittsburgh Steelers selected Hines Ward in the third round of the 1998 NFL draft.

Ward's professional career began to take off in 2001 and by 2006, he was a celebrity in Pittsburgh and Korea with his Super Bowl XL ring and MVP status. In the spring after the Super Bowl win, Ward visited South Korea for the first time since he left as a baby. In South Korea, "the number of Amerasians—those generally with white or black American fathers, often from the military—is slowly shrinking, but their mere appearance leads to harsher discrimination" (Branch, 2009). Ward was greatly impacted by his trip to South Korea, especially with the biracial children he spent time with through the Pearl S. Buck International group, and in September 2006, founded the Hines Ward Helping Hands foundation in the U.S. and later in South Korea. Ward "pledged an initial $1 million in U.S. funds ($785,000 Korean) to the Hines Ward Helping Hands Foundation" (Jin-man, 2006), a charity run through The Pittsburgh Foundation with goals in the United States to help underprivileged and inner-city youth with literacy and other programs designed to help them succeed in life. The South Korea iteration of the charity, a partnership with Pearl Buck International, aims to combat bi-racial discrimination. When asked by a journalist in 2011 what made Ward start to work for these causes, he responded:

> I decided to start my charity out of my love for kids of all ages and because of my own upbringing. In Pittsburgh, I meet kids of all ages from all walks of life. I see the desire in their eyes to be someone great and I want to do all that I can to help those without the means and/or resources to achieve their dreams. When I went to Korea and saw, firsthand, the biracial children, I could easily identify with them and they embraced me, like a hero. I do not want to let them down. I want to encourage them by providing

them with resources and programs that will enhance their lives and chances for success in life. (Ward, 2011)

Ultimately, Ward wants all the children involved to never be ashamed of who they are or where they come from and have the opportunity to thrive and "achieve their dreams." And for the biracial Amerasians, Ward wants them to embrace the opportunity to be a part of two cultures.

Hines Ward spent his entire fourteen-year career with the Steelers, retiring after the 2011 NFL season. Ward has been and continues to be much more than a professional athlete. Ward is also activist, mentor, news analyst, and even restauranteur and actor. In 2010, Ward was appointed by former President Barack Obama to the President's Advisory Commission on Asian Americans and Pacific Islanders. When asked what he wants his legacy to be, Ward said, "I want to be known as a sincere ambassador for underprivileged and biracial children worldwide. In Korea, I want to do my part in ending the biracial discrimination that is prevalent there. Football is my passion. Children are my heart. We don't choose to be the color or race we are. It is a gift from God and we should all view it that way" (Ward, 2011).

Black

Kareem Abdul-Jabbar (1947–)

The man who lives today as Kareem Abdul-Jabbar did not come into existence until 1971 while a standout for the NBA's Milwaukee Bucks. Originally named Lew Alcindor, he changed his name to Kareem Abdul-Jabbar. Lew Alcindor was born in 1947 and raised in the city of Harlem, New York. Standing seven feet two inches tall, Alcindor became the most publicized and sought-after college player in the United States. Alcindor chose to attend UCLA and, as a sophomore, joined the UCLA varsity team for the 1966–1967 season. The success of Lew Alcindor at the collegiate level had not been seen since the likes of

Wilt Chamberlain. As a UCLA Bruin, Alcindor led his teammates and Hall of Fame coach, John Wooden, to three national
championships in four years. After UCLA won its first national
title with an undefeated record, the NCAA decided to ban
the dunk. While the NCAA and some of its college coaches
cited things like "too many players got injured . . . breaking
backboards and bending rims . . . [and] no defense against the
dunk" (Smith, 2018), critics of the ban aptly referred to it as
the "Alcindor rule," and Alcindor saw the racial discrimination
through the poor explanations of the NCAA because most of
the people who dunked at the time were Black athletes.

Alcindor's acute awareness of racism and racial politics
sparked before his arrival to UCLA's campus, but his activism emerged during his time as a Bruin. In his autobiography,
Giant Steps, Abdul-Jabbar reflected that after the bombing of
the Sixteenth Street Baptist Church that resulted in the death
of four little girls in Birmingham, Alabama, occurred in 1963,
"my whole view of the world fell into place. My faith was exploded like church rubble, my anger was shrapnel. I would
gladly have killed whoever killed those girls by myself" (Lapchick, 2015). Within just a handful of years, Alcindor began to
become activated beyond sheer emotion. He became inspired
by other successful Black athletes like Muhammed Ali, Bill
Russell, and Jim Brown, admiring their activism and courage to challenge White supremacy nationally and globally. In
1967, with Muhammad Ali having publicly denounced the
Vietnam War because it didn't align with his moral beliefs and
Ali's willingness to suffer consequences for not fighting the
Vietcong, Jim Brown invited Alcindor and seven other professional Black athletes to meet with Ali after Ali had been
stripped of his heavyweight title. This meeting was called the
Cleveland Summit. At age twenty, Alcindor was the youngest
participant in the Summit, which called for him and his fellow Black athletes to determine the sincerity of Ali's claim of
being a conscientious objector. The Cleveland Summit had a
profound impact on Alcindor:

[I]t marked the first time that black athletes unified across various sports to rally behind a single cause. It also inspired Alcindor to see himself in the same light as Ali, Brown and Russell . . . he realized that day that he too had a responsibility to use his platform to speak out against racism and injustice, even at a cost. (Smith, 2018)

Shortly after the Cleveland Summit, Alcindor absolutely began to "use his platform to speak out against racism and injustice" at a cost.

The next year, 1968, was a tumultuous one nationally and internationally—Martin Luther King Jr. was assassinated, the world was denouncing South African apartheid—and Black athletes were preparing to revolt under the leadership of Dr. Harry Edwards at San Jose State University and the newly founded OPHR. Lew Alcindor was one of the first athletes to get on board with the OPHR, explaining why in an interview with *Sports Illustrated*:

I pushed to the back of my mind all the normalcies of college life and dug down deep into my black studies and my religious studies. I withdrew to find myself. I made no attempt to integrate. I was consumed and obsessed by my interest in the black man, in Black Power, black pride, black courage. That, for me, would suffice. I was full of serious ideas. I could see the whole transition of the black man and his history. And I developed my first interest in Islam. (Zirin, 2008, 163)

While "serious ideas" and the visualization of a better trajectory for Black Americans was fairly easy to do, Alcindor had been invited to play on the 1968 Olympic men's basketball team, and he was torn in making his decision. Alcindor felt that joining the team would signal support for the current state of race relations in America, but that not joining would make him appear as though he didn't love his country, and he loved the

United States. Ultimately, Alcindor chose to boycott the 1968 Olympics, instead choosing to work for Operation Sports Rescue "teach[ing] kids in New York City how to play basketball and why they should stay in school" (Abdul-Jabbar, 2018). Lew Alcindor's decision resulted in backlash that mostly characterized him as disgraceful, unpatriotic, and ungrateful. Some even called for the revocation of his scholarship to UCLA if he didn't play for the U.S. Olympic team. Although "we remember the 1968 Olympics for John Carlos and Tommie Smith's demonstration on the victory stand, Alcindor was the most famous athlete who avoided the games" (Smith, 2018).

Alcindor decided to take another risk based on his beliefs right after winning the NBA title with the Milwaukee Bucks in 1971: he publicly declared that he was Muslim and had changed his name from Lew Alcindor to Kareem Abdul-Jabbar. Upon his graduation from UCLA in 1969, Alcindor had been picked first in the 1969 NBA draft by the Bucks and earned Rookie of the Year honors. Alcindor was an instant star at the professional level, winning his first NBA title with the Bucks in his second season. Alcindor—who had converted to Islam in 1968—realized making a public statement about his name change and religious beliefs was a risk for his career. However, Kareem Abdul-Jabbar's personal authenticity outweighed his desire for endorsement deals and larger paychecks. Kareem's introduction to the world did affect his professional earning potential as "the ad men and marketers of Madison Avenue weren't too keen on him. Kareem was too aware, too serious, and, most of all, too *political*" (Bryant, 2018, 71). The businessmen of sport focused their efforts instead on the NFL's O. J. Simpson in the 1970s and 1980s, who opted to stay out of politics and steer Black athletes to focus on endorsement deals. The NBA's Michael Jordan soon took the spotlight from O. J. Simpson but followed in Simpson's footsteps in remaining apolitical and focused on selling products and increasing ticket sales. In the mid-1970s and 1980s, "Abdul-Jabbar turned inward, perhaps tired of fighting alone and disillusioned that he was the only one who had actually gone through with the 1968 Olympic boycott, [and] became a distant voice of a fading movement" (Bryant, 2018, 82). Abdul-Jabbar still remained one of the best basketball players of all time throughout his career, being acquired by the Los Angeles Lakers in 1975. In his twenty years of professional basketball, he amassed six championships and six MVP awards and appeared in nineteen All-Star Games.

Since Kareem Abdul-Jabbar's retirement from the game, however, he has become an influential writer and cultural commentator. He has written fifteen books; contributed to publications like *ESPN*, *Time*, the *Guardian*, and *Huffington Post*; was named a global cultural ambassador in 2012 by then–secretary of state Hillary Clinton; and continues to speak across the country. Abdul-Jabbar has most recently been a huge supporter of Colin Kaepernick and the Black athletic protestation in support of all types of issues related to equality and inclusiveness. In a piece about what sports have taught him about race in America, Abdul-Jabbar wrote:

> Sports energizes me and makes me hopeful about humanity. But I am even more energized and hopeful when I see those same athletes speak out against injustices because I know that in doing so, they are risking the careers that they spent their whole lives working towards. Their willingness to risk everything in order to give voice to the powerless—despite all efforts to silence them—makes me proud as an athlete and as an American. . . . Athletes who speak out are proclaiming their loyalty to a constitution that demands equality and inclusiveness. (2018)

It may have taken decades spent in the shadows, but Kareem Abdul-Jabbar has re-emerged as one among many Black athletes who is willing to risk everything for the betterment of a collective society. And this time, much of society is paying attention to Kareem's words with the reverence that he deserves.

Muhammad Ali (1942–2016)

Muhammad Ali didn't become known as Muhammed Ali until the 1960s. Muhammed Ali was born in Louisville, Kentucky, in 1942 with the birth name of Cassius Clay. Clay's father made money as a house painter, and Clay's mother was a domestic worker. "The Louisville of 1942 was a segregated horse-breeding community, where being Black meant being seen as a servant" (Zirin, 2005, 58). Clay, however, had other plans for how he'd be seen: boxing well and using his voice. His relentless talking earned him the nicknames "Cash the Brash," "Louisville Lip," "Gaseous Cassius," and "Mighty Mouth." At eighteen, Clay's boxing skills won him the gold medal in the 1960 Rome Olympics. Back at home post-Olympics, Clay often wore his medal around Louisville. One day, when attempting to patronize a restaurant with the gold medal around his neck, Clay was denied service. This moment of discrimination catalyzed something political within Clay.

Cassius Clay continued to box magnificently, but he also searched for political answers, eventually finding the words of Malcolm X most compelling at a meeting of the Nation of Islam (NOI). In 1964, after beating Sonny Liston to win the heavyweight title, Clay announced that he converted to Islam and was a follower of the Nation of Islam. For a while, he was known as Cassius X until the leader of the Nation of Islam, Elijah Muhammad, gave Cassius Clay the name Muhammed Ali. The boxer's Islamic name change was something no professional athlete had done before, and the public impact was enormously significant:

> Almost overnight, calling the champ Ali or Clay indicated where one stood on civil rights, Black Power, and eventually, the war in Vietnam. For years after the change, the *New York Times'* editorial policy was to refer to Ali as Clay. This all took place against the backdrop of a Black freedom struggle that rolled from the South to the North. During the summer of 1964, there were 1,000 arrests

of civil rights activists, thirty buildings bombed, and thirty-six churches burned by the Ku Klux Klan and their sympathizers. . . . The politics of Black Power began to emerge, and Muhammed Ali became the critical symbol of this transformation. (Zirin, 2005, 63)

Ali continued to dominate the boxing world and use his voice to stand up for his beliefs. For example, in November 1965, Ali defeated Floyd Patterson in a memorable bout. Leading up to the bought, Ali was the "villain" and Patterson was the "patriotic" African American. Patterson had refused to call Ali by his new name and told the public that he felt beating Ali was his patriotic duty. The fight was easily dominated by Ali, and throughout the nine rounds, Ali kept yelling at Patterson, "Come on, America! Come on, white America. . . . What's my name? Is my name Clay? What's my name, fool?" (Zirin, 2005, 63–64)

The next thing that Muhammad Ali did after his name change is what exiled him from boxing for three years and almost ruined him financially. In 1966, Ali became eligible for the draft. Ali was drafted to the U.S. Army, but on April 28, 1967, in Houston, Texas, he refused to be inducted into the armed forces; his refusal to fight in Vietnam was front-page news internationally. When pressed by a reporter about his views on the war, Ali explained on camera:

Why should they ask me to put on a uniform and go 10,000 miles from home and drop bombs and bullets on Brown people in Vietnam while so-called Negro people in Louisville are treated like dogs and denied simple human rights? No, I'm not going 10,000 miles from home to help murder and burn another poor nation simply to continue the domination of white slave masters of darker people the world over. This is the day when such evils must come to an end. I have been warned that to take such a stand would cost me millions of dollars. But I have said it once and I will say it again. The real enemy of my people is here. I will not disgrace my religion, my people, or myself by becoming a tool to enslave those who are fighting for their own justice, freedom, and equality. . . . If I thought the war was going to bring freedom and equality to 22 million of my people they wouldn't have to draft me, I'd join tomorrow. I have nothing to lose by standing up for my beliefs. So I'll go to jail, so what? We've been in jail for 400 years. (Zirin, 2005, 66)

Ali was clear in his stance. For Ali, fighting in Vietnam went against the teachings of the Nation of Islam—the Quran bans Muslims from fighting Christian wars—and also ignored what he felt was a dire situation for Black and Brown people in the United States in attaining "justice, freedom, and equality." Most importantly, Ali knew that speaking out and upholding his beliefs could potentially "cost millions of dollars" and even jail time.

Ali was quickly made to pay the price for refusing to serve in the U.S. Army. Less than two months after he refused his induction, he was convicted of draft evasion, fined $10,000, banned from boxing for three years, got his passport revoked, and was sentenced to five years in prison. Ali never did serve any time in jail, and on June 28, 1971, "The Supreme Court unanimously overturned his conviction, saying his draft board failed to specify why his conscientious objector application was denied" (Wolfson, 2018). However, the three years spent exiled from boxing were not easy for Ali. Though his political influence grew, Ali's treatment from many was negative:

Popular black athletes such as Jackie Robinson and Joe Louis denounced him. . . . In Chicago, where he spent much of his banishment, Mayor Richard Daley refused to call him by his Muslim name, and Illinois Gov. Otto Kerner called him "unpatriotic" . . . to pay the bills and help support his wife, Khailah, and their child, Ali embarked on a college speaking tour, earning pennies on the dollar compared to his time in the ring. (Wolfson, 2018)

The good thing about the college touring was that Muhammed Ali was able to work on his public speaking. He wasn't a very good orator at first, but his speeches improved thanks to the verbal sparring with students. Ali became more of an independent thinker and developed his own consciousness during those three years.

Eventually, Ali fought again and gave the world more of his spectacular boxing ability, reclaiming his heavyweight championship along the way. Both his prolific fights against George Foreman in Zaire and Joe Frazier in Manila took place after his boxing exile. Ali is a man who spent time with both Malcolm X and Martin Luther King and received his fair share of death threats for standing up for what he believes in. In the decades to come, his country and the world would come to embrace him as an ambassador of peace and goodwill (Wolfson, 2018). Ali retired from the sport of boxing in 1981 at the age of thirty-nine and having only lost five matches.

A few years after his retirement, Ali was diagnosed with Parkinson's Syndrome, a cluster of symptoms that resemble Parkinson's Disease. Ali's motor skills began to decline slowly, along with his speech. Yet, Ali remained committed to advocating for his religion and being an example of humanitarianism at its best. Ali served as a United Nations Messenger of Peace, was inducted into the Boxing Hall of Fame in 1990, lit the cauldron at the 1996 Olympic Games, and was awarded the Presidential Medal of Freedom in 2005. Ali died at the age of seventy-four. Ali married four times in his life and had nine children, seven daughters and two sons. He passed away in June of 2016 at the age of seventy-four.

Simone Biles (1997–) and the World Champions Centre

African American gymnast Simone Biles is the most decorated American gymnast of all time. Biles was born in Columbus, Ohio, in 1997 but spent her childhood living in Texas with her adopted parents, Ron and Nellie Biles. Ron and Nellie Biles have been the parents of Simone and her sister, Adria, since the girls were ages five and three, respectively. Ron is the maternal grandfather of Simone and Adria; Ron's daughter struggled with drugs and alcohol, so the girls came to live with Ron and Nellie. Although Biles does keep in touch with her biological mother, she has made it clear to the world that Ron and Nellie are her parents and should not be referred to as her grandparents. If it weren't for her parents, it's unlikely that Simone would be the best gymnast in the world.

It is clear that Biles's rise to the top in gymnastics is impressive, but so is the way she and her family are, perhaps, creating a gymnastics empire in Spring, Texas:

> World Champions Centre, which is owned by Ron and Nellie Biles, who built it from the ground up as their retirement venture, consulting with architects on its family-friendly design. It's a 56,000-square-foot, light-filled and color-splashed oasis for gymnasts of all ages and abilities, as well as their parents and siblings. The Biles made sure to include the amenities they would have liked during the years they took turns watching Biles practice and compete in countless gyms around the country and world. There's an observation room above the gym floor for adults, with Wi-Fi and comfortable seating. There's a café; dance and taekwondo studios for siblings who aren't interested in gymnastics but need to stay busy; classrooms for use by families who home-school their children. (Clarke, 2016)

Simone Biles began practicing in the World Champions Centre in 2014, but the Centre officially opened to the public in the spring of 2016. The road to creating the World Champions Centre was long and risky for the Biles family because gymnastics is not a sport that has historically fielded large numbers of elite Black athletes, coaches, or organizations like baseball, football, or basketball. Fortunately for Simone Biles, she grew up with parents who were financially stable and business savvy.

As professor Gary Sailes notes, "Black athletic success is not a genetic phenomenon but the result of the determination of Black individuals to overcome perceived arbitrary and deliberately contrived social barriers" (Sailes, 1991, 485). In other words, Simone Biles and her family have successfully worked at creating the athletic environment where Black gymnasts, coaches, and gym owners can thrive.

It is quite possible that there is no other Black-owned gymnastics training facility like the World Champions Centre. Former rhythmic gymnast Wendy Hilliard established the Wendy Hilliard Gymnastics Foundation in 1996 and has helped to provide free and low-cost gymnastics programs for inner-city youth in Harlem, New York, and Detroit, Michigan. However, Hilliard's foundation is a nonprofit and has to rely heavily on volunteerism and donations. The World Champions Centre employs all of its staff members—five out of fourteen who are visibly people of color (one Asian, four African American)—and earns a profit from its competitive teams, preschool and recreational programs, dance classes, taekwondo classes, and birthday parties. The five people of color among the World Champions Centre staff all hold titles of either owner, manager, director, or head coach (World Champions Centre, 2020).

Images of successful Black athletes in the United States abound, but there are far fewer images of these athletes and other Black Americans as role models for ownership. The obsession with highly visible and successful professional athletes overshadows or even negates the most common experiences of professional athletes (Beamon and Messer, 2014, 182–83). And the common experience of most elite gymnasts is to be coached by Whites, compete alongside White teammates, and train in a gym that is owned by Whites. The Biles family is changing the narrative, and over time, the World Champions Centre may become known as *the* gym to train at if one wants to become an Olympic gymnast. Most gymnasts are lucky if they make a second Olympic team, but Simone seems to be well on her way to her second, the Tokyo 2021 Olympic games. In her first competition since winning four Olympic gold medals in Rio, Simone Biles earned a "commanding all-around win with a score of 58.70 at the GK U.S. Classic on July 28, 2018 at the Schottenstein Center in Columbus [Ohio]" (Direnna, 2018) and easily came in first at the U.S. Gymnastics Championships the following month with a margin of victory of over six full points—her fifth national title in six years.

Even if Simone does compete in another Olympics, her career will be short-lived because of the nature of her sport. Ron and Nellie Biles have already secured a financial future for Simone and the rest of their family members in the World Champions Centre *and* established themselves as an example of how to own their Black athletic capital, rather than be financially exploited by the predominantly White gymnastics world. It would be useful for Black athletes in other sports to look to the Biles family and the World Champions Centre as a model for building wealth among the African American community. Despite this success, "of the dozen or so articles collected by this researcher on Biles [leading up to the 2016 Rio Olympics], only two mentioned that Biles's parents built the gym in which she trains" (Myers, 2018, 63). Simone Biles and her family's financial stability and economic promise in the gymnastics world as African Americans is an incredibly important story that needs to be told by the media.

Harry Edwards (1942–)

For many sports scholars, Dr. Harry Edwards is seen as the pioneer of the sociological study of the African American sporting experience. Dr. Edwards's research is specialized in the areas of sport, race, and protest. Edwards is not only "the first scholar to write a book [*Revolt of the Black Athlete*, 1969] about the black protest of the 1968 Olympic Games" (Lomax, 2002, 469), but also helped to organize the iconic podium protest of sprinters Tommie Smith and John Carlos at the 1968 Summer Olympics in Mexico City. And even decades later, you can now find Harry Edwards offering counsel to protesting athletes like Colin Kaepernick and other professional sports teams who wish to support activism among its players for righteous causes.

Harry Edwards was born in St. Louis, Missouri in 1942 but spent the majority of his early years in East St. Louis. The childhood that Edwards found himself living was not easy. For a while, Edwards's mother and father tried to raise their eight kids, in a neighborhood fittingly named The Bottoms, as a lower-working class family. However, life didn't go according to ideal plans and Harry's mother left, not returning until Harry was twelve years old. Of his siblings, Harry was the only one who chose to remain with his father because there was familiarity in the routine of life he already had, which included athletic success. Edwards became a star athlete at East St. Louis High, and soon after his graduation in 1960, he transferred to San Jose State University on a track and field scholarship after originally enrolling in Fresno City College.

As an undergraduate student-athlete at San Jose State University, Edwards qualified for the Olympic trials, set a school record in discus, and even captained the basketball team. Edwards quit the track team before the Olympic trails, however, when "the discriminatory treatment of black athletes [at San Jose State] left him alienated and angry" (O'Neal, 2018). Rather than flee from or succumb to these feelings of alienation and anger, Edwards chose to set his life on a path to confront the racial discrimination experienced by Black athletes like himself, despite having incredible professional athletic opportunities within his grasp:

> He was on draft boards for the San Diego Chargers and Minnesota Vikings, and the NBA's Los Angeles Lakers expressed interest too. Instead, he decided to go to Cornell to get a master's degree and, eventually, a doctorate. His father thought he was throwing away a black man's best chance, the chance he never got, and three years passed before he spoke to his son again. (O'Neal, 2018)

While at Cornell for his master's degree, Edwards began to drive into New York City on weekends to attend meetings organized by Malcolm X. According to Edwards, "Malcolm's new stimulating ideas stirred a passion in him to legitimize and act upon deeply felt convictions . . . [Malcolm X] spoke for the need for black unity and self-determination, for community control, and for the internalization of the black struggle" (Lomax, 2002, 470). Upon finishing his master's degree, Edwards accepted a position as an instructor back at San Jose State.

In 1967, Edwards assembled together a number of Black athletes to discuss the possibility of an Olympic boycott. The group called their undertaking the Olympic Project for Human Rights (OPHR) and announced their plan at a news conference in New York City, with their list of demands ready:

> The demands included the reinstatement of Ali as world heavyweight champion (illegally stripped of the title by the U.S. government), the ousting of Avery Brundage as president of the International Olympic Committee, an end to the discrimination against black and Jews by the New York Athletic Club (NYAC), the appointment of an additional black coach to the Olympic track and field team, the selection of a black man to the United States Olympic Committee, and the barring of South Africa and Rhodesia from Olympic competition. (Wiggins, 1997, 108)

Even though the OPHR boycott lost some of its numbers by the time the 1968 Mexico City Olympics arrived, due to the assassination of Martin Luther King Jr. and turmoil in Mexico City less than two weeks before the start of the Games, Tommie Smith and John Carlos raised their fists, spreading the cause of the OPHR globally through media coverage.

Two years later, Edwards was hired at the University of California, Berkeley, where he remained a sociology professor until 2001. Edwards now holds the title of Professor Emeritus at the same institution, but his journey to get there was not a smooth one. In his first seven years at UC Berkeley, Edwards taught oversubscribed classes, published widely, and "invented a field of study, the sociology of sports, and provided the foundation for all its assertions" (O'Neal, 2018). Despite these achievements, Edwards was initially denied tenure in 1977, sparking media coverage and campus protests. The decision was reversed shortly thereafter.

The scholarship of Harry Edwards has made a significant contribution to the field of sociology, as he ushered in the narrative for the history of the Black experience in sport in a way that also established a high standard for research and analysis. The chief assertion of the sociology of sport is "that sports is a recapitulation of the power relationships in society and you can't have a non-racist sports-industrial complex within the context of a racist society, 'any more than you can have a chicken lay a duck egg,' [Edwards] says" (O'Neal, 2018). Edwards's scholarship "paved the way to intellectual respectability for the sport history and sport sociology fields" (Lomax, 2002, 476).

Equally as significant is Edwards's continued commitment to supporting the activism of Black athletes and his commentary on the "wave of modern sports protest" (Moffitt, 2017). In the 1980s, Edwards began consulting on issues of diversity in professional sports organizations through holding seminars that focused on social interactions, player counseling and support, and finances. Alongside former San Francisco 49ers coach Bill Walsh, Edwards established the NFL's Minority Coaches Internship and Outreach Program in order to help produce more coaches of color within the NFL; Mike Tomlin (Pittsburgh Steelers), Marvin Lewis (Cincinnati Bengals), and Hue Jackson (Cleveland Browns) all went through this program. In a 2017 interview with a St. Louis Public Radio journalist, Edwards said of the waves of athlete activism:

It was always clear there were ongoing waves of athletic activism, framed up by historical developments of the moment. . . . Whether abject segregation with Jack Johnson, Jesse Owens and Joe Lewis; whether an effort to desegregate with Jackie Robinson, Larry Doby, Kenny Washington and Chuck Cooper; whether the Black Power Movement, which instituted a new frame of reference beyond the Civil Rights and desegregation effort. We're now in a fourth wave that was framed up by the Black Lives Matter movement. (Moffitt, 2017)

In this "fourth wave," Edwards's decades of activism have found a tangible home in the San Jose State Institute for the Study of Sport, Society and Social Change. The Institute launched in 2017 and houses the books, buttons, jackets, posters, FBI files, primary documents of Edwards' activism throughout the years, and also features research and programming on the significance of the OPHR movement.

Currently in his late seventies, Dr. Harry Edwards is still the man somewhere close by the Black athletes who choose to revolt against White supremacy and other intersectional oppressions. Edwards hopes to see Kaepernick's jersey placed in the Smithsonian's National Museum for African American History and Culture, and "he is already planning lectures on the coming battles, perhaps on female athletes and threats to reproductive rights, perhaps more about football players and President Donald Trump" (O'Neal, 2018). Edwards, the six-foot-eight-inch-tall former Black Panther Party member, is still in the fight that will benefit everyone involved in athletics, not just the Black athlete.

Curt Flood (1938–1997)

Curt Flood is an athlete unknown to most, but the late MLB St. Louis Cardinals All-Star was the catalyst for MLB players winning the power of free agency. Although born in Houston, Texas, in 1938, Flood was raised in Oakland, California, and excelled in youth baseball. Flood was drafted in 1956 by the National League's Cincinnati Reds and was traded to the

St. Louis Cardinals two years later. On the heels of the swelling Black Power movement, MLB union leader Marvin Miller, a former United Steelworkers official, began courting African American players to challenge the biggest economic obstacle faced by players: the reserve clause. The reserve clause essentially deemed players the property of the team. *The Atlantic* journalist Allen Barra perhaps best explains the trouble with the clause from the player's angle: "Simply put, a player was a team's property. Unless the team chose to trade him or release him, his first big-league team would be his only big-league team for his entire career. A player's only recourse was retirement" (Barra, 2011).

After being sent straight to the Southern minor league system, Flood faced a racially segregated reality. Flood was "fighting mad after making it through a southern minor league system of segregated hotels and eating out of the kitchen on road trips" (Zirin, 2008, 206). Of Flood's time in the South and the role it played on his worldview, Miller said, "I have always felt that when a player of [Flood's] temperament and pride was sent to the South, not being able to stay in the same hotels and motels, playing in Georgia and Mississippi, I think it made a very big difference in [Flood's] outlook on the world" (Zirin, 2008, 207). Thus, in 1969, Curt Flood was more than willing to protest his trade—which was never discussed with Flood himself due to the reserve clause—from St. Louis to the Philadelphia Phillies.

Upon the news of his trade from St. Louis to Philadelphia, Flood responded respectfully by writing a letter directly to the commissioner at the time, Bowie Kuhn:

Dear Mr. Kuhn:

After 12 years in the major leagues I do not feel that I am a piece of property to be bought and sold irrespective of my wishes. I believe that any system which produces that result violates my basic rights as a citizen and a human being. I believe that I have the right to consider offers

from other clubs before making any decisions. I, therefore, request that you make known to all the major league
clubs my feelings in this matter, and advise them of my
availability for the 1970 season. (Zirin, 2005, 103–104)

Curt Flood's letter to the MLB commissioner was a request for
free agency—the eligibility to join any team when not bound
by contract. Kuhn's response to Flood was brief; Kuhn agreed
that Flood was not a piece of property but did not see how that
applied to MLB. Unsatisfied by Kuhn response, Flood filed an
antitrust suit against Kuhn that made its way to the Supreme
Court. No active players in the MLB came to support Flood
publicly because it was just too easy for owners to retaliate
against players without free agency. Only two former players,
Jackie Robinson and Hank Greenberg, openly stood in support
of Flood.

In 1972, the Supreme Court handed down a 5–3 ruling in
favor of Kuhn and MLB in *Flood v. Kuhn*. Although Flood had
lost his case, something important came to light for the union-
ized players: "In effect, the court ruled that yes, Flood should
have the right to be a free agent, but that baseball's antitrust
exemption could only be removed by an act of Congress and
that free agency for players should be attained through collective bargaining" (Barra, 2011).

In the handful of years that followed, Marvin Miller and the
union were able to capitalize on the pressure MLB owners felt
due to Flood's suit. Players were able to successfully argue for
binding arbitration on grievances, and "in 1976, when pitchers
Andy Messersmith and Dave McNally agreed to play a season without a contract, arbitrator Peter Seitz ruled them free
agents" (Barra, 2011).

Many fans, media outlets, and owners feared the destruction of "America's pastime," but the opposite occurred. Fear
of losing players to free agency on an annual basis pushed the
owners to compromise with their players. The negotiated compromise system "allowed for players to become free under two

conditions: a) their contracts had expired and b) they had accumulated at least six years of major league service time" (Markusen, 2016). It turns out that fans found the excitement of the free agency system and the possibilities of talent acquisition it created intoxicating: MLB profits increased. The most important increase, however, came in the form of player salaries. In 1967, the average baseball salary was $19,000 a year (Zirin, 2005, 102). Although Curt Flood was an All-Star who had frowned at a salary offer of $100,000 by the Philadelphia Phillies in his trade, Flood knew that the average player in the major leagues had to work in the off-season. A decade later—a mere seven years after Curt Flood played his last professional baseball game—the average major league baseball salary rose to $76,066 (Associated Press, 2008) and it has only continued to increase with current average salaries hovering in the low millions.

As a professional athlete in the United States, Flood sacrificed his own career so that *all* major league baseball players could benefit. As a professional athlete in the United States that also happened to be Black, Flood, like other athletes before him, was never allowed to benefit personally from his fight against institutional oppression:

> By challenging the reserve clause, Flood had used the inheritance of [Jackie] Robinson, just as [Tommie] Smith and [John] Carlos and [Muhammad] Ali had done before, and at enormous cost to himself, one that would never be recouped. Flood would lose . . . much of the goodwill from the people who had attempted to give him a chance to return to the game, and all of his money. . . . Save for a short-lived TV gig with the Oakland A's and other small, unfulfilled flashes of reconciliation with Major League Baseball, there was nothing left in baseball for Curt Flood. (Bryant, 2018, 56)

Flood would go on to receive some recognition in the early 1990s, getting the NAACP Jackie Robinson Award for his contributions to Black athletes in 1992. In 1994, Flood delivered a speech to the current MLB players set to go on strike; his speech earned him a standing ovation. Diagnosed with throat cancer in 1995, Flood succumbed to the disease in January 1997. The words of Curt Flood's epitaph represent how he should be remembered by all: "Baseball didn't change Curt Flood. Curt Flood changed baseball. He fought the good fight" (Barra, 2011).

LeBron James (1984–) and the I Promise School

Like Colin Kaepernick, LeBron James is exemplifying a new wave of Black athlete activism whose voice becomes enhanced with high marketability and financial resources. James grew up with limited financial security in Akron, Ohio, raised by a mother who gave birth to him in 1984 while she was just a teenager. James started to play organized basketball in the fifth grade and honed his game to the point where he became a household name in high school, playing for St. Vincent-St. Mary in Akron. James led his high school team to two Ohio state basketball titles before he entered the 2003 NBA Draft right out of high school. James was drafted as the overall pick in 2003's draft. As a professional player in the NBA, James has played for the Cleveland Cavaliers (2004–2010 and 2014–2018), the Miami Heat (2010–2014), and the Los Angeles Lakers (2018–present). Of his many professional athletic accolades, most impressive are his three NBA titles and four NBA most valuable player honors.

James spent his early twenties as another highly successful professional Black athlete sticking to sports, mostly keeping personal politics and causes close to his chest and bank account—"his net worth is at least $440 million" (Wong, 2018). However, around 2011, LeBron James started to publicly represent social causes and hasn't stopped doing so. Initially, James partnered with State Farm insurance company in a campaign called "26 seconds," which helped to bring awareness to the statistic of American students dropping out of school every twenty-six seconds. James now "has a history of progressive political activism, and has advocated for racial justice, the Black Lives Matter movement, and gun control" (Wong, 2018). With his most recent—and most prolific—endeavor, it's clear that LeBron James has long-term invested focus in education reform in the United States.

In July 2018, it seemed that all of American media took the time to talk about LeBron James, but this time it had nothing to do with his then-recent choice to go play for the Los Angeles Lakers franchise. LeBron James and his LeBron James Family Foundation announced a partnership with the Akron Public School District; a public school would be opened in Akron, Ohio, unlike any other in the country in time for the 2018–2019 academic year. James's school, called the I Promise School (IPS), is unique for a number of reasons, but most so because of its public school status:

> Celebrities often back charter schools, like the Harlem Academy founded by Sean "Diddy" Combs and the Detroit charter named after former NBA player and ESPN analyst Jalen Rose. Or they open unorthodox private schools—think Elon Musk's 40-student school, situated in a conference room at Space X, where kids play with flamethrowers. (Zahn, 2018)

James has created a school that serves children in the same town he grew up in, in the public school system. The creation of the IPS was the next huge step in the James Family Foundation's I Promise program that already runs across dozens of schools in the district, assisting program participants with experiential activities, educational programs, and services. It is James's partnership with a public school system, and the data that can be collected over the next several years on its triumphs and tribulations, that will be absolutely vital for potential U.S. education reform. In fact, in August 2018, Democratic senators in Ohio and Maryland "introduced a bill that would set aside $45 million for federal competitive grants to fund part-nerships between schools and their communities . . . to repli-cate the I Promise model in places that don't have 'a LeBron James'" (Wong, 2018).

The vision and infrastructure of the school are also unique to most public schools, although providing access to quality education is the leading goal for the LeBron James Family Foundation and Akron Public School District. The I Promise School currently differs from most public schools in its yearly and daily schedule and its commitment to students and their families:

> Its lengthy school day runs from 9 a.m. to 5 p.m., along with an extended school year that runs from July through May. During a seven-week summer session, the school will provide STEM-based camps. Students will spend time each day on social-emotional learning, and participate in a "supportive circle" after lunch aimed at helping them refocus on work, Cleveland.com reports. (Zahn, 2018)

Through the I Promise School, the LeBron James Family Foun-dation seeks to change the troubling trajectory of the Akron Public Schools high-school dropout rate. Currently, "fewer than three in four public-school students in Akron—where about a quarter of the city's population lives below the poverty level—graduate high school within four years" (Wong, 2018), so IPS really wants to be involved in aspects of its students' lives beyond a typical academic experience.

By creating a longer school day, IPS is able to support its students, faculty, and families in significant ways. Nutrition and health are key in the IPS experience, as students receive free breakfast, lunch, drinks, and snacks each day and have access to a fitness expert. LeBron James also purchased each student a new bicycle and helmet. Parents and guardians of IPS students are also offered assistance with job placement and even GED classes because, as IPS principal Brandi Davis put it, "It is about true wrap-around support, true family integration, and true compassion" (Zahn, 2018). Students at IPS are also provided with free school uniforms, and the school has a food pantry and clothing center too. The first crop of IPS students are all third and fourth graders, but the school has plans to add grades each year through 2022, when it should serve grades first through eighth. The Akron School District "selected area students from among those who trail their peers by a year or two in academic performance" (Zahn, 2018) and then selected from the pool of students who fit the criteria at random to invite them to be a part of the revolutionary new school. The I Promise School's staff of forty-three comprises the typical classroom teachers and administrators (i.e., principal and assistant principal) and also a tutor, intervention specialists, and teachers who specialize in English as a second language (ESL) instruction, music and physical fitness.

Not many public school systems have the ability to provide for their students and community the way IPS does, and that has everything to do with LeBron James's professional marketability and money. As writer and author Howard Bryant puts it in his latest book *The Heritage: Black Athletes, A Divided America, and the Politics of Patriotism*, "Today's players are ubiquitous, shaped by the marketing muscle of some of the world's biggest corporations. . . . Their ubiquity within the culture has given black athletes a different mission: they are not expected to stand for black people but to make the world a better place" (2018, 224). Fortunately, LeBron James is doing both; he's taken a stand for Black people specifically in his support for the Black Lives Matter movement and also seeks to make the world a better place through his school. The day that James publicly announced the creation and opening of IPS, praise came from celebrities, fellow athletes, much of the media, and the general public. Yet James's efforts with the opening of the I Promise School were not immune to scrutiny by some.

Criticism of James's philanthropic efforts with IPS were targeted at his choice of location and its funding. Some critics felt that LeBron should have chosen to start a school in a different U.S. location where its community is worse off than in Akron. The majority of criticism was aimed at the actual funding of IPS, with the goal being to undercut the significance of James's efforts and have it appear "as James paying for 25 percent of the I Promise School and the other 75 percent being foisted upon the Akron taxpayers" (Barca, 2018). Journalists that spent more efforts talking directly with Akron Public Schools officials were able to combat the narrative that James had actually somehow burdened a community or that his praise should be minimalized. Jerry Barca, contributing writer for *Forbes,* shared key information about the funding of IPS and its taxpayer impact after speaking with Ryan Pendleton, Akron Public School District's chief financial officer and district spokesman Mark Williamson:

> "We've been planning this . . . the district allocated $2.5 million for the school, which has 240 students . . . that's less than one percent of the district's total budget," Pendleton said.
> "It's important for our citizens to know that they're doing something really good with LeBron James. We're not asking them for more money," district spokesman Mark Williamson said. (Barca, 2018)

In addition to the insights of the school district itself, the LeBron James Family Foundation released updated numbers on its total I Promise School contributions shortly after the school opened. The total contributions from the Foundation and its partners is about $2.8 million for the 2018–2019 school year. The following resource breakdown was also provided by the Foundation:

- $2.2 million (contributions made by the foundation and its partners):

- Renovations to the Akron Public School building on W. Market St. which originally housed classroom overflow space for the district
- Desks and furniture, teacher and staff support, wiring of technology and additional needs that are presented within the school
- Family resource center
- Food pantry
- $608,000:
  - Four additional teaching staff members to reduce class size
  - Coverage of substitute teachers
  - Tutors
  - Additional hour of school time
- After-school programs. (Abraham, 2018)

The current significance of LeBron James's I Promise School is so immense due to its long-term commitment. It's true that IPS doesn't belong to LeBron James, as he's not paying for everything. However, that is also the power of IPS because it's not meant to be a school that excludes privileges and benefits between students, their families, and the greater community. Creating a private or charter school could have meant "alienating the local teachers' union and district administrators and, potentially, families without the savvy to take advantage of public-school alternatives" (Wong, 2018). A private or charter school option would have been isolated innovation, a barrier to reaching as many at-risk students as James and his foundation sought to target. The final huge benefit James has made through the creation of the I Promise School is that if students "successfully complete the school program and graduate from high school, James will cover their full tuition at the local public college, University of Akron" (Zahn, 2018). With its oldest students currently in the fourth grade, James's finances will hopefully take huge hits around the year 2026 through his promise to cover college tuitions. Imagine how much U.S. public education could change if more professional Black athletes followed James's lead.

Paul Robeson (1898–1976)

Paul Robeson was much more than a talented athlete, great actor, and singer. In fact, "before the 1950s, Robeson was one of the world's most famous entertainers and beloved American heroes—once being named 'Man of the Year' by the National Association for the Advancement of Colored People [NAACP]" (National Archives, 2016). Paul Robeson was born in 1898 in Princeton, New Jersey, to a father who had escaped slavery and a mother who would die tragically when Robeson was only six. At the age of seventeen, Robeson earned an athletic scholarship to Rutgers University, becoming the third African American to do so. While at Rutgers, Robeson excelled athletically and academically. Athletically, Robeson earned varsity letters in baseball, track, football, and basketball. Academically, Robeson was elected Phi Beta Kappa, "won speech and debate tournaments and managed to graduate valedictorian of his class" (National Archives, 2016).

Upon graduating from Rutgers, Robeson took his academic talents to the law school at Columbia University and athletically used his talents on two professional football teams to help pay his law school tuition from 1920 to 1923. In 1921, he wed fellow Columbia student, journalist Eslanda Goode; the two would be married for more than forty years and have a son together in 1927, Paul Robeson Jr. (Biography.com Editors, 2014). Robeson's professional football career only spanned fifteen games: eight games with the Akron Pros in 1921 and seven games with the Milwaukee Badgers in 1922. Robeson attempted to begin a career as a lawyer in 1923 but ultimately could not thrive professionally and personally in the legal profession as a Black man. Fortunately for Robeson, he had other talents that were considered acceptable by White society for Blacks to make a living off: singing and acting.

With the support of his wife, Eslanda, as his manager, Paul Robeson turned to the theater. Robeson starred in plays, musicals, and films and received rave reviews from audiences of all races and nationalities. His concert career spanned the globe: Vienna, Prague, Budapest, Berlin, Paris, Amsterdam, London, Moscow, New York, and Nairobi (National Archives, 2016). As an internationally known entertainer, Paul Robeson was finally able to financially support his family, earning more money than some of his White counterparts. Robeson's exposure to different parts of the world and its people led him to a greater understanding of universal suffering and inspired him to act:

> Robeson regularly spoke out against racial injustice and was involved in world politics. He supported Pan-Africanism, sang for Loyalist soldiers during Spain's civil war, took part in anti-Nazi demonstrations and performed for Allied forces during WWII. He also visited the Soviet Union several times during the mid-1930s, where he developed a fondness for Russian folk culture. (Biography.com Editors, 2014)

While African Americans embraced Robeson's Pan-Africanism—the idea that Black people were each connected to a global Black community by a common experience, a common condition, and a common cause—it would be Robeson's relationship with the U.S.S.R. that would lead to Robeson's fall from financial stability and public adoration.

In 1949, Robeson traveled to France to attend the Soviet-sponsored Paris Peace Conference. After singing for the audience, Paul Robeson began to address the crowd, delivering an impromptu speech that addressed the reality of being Black in America and stated that "World War III was not inevitable, as many Americans did not want war with the Soviet Union" (King, 2011). Back in the United States, news of Robeson's speech had been reported inaccurately. Politicians and journalists began to dismantle Robeson's esteemed image and paint him as a communist traitor before he even returned to the United States. In an effort to discredit Robeson in the same year, the House Un-American Activities Committee asked influential Black Americans to refute Robeson's claim that Negroes wouldn't fight against Russia. Baseball legend Jackie Robinson, "the Symbol of Integration, was the prized speaker" (Rhoden 2006, 124) and testified against Robeson.

In 1950, the U.S. government revoked Robeson's passport, erasing Robeson's ability to continue to travel and earn an income abroad. Essentially trapped in the United States during the rise of McCarthyism, Robeson found himself blacklisted from domestic record labels, film studios, and concert venues. After six years of failed attempts to reinstate his passport, Paul Robeson found himself in the Eighty-Fourth Congress where the House Un-American Activities Committee held hearings titled "Investigation of the Unauthorized Use of U.S. Passports." Robeson was again attempting to have his passport reinstated. Journalist Howard Bryant aptly describes Robeson's personal situation and resilience in standing up for civil rights for Black Americans at the time of Robeson's hearing:

> The revoking of the passport wiped out Robeson financially, taking him from a person who would be a millionaire in today's dollars to one making about $60,000 annually. . . . It was Robeson's commitment to black people, both in the United States and around the world, combined with his popularity in Russia and his belief in anti-capitalist economic systems that drew the suspicion of the committee. . . . Robeson told the committee that while visiting the Soviet Union, he had never faced the type of discrimination he faced in Mississippi, or the type of hostility he now faced from them. (2018, x–xi)

Robeson only managed to infuriate the members of the House Un-American Activities Committee. Paul Robeson's passport remained revoked for another two years until the U.S. Supreme

Court ruled that the State Department could not deny citizens the right to travel based on political affiliations or beliefs.

In 1958, the same year his passport was reinstated, Paul Robeson's book *Here I Stand* was published. *Here I Stand* was Robeson's way of addressing all the questions about why his pursuit to win the freedom of all Black people incited so much fear in his own country. Paul Robeson certainly stood his ground when it came to using his public persona to try and push for a changed reality for Black people in the United States and beyond. The damage done to his legacy and reputation by White America, however, was immense. Newsreel footage of him was destroyed, recordings were erased, and there was a clear effort in the media to avoid any mention of his name (King, 2011). With his passport reinstated, Robeson began to travel again, but not with the same joy he once experienced. At the end of his life, Robeson experienced debilitating depression and passed away from a stroke at the age of seventy-seven on January 23, 1976, in Philadelphia, Pennsylvania. Despite all of his accomplishments and the efforts of various industries to try and reestablish the honor and legacy of the man, Paul Robeson is often ignored in U.S. history textbooks and conversations.

Kenneth L. Shropshire (1955–)

In July of 2017, Kenneth Shropshire became the CEO of the Global Sport Institute, first Adidas Distinguished Professor of Global Sport at Arizona State University, and a Wharton Endowed Professor Emeritus. Before his tenure at Arizona State began, Shropshire served as a professor in the Wharton School of Business and Department of Africana Studies at the University of Pennsylvania. Kenneth Shropshire is a husband, father, educator, consultant, and attorney. Born in Los Angeles in 1955, Shropshire's love of sport began at a young age, and he earned a football scholarship to Stanford University in 1973. Shropshire graduated with an undergraduate degree in economics in 1977 and then attended Columbia University, earning his JD in 1980. Shropshire "practiced law in his hometown and served for three years as an executive with the Los Angeles Olympic Organizing Committee before joining the Wharton faculty in 1986" (Bolling, 2017).

Shropshire has impacted the realm of sports in a number of ways. Shropshire is the former president of the Sports Lawyers Association, the largest organization of its kind globally, and the former program chair of the American Bar Association Forum Committee, Sports Law Section. Shropshire has also served as a consultant for a number of professional sports organizations and athletes: the NFL and its Players Association; the NCAA; the U.S. Olympic Committee; the Sixers Innovation Lab; the MLB's On Field Diversity Task Force; and PGA golfer Rory McIlroy. In addition, Shropshire has served on the Board of Directors for the Ross Initiative in Sports for Equality (RISE) since 2016, and he serves on the Board of Directors of USA Volleyball. Shropshire's biggest impact thus far has been through the sports business infrastructure he established at the University of Pennsylvania, the Wharton Sports Business Initiative (WSBI).

The Wharton Sports Business Initiative is not a degree-granting program at the University of Pennsylvania. Rather, WSBI operates as a "think tank" where students and executives can conduct research, evaluate, and learn best practices in business and sport. The WSBI even runs summer programs for high school students to introduce them to sports business and sports analytics. And in 2005, Shropshire "developed and delivered the Warton-NFL/NFLPA Player Business Education Transition Program, the first of its kind" (Bolling, 2017). Now known as the NFL-NFLPA Business Management and Entrepreneurship Program, this program helps prepare NFL players for life after football, providing them with information about financial issues and business. Shropshire also cohosted The Wharton Sports Business Show on SiriusXM Business Radio until 2018. While Shropshire remains the Emeritus Faculty Director of the WSBI, his potential to make an even greater impact on sports through a multitude of different lenses, has arisen in his new position as CEO of the Global Sport Institute at Arizona State.

The collaboration between Adidas and Arizona State was announced in 2017 with the intent of the Global Sport Institute being "to tackle big-picture issues in sports, including race and gender, that can positively affect society as a whole" (Smith, 2017). The possibilities for research supported and led by Shropshire through the Institute are far vaster than at the WSBI. When asked by a journalist what motivated the move away from Wharton and Philadelphia for the opportunity at Arizona State, Shropshire said, "[F]rankly, I want to work on podcasts, documentaries, and drill down deeper on issues, and build something across an innovative university" (Bolling, 2017). The Global Sport Institute is a way for Shropshire to build up meaningful platforms for athletes, academics, and more to dive deeply into sport and society. One of the Institute's first successful initiatives was to commemorate the fiftieth anniversary of the 1968 Olympics in a way that resonated with people today. Shropshire and his team chose to ground the commemorative gathering with the name "Raising a Fist to Take a Knee" in order to spark conversation and focus on how influential the 1968 Mexico Olympics were then to athlete activism and how that athlete activism connects and lives on in present times. Keynote speakers offered perspectives on: pre-1968 social issues and athlete activism; Olympic medal–winning moments and the athlete perspective of activism at the time; the role of art and imagery in activism; and the role of athletes in society in 1968 and 2018.

The successful fiftieth-anniversary commemoration of the 1968 Olympics was only the beginning for Shropshire and his influence on sport—and particularly race and sport. Arizona State and Adidas have seemingly unlimited resources and the right person at the helm to guide them through abundant research ideas:

In addition to the big-picture items, such as why minorities don't have the same access to coaching or executive positions, the institute will use its resources from ASU and Adidas to explore questions that range from human performance to the business side of sports. . . . The Sun-Devils' 700-plus athletes will have a role in the performance and training research, while also serving internships that could help launch their careers. . . . Shropshire has heard from faculty at ASU about unique research on the participation of Latina girls in sports, and what the future looks like for the Cuban athlete. . . . "We'll use every part of the university to find out these things, [Shropshire] said." (Smith, 2017)

Aside from serving as the CEO of the Global Sport Institute at Arizona State University, Shropshire is also a joint faculty member in the University's School of Business and School of Journalism and Mass Communication, and an affiliate faculty member in the College of Law and African and African American Studies program. Shropshire has numerous academic publications dealing with sports law, the business of sport, and sports leadership. His latest coauthored book, *The Mis-Education of the Student-Athlete: How to Fix College Sports*, promotes a "Meaningful Degree Model" that aims to ensure that college athletes are receiving meaningful educations while also being successful in athletics. And in terms of race and sport, Shropshire's 1996 work, *In Black and White: Race and Sports in America*, is considered a foundational text among scholars in the field.

Native American

Oren Lyons (1930–)

Oren Lyons, activist for Indigenous and environmental justice and principal founder of the Iroquois Nationals lacrosse team, was born and raised in upstate New York in 1930. Specifically,

"Lyons grew up at Onondaga, the capital of the Haudenosunee, which the French missionaries called the Iroquois Confederacy" (Gadoua, 2018). Like many of the Indigenous Iroquois young men around him, Oren Lyons played lacrosse on the Onondaga and Seneca reservations. At age twenty, Lyons was drafted into the U.S. Army and served for three years before returning back to upstate New York. It was then that Oren was recruited by the Syracuse University lacrosse coach to join the team. While at Syracuse, Lyons played goalie, earning All-American honors twice and serving as cocaptain in 1957 and 1958. Lyons was teammates at Syracuse with African American standout athlete Jim Brown, "playing together on the Syracuse lacrosse team that had an undefeated season and won the national championship in 1957" (Weiner, 2016). In 1993, Lyons was inducted into the Lacrosse Hall of Fame—"the second Indian out of 201 inductees to be so honored (The first was a Cherokee from Carlisle Indian School, elected in the early 1900s)" (Vennum, 1994, 283). After graduating from Syracuse in 1958 with a degree in fine arts, Lyons pursued a career in commercial art in New York City, continuing to play lacrosse for various clubs.

It seemed as though Lyons was assimilating well to the pursuit of what the majority of society defines as success: good job plus good house equals a good life. However, while working in New York City and living in his New Jersey home, Oren learned an important lesson that led to his return to Onondaga:

> He bought a house in New Jersey, he said, and for a while he took a shot at leading a typical homeowner's life. Then he grew to know a neighbor, a nice enough man who worked long hours to try to get ahead. The neighbor spent the little bit of free time that he had "always taking care of his house and always cutting his lawn and always taking care of his flowers." "One day I went by there," Lyons said, "and there was a wreath on the door." The guy was dead from the stress. Lyons sold his house and went back to Onondaga. (Kirst, 2007)

The life that Lyons had tried to lead in the city and the suburbs of New Jersey went against much of what he had known growing up a Native American in upstate New York. Lyons realized that he didn't want to spend his life "trying to get ahead"; he wanted to be accepting of humanity and ground himself in an appreciation for the environment again. So in 1970, Lyons left New York City for good. Shortly after, Lyons was approached by clan mothers of the Onondaga Nation, who asked him to be a faithkeeper.

After some thought, Oren Lyons accepted the role as faithkeeper of the Turtle Clan among the Onondaga people of western New York state. As a faithkeeper, Lyons is entrusted to uphold the history, values, and principles of the Turtle Clan. Lyons has sat on the Council of Chiefs of the Haudenosaunee—or the Six Nations, as they are sometimes known—for over four decades. As a council chief, Oren is said to be "sitting for the welfare of the people" and to be engaged in sustaining "the power of the good mind" in discussions with others on the council, all of whom are exchanging thoughts about the everyday application of the wisdom given them by the Peace Maker (Lopez and Lyons, 2007, 5). Lyons has gone on to carry out the duties of faithkeeper and council chief on behalf of *all* Indigenous people with pure dedication and a lot of recognized acclaim both in the United States and abroad. Lyons helped establish the Working Group on Indigenous Populations at the United Nations in 1982 and for more than four decades "has been a defining presence in international indigenous rights and sovereignty issues" (Lopez and Lyons, 2007, 6).

Lyons's love of lacrosse still remains deep because of the history of the game in Indigenous history, as well as his founding role of the Iroquois Nationals team. For many Native Americans, lacrosse is far more than a game. For some, lacrosse was traditionally used as a means of healing between parties when painful conflicts were imminent. In native languages of Southeastern tribes, lacrosse was called "brother to war," or "little brother of war," and most historians writing on the sport

stressed its violent nature (Vennum, 1994, xii). Even today, lacrosse ties into religious beliefs and other aspects of Indigenous
culture:

> The training of warriors, medicinal benefits, connections
> to religion, and the incorporation of social aspects are still
> engrained in modern lacrosse, despite its evolution over
> the past one hundred fifty years. One of the most cher-
> ished possessions an Iroquois boy will have is his lacrosse
> stick. There are stories of newborns having sticks placed in
> their cribs, and elders buried alongside their prized stick.
> Today, lacrosse serves as the identity of contemporary Iro-
> quois culture. (Root, 2016, 7)

Oren Lyons is a part of this preservation of Iroquois culture
through lacrosse, as he helped to found the Iroquois Nationals
team—which earned a bronze medal in the 2018 Federation of
International Lacrosse World Championships in Israel—back
in 1983. With an intent to become eligible to compete in international games and gain official recognition from the amateur
non-Indian lacrosse community, the Iroquois Nationals team
remains the only Native American team authorized to play a
sport internationally. In a 1986 *New York Times* article, Lyons
said "this team is so important because it's a place where we can
prove ourselves without all those [non-Indian] rules jammed at
us. . . . When they say you've got to be an American college boy
to be an all-American at lacrosse, that's a subtle way of controlling and directing us" (Lipsyte, 1986). Lyons has past experience coaching the Nationals team, as well as currently serving
on its Board of Directors as a founding member.

Oren Lyons is highly prized for his lacrosse career as player,
coach, and Iroquois Nationals founder. Lyons is also worthy of praise for his once-in-a-lifetime accolades for work
in international advocacy for Indigenous peoples, environmental stewardship, and human rights. In addition, Lyons is
also a significant Native American scholar. Lyons served as a

professor of American Studies at the State University of New York at Buffalo for over thirty-five years and has published numerous books and illustrated children's books authored by fellow Native Americans. Oren Lyons "has been talking about cultural identity and Native sovereignty most of his life" (Gadoua, 2018) and has created a legacy that demonstrates that race, sports, and activism are inextricably linked and powerful.

Shoni (1992–) and Jude (1993–) Schimmel

Sisters Shoni and Jude Schimmel are only two of Rick and Ceci Schimmel's eight children. Rick and Ceci got together shortly before Rick left to begin his first year at Stanford University on a baseball scholarship. Ceci had been a star basketball player in high school but reveals being overlooked and unassisted by the White coaches around her because of her Native American heritage. Ceci let Rick, who racially identifies as White, know that she was pregnant during his freshman year of college, and he quickly left Stanford to come back and start a family with Ceci on the Umatilla Indian Reservation in the northeast corner of Oregon. As Rick's mother let viewers know in the 2011 TLC documentary *Off the Rez,* her son's choice was judged harshly by their community and her own husband. Rick and Ceci went on to have eight children together, and not one of them has a relationship with their paternal grandfather. The *Off the Rez* documentary, directed by Jonathan Hook, follows the last two years of Shoni Schimmel's high school basketball career, as she and her family move off the Umatilla Indian Reservation they'd called home for the city of Portland. Shoni and Jude—who is two years younger than Shoni—are successfully coached by their mother. By the closing credits of the documentary, Shoni finally reveals her choice of college: the University of Louisville. Shoni became the first Native American from the Umatilla Reservation to earn a Division I college basketball scholarship in 2010; Jude joined Shoni on the team at Louisville two years later.

For viewers of *Off the Rez*, Shoni's mother Ceci doesn't hide her anger and what appears to be bitterness toward the limited pathways for success presented to herself growing up, most likely due to her Native American heritage. Ceci Schimmel also doesn't hide her past experiences from Shoni and Jude in the documentary and Shoni admits to feeling "mad" because of the way her mother was limited. While the documentary propelled Shoni and Jude into the national spotlight, they would have become household names for Native Americans and women's basketball fans nationwide without the film, too. Shoni helped to turn the Louisville women's team into a powerhouse program. Shoni, a four-year starter for the Cardinals, finished her career as the second all-time scoring leader in Louisville history with 2,174 points and then was drafted into the Women's National Basketball Association (WNBA) in 2014 as the eighth pick overall by the Atlanta Dream. Jude, who played in the NCAA Tournament all four years and finished as part of a senior class that is the winningest Louisville women's basketball team in history (112–31), now serves as a Nike N7 Fund Ambassador and is a published author.

Throughout their collegiate careers, Jude and Shoni Schimmel have made it a priority to positively represent Native Americans to the rest of the country and to inspire Native American youth to continue to strive for the goals they have for themselves, whether those goals keep them on the reservation or moving off it. During Shoni's sophomore at Louisville, "Schimmel traveled back to the reservation with her teammates in tow to host a Health and Wellness Camp for kids at the Nixyaawii Community School gym before touring the Tribal Center and Museum. Hundreds of Native American children turned out for the camp and autograph session. . . . [Shoni] knows that few people outside of the reservation truly understand Native American history and culture . . . the trip let her teammates get an up-close look at how important a figure she and Jude are in their community" (Schnell, 2011). The impact of the Schimmels on the Native American population of the United

States only intensified the following year when Louisville made their run all the way to the 2013 NCAA Championship game. Throughout the team's successful run, "ESPN showed pictures of a young Shoni and Jude in full tribal wear, as fans across the country became familiar with their backstory" (Schnell, 2013) and Native Americans from hours away and from different tribes physically began traveling to come support Jude and Shoni in person. Nichole Maher, a member of the Tlingit tribe of Alaska and the former executive director of the Native American Youth and Family Center in Portland, explained to *Oregonian* reporter Lindsay Schnell that "there are lots of Natives who are in visible positions, but people don't know they're Native. The great thing about Shoni and Jude is that they're willing to tell their whole story and their whole complexity. They're showing people we're here, we're growing—and we're not going anywhere" (Schnell, 2013).

Sport, specifically basketball, has been viewed as an encouraging pathway to a successful future for Native Americans living on reservations. According to Umatilla tribal member Corinne Sams in a 2013 interview with NPR host Melissa Block, basketball is used on "our reservation as a tool to promote education and to do positive things with our youth here. And so it's always been a dominant force. But since the Schimmel girls have been playing Division I basketball, it's exploded into everybody wanting to participate and get to that next level" (Sams, 2013). After their respective graduations from Louisville, Jude and Shoni have continued to play basketball in different settings and advocate on behalf of Native Americans. Shoni is the second Native American drafted to the WNBA behind Ryneldi Becenti, who was drafted in 1997. Most women in the league chose to play overseas in the offseason to improve their financial security, but Schimmel has yet to do so. Shoni's professional career has been rocky at times, and she's needed to take time off due to her now late-grandmother's health and Shoni's own health issues with concussion recovery. Shoni has played for the New York Liberty, and the Atlanta Dream, and is now with the Las Vegas Aces. While playing for the Dream, Shoni explained to a reporter with the *Atlanta Journal-Constitution*, "It's not about the money for me. It's about spending time with my family. Being here in Atlanta for six months out of the year is long enough to be away from my family" (Roberson, 2016). Shoni Schimmel is showing everyone, especially Native Americans, that there is a way to create your own professional path and balance without losing your heritage and assimilating to the path others have taken.

Jude Schimmel graduated from Louisville in only three years and won the NCAA Elite 89 Award in her final year for having the highest GPA of any player in the final four. Jude was not selected for the WNBA draft but did spend time playing overseas in Spain and published an autobiography, *Dreamcatcher*, in 2015. Her autobiography focuses on "growing up on the Umatilla Reservation in Oregon; her stories four-year collegiate basketball career . . . and helping educate non-Natives about what's important in the Native communities across the country" (Harwood, 2015). In addition to the book, Jude has traveled throughout the country, speaking to over forty Native American tribes and has been a keynote speaker at the National Unity Conference. Currently, Jude is doing a lot of work as a Nike N7 Ambassador. Nike N7 Fund Ambassadors are athletes that reflect the Native American and Aboriginal community and also influencers who choose to use their voice to inspire future generations of and celebrate the power of native youth.

White American

Dr. Richard Lapchick (1945–) and the Racial and Gender Report Card

Richard Lapchick is arguably the most important person involved in making the future of all professional sporting organizations truly diverse and equitably accessible. He is a man who uses words and numbers to grip the attention of people and tell his personal story and the story of racial and gender bias in sports. Dr. Lapchick accepted an endowed chair position at the University of Central Florida (UCF) for its DeVos Sport Management Graduate Program in 2001. Before landing at UCF, Lapchick founded the Center for the Study of Sport in Society in 1984 at Northeastern University. It was at the Center for the Study of Sport in Society, beginning in 1988, where Dr. Lapchick began regularly compiling "report cards" for sports leagues and colleges to assess diversity along the lines of race, gender, and even graduation rates. Since becoming the director of the Institute for Diversity and Ethics in Sport (TIDES) at UCF, he has become "the author of the Racial and Gender Report Card, the institute's annual project that assesses hiring practices in professional and college sports" (Rietmann, 2017), and has authored seventeen books.

Professional and collegiate athletic organizations give both praise and criticism to Lapchick's Racial and Gender Report Cards, as most organizations have a lot of work to do in improving their grades by Lapchick's standards. MLB, major league soccer, the NFL, the WNBA, and the NBA all file their league office personnel data to TIDES. In the Fall 2011 Report, "baseball received an A in racial hiring and a B-minus in gender. The N.F.L. scored an A-plus and a C, while the N.B.A. earned an A-plus and an A-minus" (Araton, 2011). In 2018, it's perhaps unsurprising that the WNBA has the highest grades in hiring women and people of color for front-office and coaching positions, compared to the rest of the professional sports organizations that submit personnel data to Lapchick and his team at TIDES. The Institute has awarded the WNBA with "an A or an A-plus for its overall race, gender and combined grade in each of the last 14 years" (Associated Press, 2018) and rated it 97.6 points in the TIDES rating system. While professional sports leagues are forging ahead in their improvement on the Racial and Gender Report Cards, college athletics has stammered at the start. For example, the 2018 D1 FBS Leadership College Racial and Gender Report Card found that "85.4

percent of our presidents, 84.6 percent of our athletic directors, and 85.3 percent of faculty athletics representatives were white and 100 percent of our conference commissioners were white. In those positions, 73.1, 76.9, and 56.6 and 90 percent were white men, respectively" (Lapchick, 2018). The leadership in collegiate athletics at the top level received a C for racial hiring practices, an F for gender hiring practices, and a D overall. In response to these grades, Lapchick ignites readers of his October 3, 2018 article on ESPN.com, reminding them that "a student in any of these institutions of higher education would either be expelled or put on probation with this record" (Lapchick, 2018).

Aside from the weight with which his quantitative data hits the sports industry and the people who keep it running and profitable, Richard Lapchick makes an impact with his personal journey of race and sports. Lapchick's father, Joe Lapchick, was the coach of the New York Knicks from 1947 to 1956 "and, in 1950, signed Nat 'Sweetwater' Clifton, one of the first African-American players in the league. As a 5-year-old, Richard saw his father's image hanged in effigy near their Yonkers, New York, home because of his [father's] moves to integrate the NBA" (Rietmann, 2017). Then, as a fifteen-year-old, Richard Lapchick found himself standing up for a young Kareem Abdul-Jabbar—known as Lew Alcindor back then—at a basketball camp in upstate New York. As Abdul-Jabbar remembers it, one of the White kids at the camp whom he knew from Power Memorial Academy enjoyed using the N-word; "Richard confronted him and got beat up" (Araton, 2011). Lapchick and Abdul-Jabbar remained friends, both coming of age in the time of the civil rights movement, Black Power movement, and the protestation of South African apartheid.

While Abdul-Jabbar's athletic career took off in one direction, Lapchick continued to fight for equal opportunity, human rights, and an understanding of the national and global racial climate. Unfortunately, Lapchick's pursuit put him directly in the path of some filled with hatred for his values:

In his battle for fairness for all, Lapchick himself became a victim of hate. In 1978, he was teaching at a Virginia college but also had grown to be a formidable voice in the struggle against apartheid. As Lapchick worked one night in his college office, two masked intruders attacked him, leaving him with a concussion, kidney and liver damage, and a racial epithet carved into his stomach. (Rietmann, 2017)

Whereas most would give up any fight for social change after such a brutal attack, Lapchick used it as a catalyst to continue forward. Lapchick didn't speak publicly about the attack for ten years, but legendary tennis player Arthur Ashe persuaded Lapchick to write about his story, telling Lapchick "to start telling the story . . . so people can understand why you're doing the things you're doing" (Araton, 2011). From his professorship in Virginia, Lapchick moved on to a position with the United Nations (UN), which brought him in direct contact with Nelson Mandela. Nelson Mandela shared with Lapchick his feelings toward the end of apartheid; Mandela believed the boycott of South African sports helped to end apartheid and put Mandela into office. After his time with the UN, Lapchick landed at Northeastern and began to found the Center for Sport and Society.

From Lapchick's personal and professional backstory, it becomes clear how he emerged into a human rights activist, pioneer for racial equality, scholar, author, founder, director, and internationally recognized expert on sport issues. When accepting the 2017 NCAA Champion of Diversity and Inclusion award, Lapchick remarked, "I have personally experienced the power sport has to unite people of all cultures and backgrounds . . . I believe colleges and universities must take advantage of the power they have to foster camaraderie and continue to fight for equality. Student-athletes have a major role to play in standing up for justice so the establishment cannot block its path" (Rietmann, 2017). Lapchick has done more than create a legacy for himself; he has created multiple pathways for others to see the issues of race, gender, and sport and address those issues head on.

Organizations

American Tennis Association (ATA) (1916–)

The American Tennis Association (ATA) is the oldest African American sports organization in the United States. The ATA is responsible for the rise of African American tennis pioneers like Althea Gibson, Arthur Ashe, and Zina Garrison. In 1950, Althea Gibson became the first African American to compete at the U.S. National Championships and the first African American to win a major tennis tournament. Arthur Ashe is the only African American man to win singles titles at the Australian Open in 1970, the U.S. Open in 1968, and Wimbledon in 1975. Zina Garrison excelled at the national and international level in the late 1980s and early 1990s, winning fourteen singles titles and twenty doubles titles.

The key to the longevity of the ATA, which held its centennial national championships in 2017, are the economically elite members of the African American community who have continued to financially support the costs associated with the sport of tennis. Tennis has traditionally been known as a middle-class and upper-class sport, where verbal and physical acts of intimidation are frowned upon (unlike sports like ice hockey and football). With known racial, gender, and class disparities plaguing the United States historically, one would think African Americans would avoid involvement in a sport that seemed financially inaccessible to most African Americans in the twentieth century. Yet, as scholar Eric Allen Hall shares, this was not the case:

> As early as 1898, an interstate tennis tournament held at the Chautauqua Tennis Club in Philadelphia featured the region's best African American players. By 1916 African

American players from Washington, DC, New York, New Jersey, Massachusetts, and Pennsylvania, representing fifty-eight tennis clubs, competed at various times through the year. To the sport's backers, however, the occasional tournament was not enough. African Americans needed more tournaments, greater financial support, and additional player development programs. (Hall, 2011, 479)

It was this acknowledgment—that more was needed—that led to twenty of the region's tennis clubs to act.

On Thanksgiving Day, 1916, representatives from twenty of the African American tennis clubs met and officially birthed the American Tennis Association. During this meeting, the founders of the ATA were able to write official standards and establish short-term and long-term goals, "including founding new clubs, consolidating local and regional tournaments . . . and hosting an annual championship tournament" (Hall, 2011, 479). The first championships were held in Baltimore, Maryland, at Druid Hill Park in 1917, the park where the centennial championships were fittingly held in 2017. The tournaments and annual championships held by the ATA were transformative in many ways for eager young Black tennis players. In the early years, "all minorities at that time were barred from competitions run by the United States Lawn Tennis Association" (Rothenberg, 2017), so the tournaments and championships offered access to play and an avenue for real development. Over the century since then, the ATA has continued to be transformative in intangible ways. For example, in her autobiography, Zina Garrison recalls what the ATA provided her and other Black tennis players beyond skill development:

The other black juniors from MacGregor Park and I never felt wanted or comfortable socially at Texas events, but we enjoyed playing the ATA...I remember getting there and seeing for the first time all these black kids who looked just like me. I never realized that there were so many black people from all part of the country playing tennis. (Garrison, 2001, 49–50)

Garrison expresses the intangible benefits of the existence of the ATA: comfort, belonging, and community. And these benefits are in direct alignment with the mission and core values of the ATA. According to the ATA website, its mission is "To Promote Black Tennis in America" and its core values are respect, family, passion, integrity, and excellence.

The United States Lawn Tennis Association (USTA), of course, ended its ban against Black tennis players long ago, but racism in tennis at times still manifests itself in other ways: inequitable media coverage, hostile fans, and biased officiating. As Serena Williams points out in her memoir, *On The Line*, "for whatever reason there's this notion that if you didn't grow up around the game, if it wasn't in your blood to begin with, you had no real claim on it. Tennis is like that, I'm afraid. There's a sense of entitlement, of belonging. Like you have to be born into it" (Williams, 2009, 12). The ATA helps give African Americans that sense of entitlement and belonging. Tennis is a sport for African Americans, too, and the ATA has endured for generations. Thanks to the ATA, African Americans *are* born into tennis.

Black Coaches Association (BCA) (1988–2015) / National Association for Coaching Equity and Development (2015–)

In 1988, the Black Coaches Association (BCA) was established by a group of notable African American men "as a membership and advocacy group for Black coaches to improve coaching opportunities" (Hallman, 2016) at professional levels. The original leadership of the BCA was comprised of prolific coaches like Nolan Richardson (University of Arkansas), John Chaney (Temple University), John Thompson Jr. (Georgetown University), and Clem Haskins (University of Minnesota). In the early decades of its inception, those coaches helped to increase the membership of the BCA, particularly with respect to African American coaches in college basketball. Between 2001 and 2013, the BCA continued to live up to its goals under the Executive Directorship of Floyd Keith, an African American man with thirty years of Division I football coaching experience. Keith's tenure brought membership numbers "from 172 to over 5,500 . . . [and] Keith helped develop the BCA Hiring Report Card that measured colleges' hiring practices on college football and basketball coaches for 10 years" (Hallman, 2016). The BCA also started the Achieving Coaching Excellence (ACE) professional development program, which is currently run by the NCAA.

Unfortunately, the success of the BCA began to decline in its later years. As many of "the greats" like Chaney and Thompson Jr. retired, the pipeline of African American basketball coaches dwindled, allegedly due to reasons such as "discriminatory search firms, white coaches given multiple chances by their bosses, [and] financially hungry colleges preferring non-minority coaches to entice money from non-minority donors" (Moore, 2018). In addition, when interviewed by a journalist from the *Undefeated* in 2018 at the age of seventy-six, Nolan Richardson stated that many of the coaches involved in the National Association for Coaching Equity and Development (NACED)—the organization that replaced the BCA in 2015—are "a bunch of go-along and get-along guys . . . I don't think these black coaches have backup anymore to keep their jobs" (Moore, 2018). As the BCA approached the late 1990s, it ambitiously added football coaches, adding another focus to its work. Then, in 2007, the BCA sought to help more African American administrators join the world of college athletics, adding even more to the mission of the organization.

In March 2013, Floyd Keith announced his resignation as the BCA's executive director. Keith noted that he felt like twelve years with the organization was plenty, and also that the BCA had been suffering from financial hardship. It was whispered about quietly that the real reason for the financial difficulty wasn't because the 501(c)(3) tax-exempt nonprofit organization was "always looking for money . . . a very difficult task" (Miller, 2014) as Keith stated in a 2014 interview; the real reason was scandal. According to those in the shadows and to Nolan Richardson, so many funds were drained illegally from the organization during the late 1990s by those in charge of its checkbook that the NCAA placed what was a private group under its corporate umbrella to help it survive (Moore, 2018). This BCA survival mode only lasted about a year before some of the BCA coaches formed the NACED and the NCAA's restructured group, Advocates for Athletic Equity, ceased its operation due to a lack of financial support in 2016.

The important lesson to be absorbed from the legacy of the BCA is about the real power of having African Americans in leadership positions within sports organizations; the ability to have a seat at the coveted coaching and administrative tables. The increase in hiring of Black coaches in the NCAA didn't happen overnight, but between 2003 and 2015, "a 117 increase in Black Division I men and women head coaches (363–480); an increase of 72 Black Division II men and women head coaches (116 to 188); and an increase of 128 Black Division III men and women head coaches (254–382)" (Hallman, 2016) occurred. Progress since 2015 has often been short-lived, with poor results from the College Sport Racial and Gender Report Cards issued by Dr. Richard Lapchick and his team at the Institute for Diversity and Ethics in Sport. While Lapchick, a White man, continues to push a more diversified coaching pool through encouraging drastic change to hiring policy and practices, there remains a clear need for current and aspiring Black coaches and administrators to have a racial affinity support network to thrive collectively. It will be up to current Black coaches and administrators to decide whether collectivism will be a priority again over individual success.

"Change the Mascot" Campaign (2013–)

In September 2013, the Oneida Indian Nation, under the leadership of Ray Halbritter, launched the "Change the Mascot" campaign to pressure the NFL's Washington Redskins to change their team name and mascot. Although the "Change the Mascot" campaign is fairly recent, the controversy and contestation over the use of Redskins—a racial slur toward Native Americans that is the equivalent of calling an African American "nigger"—is decades old. The NFL team actually began in Boston. In 1933, former owner George P. Marshall changed the team name from the "Braves" to the "Redskins" to avoid confusion with a baseball team in Boston that also used the "Braves" moniker, and then he moved the team to Washington, D.C., in 1937. Three decades later, in 1968, the National Congress of American Indians (NCAI) launched the first organized effort to end negative stereotypes about Native Americans in pop culture, sports, and the media. The media began to expend time covering the controversy over the team name in the early 1970s, and since that time, there has been both progress and frustration over the "R-word." On the progressive side, lawsuits to strip the NFL team of its name registrations were filed in 1992 and 2006; "decades of controversy ended when Ohio's Miami University decided to drop its Redskins nickname, later changing the school's mascot to Redhawks" (Cox, 2016) in 1996, and the NCAA "ruled that teams with nicknames or mascots deemed 'hostile or abusive' could no longer participate in post-season play" (Cox, 2016) in 2005.

With all the progress that has been made at both the national youth and collegiate levels in the abandonment of offensive names and mascots toward Native Americans, it can seem surprising that the Washington team still refused to budge until faced with detrimental financial losses. After a lost appeal by a group of Native Americans challenging the Redskins trademark in 2009, the fight against the team calmed down for a few years. Then, in February = 2013, a symposium was held at the

Smithsonian National Museum of the American Indian. At the symposium, Native Americans "demanded that the team change [the name], reigniting the debate" (Cox, 2016). In May of the same year, Washington team owner Dan Snyder vowed to never change the name; just a few months later, the Oneida Indian Nation launched the "Change the Mascot" campaign. Change the Mascot is "a campaign of radio ads, polls, opposition research, academic studies, YouTube videos, Twitter hashtags, and media interviews" (Sabar, 2015). Change the Mascot's ability to utilize all of those different platforms to create change points to what differentiates the campaign from a long line of activists who came before: money—specifically, Ray Halbritter's money.

In February 2018, at the Twentieth Annual Leadership Awards Ceremony of the National Congress of American Indians (NCAI) in Washington, D.C., Ray Halbritter was presented with the Native Voice Award. The Native Voice Award is given in appreciation of an individual's commitment and leadership to create equality, fair representation, and increased opportunity for Native Americans and future generations (*Oneida Daily Dispatch*, 2018). Halbritter was chosen for being a champion of respectful and truthful portrayals of Native Americans through the Change the Mascot campaign and for Indian Country Today Media Network, which celebrates Native voices. Ray Halbritter is a multimillionaire CEO and Oneida Nation representative who attended Syracuse University and then Harvard Law School. Once an ironworker, Halbritter began to question the future and quality of life for Native American people as long as it was dependent on the benevolence of white men. Thus, in his early 30s, Halbritter began college at Syracuse. Under the leadership—sometimes considered controversial leadership—of founder Halbritter, the Oneida Nation Enterprises, a commercial empire, "is one of the largest employers in central New York" (Sabar, 2015).

In its first two years of existence, Change the Mascot made sure that anti-Redskins radio ads aired in every city where the team played. The campaign has been powerful enough to really get people to listen:

> Marquee sports journalists such as Bob Costas said they would stop using the name, as did more than a dozen news outlets and the editorial board of the Redskins' hometown paper, *The Washington Post* . . . 50 U.S. senators signed a letter to NFL Commissioner Roger Goodell, who admitted that the league needed to listen to "different perspectives." . . . President Obama (who overlapped with Halbritter at Harvard Law, though the two didn't know each other) told reporters that if he were the team owner, he'd "think about changing" the name. The controversy even landed on episodes of *South Park*, *The Daily Show*, and *Jeopardy!* (Sabar, 2015)

In response to all the controversy, Dan Snyder tried to quell some of the national criticism by starting a foundation that aids Native Americans, but he continues to refuse a change in the Washington football team's name. Change the Mascot and the NCAI continue to oppose the use of the R-word and the team's ability to return the District of Columbia to play its football games; the team's "home stadium" is currently located in Maryland.

In October 2018, the Change the Mascot campaign praised a resolution by the NCAI at their Annual Convention and Marketplace that "reaffirms [NCAI's] categorical opposition to the use of the demeaning R-word by the Washington NFL team" (*Change the Mascot*, 2018) and asks Washington D.C. political leaders to refuse the approval of the franchise to return to play back in the District until it changes its name to something inoffensive. Just a few weeks before the NCAI resolution, Matt Hoyer, the grandson of a Menominee Indian and medical student at the Johns Hopkins University School of Medicine, had an op-ed piece published in the *Washington Post* that focused on the psychological toll of the R-word. Hoyer importantly shares:

> [P]eople internalize imagery that reinforces their world-view, and it can be difficult to distinguish between carica-tures trading blows from a distance and a confrontation to be had when they meet that image themselves. For Na-tive American children, this is an unfortunate reality that plays out in schools across the United States. According to the American Psychological Association, Native American mascots "establish an unwelcome and often times hostile learning environment for American Indian students that affirms negative images/stereotypes that are promoted in mainstream society." . . . Reliance on these images not only hinders the public's understanding of Native Ameri-cans but also limits the ways that Native Americans see themselves. (Hoyer, 2018)

It is through continued research studies and reliance on the sharing of compelling public opinions like that of Matt Hoyer, which Ray Halbritter and the Change the Mascot campaign re-lies on. Change the Mascot has the money to invest in the turn of public morals and values towards uplifting Native Ameri-cans, unlike earlier anti-Redskins activists who had to put all of their hopes into court rulings. In 2015, Halbritter stated that change will come "not because of the benevolence of a team owner, but because a critical mass of Americans will no longer tolerate, patronize, and cheer on bigotry" (Sabar, 2015). Halbritter was correct. In July 2020, in the wake of a nation confronting heightened systemic and interpersonal racism, and threatened with billion dollar losses from investors, Washington owner Dan Snyder and the NFL finally dropped the R-word.

Ross Initiative in Sports for Equality (RISE) (2015–)

The Ross Initiative in Sports for Equality (RISE) was founded in 2015 by accomplished businessman and owner of the NFL's

Miami Dolphins, Stephen Ross. The catalyst for the creation of RISE, however, began in 2013 after his team came under national scrutiny for its alleged internal culture of bullying and harassment. In 2013, lineman Johnathan Martin quit mid-season, claiming he was frequently dealing with inappropriate sexual and racially charged messages from teammates. Ross created RISE in the wake of the scandal as a pathway to improve race relations and drive social progress in the United States. Partnering with sports leagues and associations, organizations, athletes, coaches, schools and policy makers, RISE seeks to spread awareness and drive dialogue through a social media and public service announcements (Lee, 2015).

RISE looks to create change primarily through three methods: educational programming, working with professional athletes, and engaging sports fans through action. One such professional athlete working with RISE is the NBA's Draymond Green. The Golden State Warriors star, with the assistance of RISE, designed and sported a pair of basketball shoes with the phrase "sideline racism" written on the sides in order to make a very public statement about the persistent problem of racism in the country. Green, along with his teammate Stephen Curry, serve on RISE's advisory board—a board that is comprised of other professional athletes, university professors, politicians, and media and organizational executives. RISE's educational programming is designed for high school and collegiate athletes so that the next generation of athletes learn how they can use their platform as athletes to create positive change. Some universities, such as Michigan State University and the University of Michigan, actually require all of their freshman student-athletes to participate in RISE's educational curriculum. Former RISE CEO Jocelyn Benson described the curriculum in a phone call with a reporter from the *Detroit Free Press* in 2017:

> We talk about implicit bias, microaggressions, and the importance of recognizing and celebrating diversity as

a tool for not just improving our world but also improving winning percentages on a team . . . it certainly makes it easier for a team to come together and perform better on the field if off the field they're united and in support of each other's varying perspectives and realities. (Sang, 2017)

RISE aims to eventually instill its educational programming at high schools in all 50 states. The curriculum can be easily administered to student-athletes by their coaches. In terms of engaging its fans through action, RISE may encourage fans to take a pledge to stand up against racism or engage in some other activity at a sporting event to show their support of athletes and activism. As of July 2017, only twenty months into its existence, RISE had "provided events and programs in 15 states, engaging more than 6,600 student-athletes, coaches and athletic staff through its leadership program and more than 25,000 fans through public awareness campaigns at live sporting events" (Benson, 2017). Additionally in 2017, at ESPN's Sports Humanitarian Awards, RISE received the Stuart Scott ENSPIRE Award. Candidates for the Stuart Scott ENSPIRE Award personify the ethos of the ethics, fairness, respect, and fellowship with others; the award is meant to celebrate people and organizations that have taken risks and used innovative approaches to help the disadvantaged through the power of sports.

Since receiving the ENPSIRE Award, RISE has continued to grow in its outreach and impact, even when Stephen Ross has undermined his own initiative. With the NFL kneeling that has continued to occur during the national anthem, years after former NFL player Colin Kaepernick began the act of protestation against police brutality and racial inequality, the owners of NFL teams nationwide have remained under pressure to make statements about the players protests. In March 2018, when many media outlets and the general public were interpreting the kneeling during the national anthem as anti-American and unsupportive of the military, Stephen Ross changed his initial support of his and other players' kneeling and told reporters, "All our players will be standing this coming season" (Adelson, 2018). Ross's strong words did not go unnoticed by the media and public. Ross quickly amended those comments and his stance as he realized that coming off as though he were going to force his players to stand was completely against everything the RISE stands for. Ross has stuck to his amended stance, as some of his players continue to kneel during the anthem and remain outspoken in their support for Kaepernick's call for Americans to re-evaluate policing, racial discrimination, and the social justice system. One such outspoken player is Dolphins wide receiver Kenny Stills, who in addition to continuing to kneel during the national anthem in the 2018–2019 NFL season, has done things like "rented an RV and traveled across the South for everything from learning about prison reform to attending a women's march to speaking to high school classes" (Adelson, 2018).

Ross's personal stumbles with his own initiative actually emphasize how well RISE is structured in creating meaningful change. Rather than being a lone decision-maker, Ross knew that RISE's success depends on a community model and multiple perspectives. Most recently, RISE hired a new CEO in Diahann Billings-Burford to replace Jocelyn Benson, who moved on from RISE in order to pursue a political career in Michigan. Billings-Buford has experience in New York City government and with Time Warner, but most importantly, she has the belief in the power of RISE:

> With RISE, we have this ability to galvanize people across all races and all classes and, in particular, people across tons of sports leagues in the United States to address racism, to address social justice and improve race relations. . . . We're going to be a vehicle to do that, and to amplify that, to help give athletes a platform. I love that we're seeing so many more athletes empowered and educated. We're

going to help in that space. We're going to help in the platform space and really figure out what are some things we can put in front of them to move the needle on these topics. That's a big order. But I think RISE is up to doing all of that. (Reid, 2018)

It's clear thus far that RISE does in fact have the "ability to galvanize people across all races and all classes" through the realm of sports because it's an organization that seeks to reach athletes, coaches, youth, and all sports fans. There is something for everyone to educate themselves about and take a stand for through RISE and its initiatives: voting, dismantling racism, civil rights, diversity and inclusion, and sports advocacy. With solid leadership, funding, and thoughtful programming, RISE's trajectory will continue to live up to its own acronym.

References

Abdul-Jabbar, Kareem. 2018. "Kareem Abdul-Jabbar: What Sports Have Taught Me about Race in America." *The Guardian* (August 28). https://www.theguardian.com/sport /2018/aug/28/notes-from-an-ungrateful-athlete-why-race -and-sports-matter-in-america.

Abraham, Amani. 2018. "Where the Money Goes: Breakdown of Funding for Lebron James' I Promise School in Akron." *wkyc.com* (August 28). https://www.wkyc.com /article/news/education/where-the-money-goes-breakdown -of-funding-for-lebron-james-i-promise-school-in-akron/95 -588377750.

Adelson, Eric. 2018. "Dolphins' Stephen Ross Undermines His Initiative in Dustup Involving Anthem and Protesting Nfl Players." *Yahoo Sports* (March 6). https://sports.yahoo .com/dolphins-owner-stephen-ross-undermines-initiative -latest-dustup-involving-national-anthem-protesting-nfl -players-042810461.html.

Araton, Harvey. 2011. "A Lifetime of Battling Bias." *The New York Times* (November 14): D1. https://www.nytimes.com /2011/11/14/sports/a-lifetime-of-battling-bias.html.

Associated Press. 2008. "Average Baseball Salary." *ESPN News Wire* (December 4). http://www.espn.com/espn/wire/_/ section/mlb/id/3744821.

Associated Press. 2018. "WNBA Receives Straight A+ Grades on Diversity Report Card." *Yahoo Sports* (October 25). https://sports.yahoo.com/wnba-receives-straight-grades -diversity-report-card-171409211--wnba.html.

Barca, Jerry. 2018. "Stunning Criticism of Lebron James and the Funding for the I Promise School." *Forbes* (August 12). https://www.forbes.com/sites/jerrybarca/2018/08/12 /stunning-criticism-of-lebron-james-and-the-funding-for -the-i-promise-school/?sh=17ed438822d5.

Barra, Allen. 2011. "How Curt Flood Changed Baseball and Killed His Career in the Process." *The Atlantic* (July 12). https://www.theatlantic.com/entertainment/archive/2011 /07/how-curt-flood-changed-baseball-and-killed-his-career -in-the-process/241783/.

Beamon, Krystal, and Chris Messer. 2014. "Professional Sports Experiences as Contested Racial Terrain." *Journal of African American Studies* 18, no. 2 (June): 181–91.

Benson, Jocelyn. 2017. "How Sports Can Bridge America's Racial Divide." *HuffPost* (July 12). https://www .huffingtonpost.com/entry/how-sports-can-bridge-americas -racial-divide_us_5964e8c0e4b0deab7c646bda.

Biography.com Editors. 2014. "Paul Robeson Biography." *Biography.com*. A&E Television Networks.

Bolling, Louis. 2017. "America's Most Innovative University Hires First Adidas Distinguished Professor of Global Sport." *HuffPost* (April 28). https://www.huffingtonpost .com/entry/americas-most-innovative-university-hires-first -adidas_us_590351e2e4b03b105b44b7cb.

Branch, John. 2009. "Ward Helps Biracial Youths on Journey toward Acceptance." *The New York Times* (November 9). https://www.nytimes.com/2009/11/09/sports/football /09ward.html.

Branch, John. 2017. "The Awakening of Colin Kaepernick." *The New York Times* (September 7). https://www.nytimes .com/2017/09/07/sports/colin-kaepernick-nfl-protests .html.

Bryant, Howard. 2018. *The Heritage: Black Athletes, a Divided America, and the Politics of Patriotism.* Boston, MA: Beacon Press.

Change the Mascot. 2018. "National Congress of American Indians Passes Resolution Opposing Washington NFL Team's Return to D.C. until R-Word Name Is Changed." http://www.changethemascot.org/wp-content/uploads /2018/10/Change-the-Mascot-Release-re-NCAI -Resolution-Oct-30-2018.pdf.

Clarke, Liz. 2016. "Four Years after Olympic Gold, Gabby Douglas's Reality Remains Riveting." *The Washington Post* (May 22): 1–5. https://www.washingtonpost.com/sports /olympics/four-years-after-olympic-gold-gabby-douglass -reality-remains-riveting/2016/05/22/073a79e6-1eb7-11e6 -b6e0-c53b7ef63b45_story.html.

Cox, John Woodward. 2016. "Timeline: The Furor over the Redskins Name." *The Washington Post.* https://www.washingtonpost.com/apps/g/page/local /timeline-the-furor-over-the-redskins-name/2035 /?noredirect=on.

Direnna, Frank. 2018. "Simone Biles Is Victorious at U.S. Classic in First Competition since Rio." *TeamUSA.org.* United States Olympic Committee.

Gadoua, Renee K. 2018. "Honoring Onondaga's Oren Lyons, Le Moyne Grapples with Jesuit History." *National Catholic Reporter* (May 18). https://www.ncronline.org/news/justice

/honoring-onondagas-oren-lyons-le-moyne-grapples-jesuit
-history.

Garrison, Zina. 2001. *Zina: My Life in Women's Tennis*. Berkeley, CA: Frog, Ltd., 2001.

Graham, Bryan Armen. 2018. "Colin Kaepernick Is Out of the Nfl but He Is More Powerful Than Ever." *The Guardian* (September 4). https://www.theguardian.com/sport/2018 /sep/04/colin-kaepernick-nfl-nike-ad-campaign.

Hall, Eric Allen. 2011. ""I Guess I'm Becoming More and More Militant": Arthur Ashe and the Black Freedom Movement, 1961–1968." *The Journal of African American History* 96, no. 4 (Fall): 474–502.

Hallman, Charles. 2016. "What Happened to the Black Coaches and Administrators (Bca)?" *Minnesota Spokesman-Recorder* (May 4). http://spokesman-recorder.com/2016/05 /04/778248/.

Harwood, Rodney. 2015. "Jude Schimmel's Book: 'You Don't Have to Leave the Reservation to Be Successful.'" *Indian Country Today* (April 16). https://newsmaven.io /indiancountrytoday/archive/jude-schimmel-s-book-you -don-t-have-to-leave-the-reservation-to-be-successful -kovGZxJsRUqtYWiUtTZ7MQ/.

Hoyer, Matt. 2018. "The Psychological Toll of That Name." *The Washington Post* (October 5).

Jin-man, Lee. 2006. "Ward Kicks Off His New Charity: Korea's Mixed Race Kids to Reap Benefit." *Pittsburgh Post-Gazette* (May 30). https://www .post-gazette.com/sports/steelers/2006/05/30 /Ward-kicks-off-his-new-charity/stories/200605300131.

King, Gilbert. 2011. "What Paul Robeson Said." *Smithsonian Magazine* (September 13). https://www.smithsonianmag .com/history/what-paul-robeson-said-77742433/.

Kirst, Sean. 2007. "Onondaga Faithkeeper Oren Lyons: 'You Want to See What You Can Do.'" *Syracuse.com* (August 8).

https://www.syracuse.com/kirst/index.ssf/2007/08/oren
_lyons_to_onondaga_faithkeeper_history_means.html.

Lapchick, Richard. 2015. "The Enduring Humanity of
Kareem Abdul-Jabbar." *ESPN.com* (September 24). http://
www.espn.com/espn/print?id=13732955.

Lapchick, Richard. 2018. "Ncaa Leaders Get Poor Marks for
Diverse Hiring Practices." *ESPN News* (October 3). http://
www.espn.com/college-sports/story/_/id/24881558/ncaa
-continues-get-poor-grades-diversity-their-hiring-practices.

Lee, Rebecca. 2015. "Owner of Miami Dolphins Stephen
Ross Creates Non-Profit, Rise to Fight Bullying and
Racism." *CBS News* (October 16). https://www.cbsnews
.com/news/owner-of-miami-dolphins-stephen-ross-creates
-non-profit-rise-to-fight-bullying-and-racism/.

Lipsyte, Robert. 1986. "Lacrosse: All-American Game." *New
York Times Magazine*: 29–68.

Lomax, Michael E. 2002. "Revisiting "the Revolt of the Black
Athlete": Harry Edwards and the Making of the New
African-American Sport Studies." *Journal of Sport History*
29, no. 3 (Fall): 469–79.

Lopez, Barry, and Oren Lyons. 2007. "The Leadership
Imperative: An Interview with Oren Lyons." *Mānoa* 19,
no. 2 (Winter): 4–12.

Markusen, Bruce. 2016. "Four Decades Later, Free Agency
Still Fuels Baseball." *National Baseball Hall of Fame and
Museum*. https://baseballhall.org/discover/short-stops/free
-agency-still-fuels-baseball.

Miller, Ted. 2014. "BCA in Flux after Staff Change."
ESPN.com (February 20). http://www.espn
.com/college-football/story/_/id/10467085
/future-bca-uncertain.

Moffitt, Kelly. 2017. "Meet St. Louis Native Harry Edwards, the
Man behind the Black Power Protest at the '68 Olympics."
St. Louis Public Radio (February 24). https://news.

stlpublicradio.org/show/st-louis-on-the-air/2017-02-24
/meet-st-louis-native-harry-edwards-the-man-behind-the
-black-power-protest-at-the-68-olympics.

Moore, Terence. 2018. "The Loss of the Black Coaches
Association Is Still Being Felt Today." *The Undefeated*
(March 16). https://theundefeated.com/features/the-loss-of
-the-black-coaches-association-is-still-being-felt-today/.

Myers, Rachel Laws. 2017. "More Than One: What
Happened When Multiple Black Female Athletes Excelled
in Predominantly White Sports at the Rio Olympics." In
Women in Sports: Breaking Barriers, Facing Obstacles, edited
by Adrienne N. Milner and Jomills Henry Braddock II,
59–75. Santa Barbara: ABC-CLIO, LLC.

National Archives. 2016. *The Many Faces of Paul Robeson*.
Washington, D.C.: The U.S. National Archives and
Records Administration.

O'Neal, Lonnae. 2018. "Harry Edwards, a Giant of Sports
Activism, Still Has People Shook." *The Undefeated*
(October 15). https://theundefeated.com/features/harry
-edwards-mexico-city-olympics-sports-activism-john-carlos
-tommie-smith-1968/.

Oneida Daily Dispatch, The. 2018. "Oneida Indian Nation's
Ray Halbritter Receives Native Voice Award." *The Oneida
Daily Dispatch* (February 17). https://www.oneidadispatch
.com/news/oneida-indian-nation-s-ray-halbritter-receives
-native-voice-award/article_3ffb0291-fbcc-5286-848f
-ddcb74f8eda5.html.

Reid, Jason. 2018. "Ross Initiative in Sports for Equality
Hires Diahann Billings-Burford as New CEO." *The
Undefeated* (September 20). https://theundefeated.com
/features/ross-initiative-in-sports-for-equality-rise-hires
-diahann-billings-burford-as-new-ceo/.

Rhoden, William C. 2006. *Forty Million Dollar Slaves: The
Rise, Fall, and Redemption of the Black Athlete*. New York:
Three Rivers Press.

Rietmann, Tom. 2017. "Lapchick Recognized as Champion of Diversity: Human Rights Activist and Author Is a Leading Voice for Equity in Sports." *NCAA* (April 7). http://www.ncaa.org/about/resources/media-center/news /lapchick-recognized-champion-diversity.

Roberson, Doug. 2016. "Dream's Cooper Disappointed in Schimmel." *The Atlanta Journal-Constitution* (April 26). https://www.ajc.com/sports/basketball/dream-cooper -disappointed-schimmel/r9nSLCLVoRbJDuag6YqMbJ/.

Root, Christopher P. 2016. *An Examination in the Evolution of Iroquois Lacrosse*. Buffalo, NY: State University of New York College.

Rothenberg, Ben. 2017. "African-American Tennis, Fostered for 100 Years." *The New York Times* (August 27): SP5.

Sabar, Ariel. 2015. "The Anti-Redskin: In the Fight over the Team's Name, Ray Halbritter Is an Adversary Unlike Any the NFL Has Faced Before." *The Atlantic* (October 2015). https://www.theatlantic.com/magazine/archive/2015/10 /the-anti-redskin/403213/.

Sailes, Gary A. 1991. "The Myth of Black Sports Supremacy." *Journal of Black Studies* 21, no. 4 (June): 480–87.

Sams, Corinne. 2013. "Two Sisters Bring Native American Pride to Women's Ncaa." By Melissa Block. *NPR* (April 8).

Sang, Orion. 2017. "Billionaire, Michigan Alum Stephen Ross Working to Make Rise Part of Legacy." *Detroit Free Press* (July 10). https://www.freep.com/story/sports/college /university-michigan/wolverines/2017/07/11/michigan -wolverines-stephen-ross-rise/466990001/.

Schnell, Lindsay. 2011. "Shoni Schimmel Returns to Umatilla Reservation with Her Teammates, Inspires Native American Children." *The Oregonian* (August 6). Published electronically November 5, 2011. https://www.oregonlive .com/collegebasketball/index.ssf/2011/08/shoni_schimmel _returns_to_umat.html.

Schnell, Lindsay. 2013. "Shoni and Jude Schimmel of Louisville Helping Natives Win a Bigger Game." *The Oregonian*. https://www.oregonlive.com /march-madness/index.ssf/2013/04/shoni_and_jude _schimmel_of_lou.html.

Smith, Johnny. 2018. "The Reign of Lew Alcindor in the Age of Revolt." *The Undefeated* (March 30). https:// theundefeated.com/features/lew-alcindor-kareem-abdul -jabbar-ucla-boycot-1968-olympics/.

Smith, Michael. 2017. "Adidas-Arizona State Alliance Gives Shropshire a Platform for Change." *Sports Business Journal* (June 19). https://www.sportsbusinessdaily.com/Journal /Issues/2017/06/19/Colleges/Arizona-State-Adidas.aspx.

Vennum, Thomas, Jr. 1994. *American Indian Lacrosse: Little Brother of War*. Washington, D.C.: Smithsonian Institution Press.

Ward, Hines. "Hines Ward Lends Helping Hand to Literacy, Mixed-Race Kids." By Eric Kuhn. *NBC News* (2011).

Weiner, Mark. 2016. "Onondaga Nation's Oren Lyons Invited to Eulogize Muhammad Ali." *Syracuse.com* (June 9). https://www.syracuse.com/news/index.ssf/2016/06 /onondaga_nations_oren_lyons_invited_to_eulogize _muhammad_ali.html.

Wiggins, David. 1997. *Glory Bound: Black Athletes in a White America*. 1st ed. Syracuse, NY: Syracuse University Press.

Williams, Serena. 2009. *On the Line*. 1st ed. New York: Grand Central Publishing.

Wolfson, Andrew. 2018. "Muhammad Ali Lost Everything in Opposing the Vietnam War. But in 1968, He Triumphed." *USA Today* (February 19). https://www.usatoday.com/story/news/2018/02/19 /1968-project-muhammad-ali-vietnam-war/334759002/.

Wong, Alia. 2018. "5 Reasons Lebron James's School Really Is Unique." *The Atlantic* (August 24). https://

www.theatlantic.com/education/archive/2018/08
/lebron-james-school-unique/568243/.

World Champions Centre. 2020. "World Champions Centre
Staff." https://www.worldchampionscentre.com/staff.

Zahn, Max. 2018. "Inside Lebron James's New $8
Million Public School, Where Students Get Free
Bikes, Meals, and College Tuition." *Money Magazine*
(July 31). http://time.com/money/5354265
/lebron-james-i-promise-school-akron/.

Zirin, Dave. 2005. *What's My Name, Fool?: Sports and
Resistance in the United States*. Chicago, IL: Haymarket
Books.

Zirin, Dave. 2008. *A People's History of Sports in the United
States: 250 Years of Politics, Protest, People, and Play*. New
York: The New Press.

5 Data and Documents

This chapter will analyze data gathered from discussions about race and sports at the youth, college, and professional levels. In addition, important documents on race and sports are included. Readers should conclude this chapter with a general understanding of the answers to the following essential questions: Who is participating in athletics? What are the demographics of athletes of color in professional and amateur sports? What sports are inclusive of athletes of color and which sports challenge their ability to participate and why? Is the participation in sports by athletes of color increasing or decreasing? What can be done to engender equality in sports as a whole for athletes of color?

Data

Race and Sport: Youth Level

Youth sport in the United States is a multibillion-dollar industry, yet "no one agency or organization monitors youth sports either as a central part of American childhood or as an industry" (Kelley and Carchia, 2013). This lack of oversight has caused scholars, journalists, and sporting and health organizations to increase their attention and study of youth involved in sport. With limited regulation of youth sport, economics, access to sport, and physical safety have become the most recent areas of focus. And when coupled with how race intersects in these

---

Happy team members of a youth basketball team. According to researchers, participation in organized sports is a valued part of the American youth experience. (Monkey Business Images/Dreamstime.com)

areas, looking at the data and hypothesizing about future rami-fications is crucial to the study of race and sport. In discussing race and sport at the youth level, data from three resources will be drawn upon and analyzed to answer the essential questions of this chapter. These three resources are: "Teen Sport in America: Why Participation Matters" (Zarrett et al., 2018); "Youth Athletes' Sustained Involvement in Elite Sport: An Exploratory Examination of Elements Affecting Their Athletic Participation" (Wendling, 2018); and "Hey, Data Data—Swing!" (Kelley and Carchia, 2013).

The Women's Sports Foundation's January 2018 report focusing on the participation of teenagers in sport in the United States used cross-sectional data collected over a five-year period between 2010-2015 in the Monitoring the Future (MTF) survey; a sample size of 14,049 twelfth graders. These high schoolers were asked questions about their participation in 20 different types of competitive sports. The sample was predominantly female (50.2%) and White (55.3%), but also included respondents who identified as male (49.8%), Black (12%), Hispanic (14.8%), and "other race" (17.9%). Geographically, the majority of the sample resided in the Southern region of the United States (36.6%) and roughly evenly split from the Northeastern region (22.7%), Midwestern region (22.7%) and Western region (22.8%). In addition, the respondents identified themselves as residing in rural (19.9%), urban (30.7%), and suburban (49.3%) areas. While the full study by the Women's Sports Foundation sought to provide insights into health behaviors, academic achievement, and psychological behavior, the dataset provided also helps to consider patterns in sports participation through the lens of race.

Table 5.1 presents the racial differences in sport participation of twelfth graders in the United States. Fifteen of the twenty sports represented reveal a significant percentage variance between races. These fifteen sports are distinguished with gray shading. The five sports—crew, gymnastics, swimming and diving, and volleyball—distinguished without shading show

Table 5.1   Racial Differences in Sport Participation of Twelfth Graders in the United States (2010–2015)

Overall	White	Black	Hispanic	Other
Does not participate in sport	30.7%	34.7%	34.9%	32.5%
Participates in at least one sport	69.3%	65.3%	65.1%	67.5%
Listing of Sports (alphabetical)				
Baseball/Softball	15.8%	8.3%	12.7%	10.1%
Basketball	17.4%	30.3%	15.8%	18.7%
Cheerleading	5.3%	8.2%	3.0%	5.5%
Crew	0.7%	0.8%	0.5%	0.9%
Cross Country	5.8%	2.8%	4.9%	4.9%
Equestrian	1.8%	0.4%	0.2%	1.1%
Field Hockey	1.2%	0.4%	0.6%	1.0%
Football	13.8%	17.6%	11.9%	15.3%
Golf	6.8%	1.4%	1.6%	4.3%
Gymnastics	1.5%	1.3%	1.8%	1.9%
Ice Hockey	2.3%	0.5%	0.6%	1.0%
Lacrosse	3.2%	1.1%	1.1%	2.8%
Soccer	12.4%	5.8%	22.9%	11.1%
Swimming and Diving	6.5%	5.1%	6.3%	8.3%
Tennis	6.2%	2.9%	3.5%	8.5%
Track and Field	11.5%	17.0%	8.6%	12.7%
Volleyball	8.5%	7.4%	6.9%	8.4%
Water Polo	1.0%	0.2%	1.0%	1.0%
Weightlifting	11.4%	9.2%	9.4%	11.2%
Wrestling	4.1%	3.4%	5.2%	5.7%

Shaded sports = significant % variance among racial groups.
Unshaded sports = similar % distribution between racial groups.

Source: Data from Table 2 in "Teen Sport in America: Why Participation Matters" (Zarrett et al., 2018).

similar percentage distributions in participation among racial groups within each respective sport. It's clear from this data set that sports participation is valued among all of the racial groups recognized in the study, with roughly 65–70 percent of twelfth graders participating in sport across racial identities. However, those fifteen sports highlighted in grey reveal a need for deeper investigation into how race plays a role in specific sports. The Women's Sports Foundation report stated the following regarding this variation in racial diversity by type of sport:

> [T]he MTF data indicated significant differences in participation rates by race/ethnicity in almost all types of sports, with a few popular sports having particularly large differences. Baseball/softball and weightlifting had particularly high participation rates among white youth compared to black or Hispanic youth, while basketball, football, and track and field had significantly higher participation rates among black youth than among white and Hispanic youth. Participation rates for soccer were significantly higher among Hispanic youth than among either black or white youth. Among all sports, only volleyball, crew, and gymnastics showed no significant differences in the race/ethnicity composition of participating youth. (Zarrett et al., 2018, 13)

The addition of swimming and diving to the list of sports that showed no significant differences because the highest percentage fell into the racial category of "Other." Thus, this racially ambiguous category could likely have been broken down further if other groups, such as Asian Americans and Native Americans, had been included in the options for racial self-identification for twelfth graders. Overall, Table 5.1 helps to confirm that sports are racially diverse, but there are also very clear differences in the racial and ethnic compositions of *each sport*. What are the reasons for varying percentages of racial diversity in individual sports? The answer to this question is two-fold: (1) Socioeconomic factors; and (2) Racialized sport culture affect access to certain sport participation.

Socioeconomic Factors Affecting Access of Youth to Sport
Unsurprisingly, young people from families with more substantial financial resources tend to have increased participation rates in youth sport. Table 5.2 displays the "Differences

Table 5.2   Differences in Sport Participation by Socioeconomic Status of
Twelfth Graders in the United States (2010–2015)

	Socioeconomic Status	
Overall	**Parents have less than a college degree**	**At least one parent has a college degree**
Does not participate in sport	37.5%	27.0%
Participates in at least one sport	62.5%	73.0%
Number of Sports		
Does not participate in sport	37.5%	27.0%
Participates in one sport	30.1%	31.0%
Participates in 2+ sports	32.4%	42.0%
Sports		
Baseball/Softball	13.1%	14.0%
Basketball	17.2%	20.3%
Cheerleading	5.2%	5.4%
Crew	0.5%	0.9%
Cross Country	3.6%	6.6%
Equestrian	1.0%	1.5%
Field Hockey	0.8%	1.2%
Football	14.3%	14.2%
Golf	3.0%	7.0%
Gymnastics	1.6%	1.6%
Ice Hockey	1.1%	2.1%
Lacrosse	1.7%	3.4%
Soccer	12.2%	13.7%
Swimming and Diving	5.6%	7.5%
Tennis	4.3%	7.1%
Track and Field	9.9%	13.7%
Volleyball	7.6%	8.6%
Water Polo	0.8%	1.1%
Weightlifting	10.2%	11.3%
Wrestling	4.9%	4.0%

Shading = significant % variance among participation based on socioeconomic status.
Unshaded sports = similar % of participation based on socioeconomic status.

Source: Data from Table 3 in "Teen Sport in America: Why Participation Matters" (Zarrett et al., 2018).

in Sport Participation by Socioeconomic Status of 12th Graders in the United States (2010–2015)" based on the level of education youths' parents have attained. The data shaded in gray depicts variation in percentage of participation based on socioeconomic status that is 0.5 percent or greater. The unshaded data depicts similar percentages of participation in specific sports, even with differing socioeconomic backgrounds (0.4% difference or less). In every sport aside from wrestling and football, the participation rate was higher for twelfth graders who had at least one parent with a college degree. The higher level of education a person receives usually equates to the ability to earn a higher level of income. A former study, also done for the Women's Sports Foundation, corroborates this notion. Professor Don Sabo of D'Youville College, in 2007, queried a sample of 2,185 male and female students ages eight through seventeen and found that "the biggest indicator of whether kids start [sport] young are whether their parents have a household income of $100,000 or more" (Kelley and Carchia, 2013).

The highest rates of participation for twelfth graders of color, according to Table 5.1, are in sports that either require very little equipment (baseball/softball, basketball, track and field, soccer) or sport that schools tend to provide equipment to the athletes (football, weightlifting). As for the spending that occurs on sports that require more equipment and other fees? In July 2016, a TD Ameritrade investor survey revealed that:

[N]early two-thirds of the parents surveyed claimed to spend up to $500 monthly per child on youth sport activities. Another 20% of parents surveyed spent more than $1,000 monthly, per child, with most of the expenditures allocated to travel and team fees. Parents justify the substantial financial sacrifice and uncountable hours spent on their children's sport pursuits, as the quest for a college scholarship or professional career. Parents have also indicated that they believe the benefits of sport participation supersede the costs. (Wendling, 2018, 659)

Table 5.2 appears to support the TD Ameritrade investor survey's findings about parents' justification of spending as twelfth graders who have at least one parent with a college degree are involved in two or more sports at a roughly 10% higher rate of participation. Thus, the more money the families of young athletes have, the more access to sports participation there is.

Racialized Sport Culture

Aside from the socioeconomic and geographic factors that have affected access to sports for various racial groups in the United States, the racialized culture that has developed around each sport also matters greatly in participation rates. Black athletes in particular "always had a cultural heritage that gave meaning to their blackness, even in the eyes of whites" (Schutte, 1995, 339) which included an involvement in sport. U.S. athletes of color struggle to carve out legitimate and respected spaces in a country that sought to oppress them in various ways (i.e., stolen land, enslavement, internment camps, etc.). Therefore, as Schutte also points out, there is a need "for an understanding of the meanings White people attach to the phenomenon of the racial other and of the motivations that lead them to act in ways, or establish structures, that have discriminatory consequences" (1995, 338). In 2009, doctoral candidate Rachel Laws, set about conducting her ethnographic and comparative dissertation research focused on the experiences of Black female athletes in South Africa and the United States through the lenses of image, perceptions, and narratives. The research sample was made up of twenty-nine purposefully selected informants in South Africa and the United States and most interviews were microcassette recorded and transcribed verbatim. With regard to perceptions, informants from South Africa and the United States were asked a few questions that dealt with racial perceptions including being asked to name what they feel are the "main" sports Black female athletes participate in. The U.S. informants of this study, most of whom were female athletes themselves, identified the sports of track and field, basketball, tennis, and volleyball as the main sports Black female athletes choose to participate in. Moreover, nine out of ten U.S. informants agreed with the statement that sports are considered and labeled "White" and "Black." According to informants in Laws's study, the following sports are associated with each race in the United States:

> _Black_—Basketball, Track & Field
> _White_—Soccer, Field Hockey, Softball, Tennis, Golf, Swimming, Lacrosse
> One informant also stated that the sport of volleyball is considered racially mixed with fairly equal amounts of Blacks and Whites participating. (Laws, 2012)

In looking back at Table 5.1, Laws's small group of informants' perceptions are supported by the racialized participation rates of twelfth graders in sports between 2010–2015 as reported by the Women's Sports Foundation (2018). Twelfth graders who self-identified as Black had highest percentages among other races in the sports of basketball and track and field, and volleyball is a sport whose racial participation rates are fairly equal.

The racialized labeling of certain sports can absolutely impact youth's decisions to begin playing certain sports. It's unclear whether these racial perceptions impact one race more than another—a consideration deserving of further investigation—but there is evidence that the perceptions impact young athletes regardless of racial identity. Research has indicated potential negative impacts of participation, including exclusion, external pressures, and barriers to participation, which may lead to athlete attrition (Wendling, 2018, 658). Informants in Laws' dissertation provide good examples of this negative impact regardless of race. A Black female informant named Victoria discussed her personal experience persisting in athletic career in a perceived "White" sport:

> I think Tennis is considered a "White" sport and for the longest time I had always wondered why I was only one of a few girls playing tennis and everyone else was White. I feel like basketball and track & field are labeled as more "Black" sports and that to me is why you see more Black boys and girls playing them. I guess what I'm trying to say is that sports that some people may call "country club" sports—such as tennis, golf, swimming etc.—are considered "White." (2012)

Similarly, White athletes are also impacted by racialized perceptions of certain sports. Two former high school basketball standouts, Jillian and Kelly, shared their experiences with Laws. Kelly felt like some of her teammates lacked confidence in her, while Jillian said, "playing basketball, some Black athletes think I am 'only a shooter' because I am White, but that is not true, as they found out" (2012). What informants Victoria, Jillian and Kelly all allude to, are instances where *stereotype threat* can emerge for young athletes choosing to play sports that are perceived to be labeled for a different racial group than their own.

In their 1995 article, "Stereotype Threat and the Intellectual Test Performance of African Americans," first published in the *Journal of Personality and Social Psychology*, scholars C.M. Steele and J. Aronson defined *stereotype threat* as a "socially premised psychological threat that arises when one is in a situation or doing something for which a negative stereotype about one's group applies." This threat isn't about belief in the stereotype and can affect anyone with a group identity about which some negative stereotype exists. Stereotype threat "focuses on the immediate situational threat that derives from the broad dissemination of negative stereotypes about one's group—the threat of possibly being judged and treated stereotypically, or of possibly self-fulfilling such a stereotype" (Steele and Aronson,

1995, 798). White basketball players Kelly and Jillian's feeling of Black teammates "lacking confidence" in them and assuming limited skill set due to their being White people playing a perceived "Black sport" like basketball is an example of stereotype threat, as is Black tennis player Victoria's pondering about why she was one of few Black girls playing tennis.

In addition, the 2018 study conducted by Wendling revealed that race plays a significant factor in youth participation in sport. Their study sample size was 1,258 travel/elite youth sport athletes from the United States between the ages of ten and eighteen. The racial group demographics consisted of Whites (71%), African Americans (17%), Hispanic (7%), Asian (2%) and Other (3%):

> Notable differences were observed between White and non-White children with the latter having higher aspirations to play at the next level; non-self-determined extrinsic motivation, such as getting noticed and being praised by others; and perceived pressures from parents and coaches. (Wendling, 2018, 669)

Researchers of this particular study concluded that future research needs to be done to investigate why these racial differences are evident because "dropout is more likely to occur during early adolescence and . . . it is critical that teammates and coaches value the contribution the athlete makes to the team, outbalancing barriers to participation that may be particularly exacerbated by the high-intensity environments in elite youth sport" (Wendling, 2018, 669).

Race and Sport: College Level

For the young athletes that don't quit their elite youth sports, there are opportunities to earn full athletic scholarships at the NCAA Division I and Division II levels. The ability to earn an athletic scholarship at the collegiate level is not, however, solely based on athletic talents. Prospective college athletes need to register online with the NCAA Eligibility Center, a process that could be construed as another way that college sports financially profits from young, prospective athletes. The NCAA Eligibility Center requires a nonrefundable $90 registration fee for U.S. and Canadian students, and it's a $150 nonrefundable registration fee for international students. You *must* be certified by the NCAA Eligibility Center to compete at an NCAA Division I or II school before you can make official visits, or even sign a National Letter of Intent in Division I or II. For families that are socioeconomically vulnerable and that have lower levels of schooling (i.e., one or both parents have not attended college), navigating the process of whether their student-athlete can get an athletic scholarship can be confusing and pose financial hardship. For example, the NCAA does offer a "fee waiver" for the Eligibility Center registration, but it still requires the parent(s)/guardian(s) of the student-athlete to have to figure out who the right adult to speak with in their child's high school is. On their online FAQ page regarding the waiver, the NCAA states:

> If you are unable to pay the registration fee for the NCAA Eligibility Center due to financial considerations, there is an option in the payment section to indicate you are eligible to receive a fee waiver. You are eligible for a waiver of the registration fee if you have received a waiver of the SAT or ACT fee. (This is not the same as a U.S. state voucher.) You must ask an authorized high school official to submit your fee waiver verification online after you complete your registration. If you request a fee waiver and are unable to receive the fee waiver, you can simply log back in to your account at eligibilitycenter.org and make a payment with a credit card or e-check.

There is no guidance about who might be the "authorized high school official," and there is no other option but to pay the full fee if a student-athlete is unable to receive a fee waiver. And let's take a step back because there's another important facet of becoming an NCAA scholarship qualifying athlete that isn't related to socioeconomic status or one's parents' education level: the high school educational curriculum itself.

It isn't common knowledge that the National Collegiate Athletic Association (NCAA) plays a significant role in determining the curriculum offered in public, religious, charter and independent high schools in the United States. The NCAA has its own prescribed set of academic rules and requirements that prospective student-athletes must adhere to and attain in order to have a chance at NCAA college athletics. In his 2016 piece for *Education Week*, entitled "The NCAA's Hidden Influence on High Schools," author James Lytle, explains how the burden of compliance with these academic rules—outlined for young student-athletes aspiring for scholarships at the Division I level in Table 5.3—rests with high schools, rather than on the NCAA to acknowledge and understand differentiated curriculums:

> [H]igh school principals must provide the NCAA with the following documentation: a course catalog from the current academic year; an academic-year calendar; a master schedule of courses; an official grading scale; a sample student transcript; and an official policy on repeated courses, graduation requirements, and academic integrity . . . the NCAA site stipulates "The review process is necessary regardless of accreditation or inclusion in a district with other schools registered with the NCAA Eligibility Center" . . . the NCAA reserves the right to review individual core courses…Completing a school's registration process requires a great deal of administrative time—at least 40 hours for the initial application. And providing assistance to students choosing to apply for eligibility requires substantial amounts of counselor time. (Lytle, 2016)

This means that a high school student-athlete, regardless of racial identity, has to meet the set academic requirements as

Table 5.3   NCAA Eligibility Center Division I Academic Requirements

Core-Course Requirement

4 years of English	+ 3 years of Math (algebra or higher)	+ 2 years of Science	+ 1 additional year of (English, math or science)	+ 2 years of Social Science	+ 4 years of additional courses (English, math, science, language, or philosophy/religion)	= 16 Core Courses

FULL QUALIFIER

- Complete 16 core courses.

- Ten of the 16 core courses must be completed before the seventh semester (senior year) of high school.

- Seven of the 10 core courses must be in English, math or natural/physical science.

- Earn a core-course GPA of at least 2.300.

- Earn an SAT combined score or ACT sum score matching the core-course GPA on the Division I sliding scale.

- Graduate high school.

ACADEMIC REDSHIRT

- Complete 16 core courses.

- Earn a core-course GPA of at least 2.000.

- Earn an SAT combined score or ACT sum score matching the core-course GPA on the Division I sliding scale.

- Graduate high school.

Source: Based off of data provided by the NCAA Eligibility Center.

determined by the NCAA. In terms of access, this puts students who may thrive in nontraditional schooling systems (e.g., schools that don't use grades and/or build curriculum around experiential learning) in a potentially heightened stressful position in choosing whether to continue in the nontraditional academic high school setting if the NCAA is more likely to reject the school's registration. And for high schools that see the deep value of athletics for its student population, those school administrators are more likely to continue to bend and shape curriculum based on NCAA rules, rather than on best practices within education. In the end, it's only "6 percent of high school athletes who go on to play Division I varsity college sports"

(Lytle, 2016), so it seems negligent that the NCAA should have such power over who gains access to the privilege of an athletic scholarship to college.

According to the NCAA Division I and II student-athlete and coaching racial demographics available online via the NCAA Demographics Database (data available from this database was used to create Tables 5.4 and 5.5), there are clear differences in racial demographics among college sports in the United States. Many of these differences are also evidenced in the data examined in the subheading of youth sports. For example, in looking at Table 5.4 and the student-athletes involved in NCAA men's Division I and II baseball and basketball, one can comprehend why baseball is presently perceived as a "White sport" and basketball is perceived as a "Black sport." Within the sport of baseball at youth level, twelfth graders who identify as White participated in baseball at a roughly 7 percent higher rate than youth who identify as Black. At the college level, this higher yield of Whites in baseball is present at the student-athlete level *and* at the coaching level. In fact, the number of NCAA Division I and II Black baseball coaches has decreased by ten at the head coach and assistant coach positions between 2008 and 2018. This data creates a research question to be potentially pursued about what has/ is happening to the development of and current experiences of Black coaches in NCAA baseball? Additionally, in baseball, at the youth and college levels, Hispanic/Latinx–identifying student-athletes are competing in greater numbers than those who identify as Black. In Division I and II men's basketball, for the student athletes, Blacks are by far more represented, similar to the participation rates shown at the youth level in Table 5.2 for the sport. In fact, at the college level over the ten-year span between 2008 and 2018, White basketball player numbers dropped by 372 and Black players increased by 397. At the college coaching level for men's basketball, interestingly, as of 2018 there are far more White head coaches (488) than Black head coaches (149), but the increase in number of Black

Table 5.4 Men's NCAA Division I and II Coaches and Student-Athlete Racial Demographics from Eight Sports (2008–2018)

Sport	Position at Institution	Racial Identity	Gender	2008	2018	Change over 10 years (+/-)
Baseball	Head Coaches	White	Male	459	498	+39
			Female	0	1	+1
		Black	Male	33	23	-10
		Hispanic/ Latino	Male	16	21	+5
		Asian	Male	6	5	-1
		Multiracial	Male	0	5	+5
		Am. Indian/ Alaska Native	Male	1	1	—
	Assistant Coaches	White	Male	1,092	1,316	+224
			Female	0	7	+7
		Black	Male	52	42	-10
		Hispanic/ Latino	Male	64	71	+7
		Asian	Male	8	8	—
		Multiracial	Male	7	24	+17
		Am. Indian/ Alaska Native	Male	4	2	-2
	Student-Athletes	White	Male	15,316	16,399	+1,083
		Black	Male	1,072	1,263	+191
		Hispanic/ Latino	Male	1,103	1,701	+598
		Asian	Male	198	230	+32
		Multiracial	Male	34	724	+690
		Am. Indian/ Alaska Native	Male	83	110	+27

(continued)

Table 5.4 *(continued)*

Sport	Position at Institution	Racial Identity	Gender	2008	2018	Change over 10 years (+/-)
Basketball	Head Coaches	White	Male	450	488	+38
		Black	Male	143	149	+6
		Hispanic/ Latino	Male	7	8	+1
		Asian	Male	1	2	+1
		Multiracial	Male	1	7	+6
		Am. Indian/ Alaska Native	Male	1	2	+1
	Assistant Coaches	White	Male	918	940	+22
			Female	3	15	+12
		Black	Male	623	742	+119
			Female	0	2	+2
		Hispanic/ Latino	Male	30	29	-1
		Asian	Male	10	7	-3
		Multiracial	Male	3	28	+25
		Am. Indian/ Alaska Native	Male	1	4	+3
	Student-Athletes	White	Male	3,439	3,067	-372
		Black	Male	5,416	5,813	+397
			Female	0	25	+25
		Hispanic/ Latino	Male	243	279	+36
		Asian	Male	44	53	+9
		Multiracial	Male	40	528	+488
		Am. Indian/ Alaska Native	Male	25	38	+13

Table 5.4 (*continued*)

Sport	Position at Institution	Racial Identity	Gender	2008	2018	Change over 10 years (+/-)
Football	Head Coaches	White	Male	327	347	+20
			Female	0	1	+1
		Black	Male	56	62	+6
		Hispanic/ Latino	Male	2	2	—
		Asian	Male	1	4	+3
		Multiracial	Male	0	2	+2
		Am. Indian/ Alaska Native	Male	3	3	—
	Assistant Coaches	White	Male	1,476	1,587	+111
			Female	9	37	+28
		Black	Male	793	1,009	+216
			Female	0	3	+3
		Hispanic/ Latino	Male	28	44	+16
		Asian	Male	23	42	+19
		Multi-Racial	Male	4	34	+30
		Am. Indian/ Alaska Native	Male	3	2	-1
			Female	0	1	+1
	Student-Athletes	White	Male	19,833	18,514	-1,319
		Black	Male	18,292	22,872	+4,580
		Hispanic/ Latino	Male	1,058	1,514	+456
		Asian	Male	563	753	+190
		Multiracial	Male	86	2,495	+2,409
		Am. Indian/ Alaska Native	Male	222	240	+18

(*continued*)

Table 5.4 (*continued*)

Sport	Position at Institution	Racial Identity	Gender	2008	2018	Change over 10 years (+/-)
Golf	Head Coaches	White	Male	435	472	+37
			Female	10	7	-3
		Black	Male	30	23	-7
		Hispanic/ Latino	Male	3	1	-2
			Female	1	0	-1
		Asian	Male	8	6	-2
			Female	0	1	+1
		Multiracial	Male	1	1	—
		Am. Indian/ Alaska Native	Male	1	1	—
	Assistant Coaches	White	Male	210	316	+106
			Female	19	37	+18
		Black	Male	11	4	-7
		Hispanic/ Latino	Male	0	5	+5
			Female	0	1	+1
		Asian	Male	8	7	-1
			Female	1	3	+2
		Multiracial	Male	1	4	+3
		Am. Indian/ Alaska Native	Male	1	0	-1
	Student- Athletes	White	Male	4,383	3,675	-708
		Black	Male	160	139	-21
			Female	1	0	-1
		Hispanic/ Latino	Male	142	158	+16
		Asian	Male	128	227	+99
		Multiracial	Male	9	101	+92
		Am. Indian/ Alaska Native	Male	21	16	-5

Table 5.4   (*continued*)

Sport	Position at Institution	Racial Identity	Gender	2008	2018	Change over 10 years (+/-)
Gymnastics	Head Coaches	White	Male	13	14	+1
		Black	Male	1	0	-1
		Asian	Male	2	1	-1
	Assistant Coaches	White	Male	20	25	+5
		Black	Male	1	1	—
		Hispanic/ Latino	Male	1	3	+2
		Asian	Male	2	3	+1
	Student-Athletes	White	Male	250	216	-34
		Black	Male	15	19	+4
		Hispanic/ Latino	Male	14	19	+5
		Asian	Male	27	25	-2
		Multiracial	Male	0	22	+22
		Am. Indian/ Alaska Native	Male	2	0	-2
Ice Hockey	Head Coaches	White	Male	58	58	—
	Assistant Coaches	White	Male	133	136	+3
		Asian	Male	0	1	+1
		Am. Indian/ Alaska Native	Male	1	0	-1
	Student-Athletes	White	Male	1,462	1,225	-237
		Black	Male	7	11	+4
		Hispanic/ Latino	Male	12	17	+5
		Asian	Male	10	7	-3
		Multiracial	Male	4	25	+21
		Am. Indian/ Alaska Native	Male	6	2	-4

(*continued*)

Table 5.4   (*continued*)

Sport	Position at Institution	Racial Identity	Gender	2008	2018	Change over 10 years (+/-)
Lacrosse	Head Coaches	White	Male	85	128	+43
		Black	Male	1	7	+6
		Hispanic/ Latino	Male	0	1	+1
		Am. Indian/ Alaska Native	Male	0	1	+1
	Assistant Coaches	White	Male	175	295	+120
			Female	0	2	+2
		Black	Male	6	6	—
		Hispanic/ Latino	Male	1	1	—
		Asian	Male	1	1	—
		Multiracial	Male	0	1	+1
		Am. Indian/ Alaska Native	Male	1	0	-1
	Student-Athletes	White	Male	3,336	4,860	+1,524
		Black	Male	66	234	+168
		Hispanic/ Latino	Male	44	172	+128
		Asian	Male	22	42	+20
		Multiracial	Male	7	159	+152
		Am. Indian/ Alaska Native	Male	10	33	+23
Rowing	Head Coaches	White	Male	33	30	-3
			Female	0	2	+2
		Hispanic/ Latino	Male	1	0	-1
	Assistant Coaches	White	Male	55	64	+9
			Female	8	4	-4

Table 5.4 (continued)

Sport	Position at Institution	Racial Identity	Gender	2008	2018	Change over 10 years (+/-)
		Black	Male	0	1	+1
			Female	0	1	+1
		Asian	Male	0	1	+1
	Student-Athletes	White	Male	1,182	966	-216
			Female	30	33	+3
		Black	Male	29	16	-13
			Female	2	0	-2
		Hispanic/ Latino	Male	44	63	+19
			Female	2	6	+4
		Asian	Male	55	30	-25
			Female	5	9	+4
		Multiracial	Male	4	42	+38
			Female	0	5	+5
		Am. Indian/ Alaska Native	Male	10	2	-8

Source: Data sample from the NCAA Demographics Database collected for 2008 and 2018, which can be found at http://www.ncaa.org/about/resources/research /ncaa-demographics-database.

assistant coaches (+119) over the ten-year span is far greater than that of White assistant coaches (+22). Could this mean a future trend for NCAA Division I and II men's basketball programs to be headed by Black males? Another important thing to note about Table 5.4 in terms of Division I and II male student athletes is that in every sport included, the number of multiracial-identifying athletes has increased over the ten-year span between 2008 and 2018. This universal increase among a racial identity group of student-athletes is only evident among those who identify as multiracial. This increase in multiracial identifying athletes seems to correspond to the 2018 U.S. Census release number CB18-41, which states that higher multiracial growth rates "are largely the result of high rates of natural increase" and "the share of children who are two or more races is projected to more than double in the coming decades, from 5.3 percent today to 11.3 perfect in 2060" (United States Census Bureau, 2018). Thus, one can expect the numbers of Multi-Racial college student-athletes—and perhaps coaches—to increase over the next four decades unless something drastically shifts in terms of how this racial demographic gains access to sport broadly or targeted individual sports.

Women's place in NCAA college sport was solidified in 1982, when it began to offer women's championships in all sports. Prior to the NCAA's jurisdiction over women's collegiate athletics, an organization called the Association for Intercollegiate Athletics for Women (AIAW) governed women's college sport. In fact, the NCAA had stood in opposition of bringing women's athletics into its male-centered fold. Title IX legislation was passed a decade earlier, but the NCAA was slow moving to support the legislation because there was nothing that required female participation at a national level. Title IX of the Education Amendments Act of 1972 is only thirty-seven words long and reads in full: "No person in the United States shall, on the basis of sex, be excluded from participation in, be denied the benefits of, or be subjected to discrimination under any education program or activity receiving Federal financial assistance" (Ware, 2007, 3). Thanks in part to Title IX and the intense pressure placed on the NCAA by numerous women's and feminist groups, the NCAA eventually offered to create financial aid, recruitment, and eligibility rules equal to those offered to men; pay all expenses for teams competing in a national championship; and guarantee television coverage for women's sport.

Yet, when examined through a critical racial lens, the NCAA has not come very far in terms of creating inclusion and access for people of color as athletes and coaches in the women's realm. In 2001, *Chronicle of Higher Education* sports journalist Welch Suggs published an article entitled "Left Behind," which provides significant research focused on the experiences of Black American women in college athletics and lesser depth to the experiences of Latinx, Asian, and Native American women in college sport following Title IX legislation. Regardless of its shortcomings in depth of racial perspectives and research, Suggs offers data spanning the years 1972–2001 that remains significant in today's understanding of women's college sport:

Since 1987, when Congress passed a law that strengthened the enforcement of Title IX, the fastest growing sports in the NCAA have been women's soccer, rowing, golf, and lacrosse. The numbers of teams and of athletes have doubled and in some cases tripled in all four sports. However, the number of women's basketball and track teams has risen only about 26 percent. . . . (Of course, black women in basketball and track have benefited from Title IX in other ways, as colleges have spent money on those programs to improve their facilities, their coaching, and their visibility). College fields, courts, and rivers are now teeming with equestriennes, female soccer players, rowers, and other athletes, but almost all of them—70 percent—are white. . . . Only 1.8 percent of all female athletes are Asian, and only 3 percent are Hispanic. . . . And members of all minority groups except black women have been going out for Division I sports in increased numbers since 1990–91, according to NCAA statistics. The proportions of American Indian, Asian, Hispanic and foreign athletes on women's teams have skyrocketed, while the proportion of black women has remained steady between 13.9 and 15.6 percent over the past decade [1990–2000]. Even so, black women continue to outnumber women of all other races except white. (Suggs, 2001)

Taking into account the statistics offered by Suggs in 2001 alongside some of the NCAA statistics available via the Demographics Database—like those presented for eight women's sports in Table 5.5 between the years 2008–2018—and valuable deductions can be made about the progress (or lack thereof) and trends in collegiate women's athletics through a racial lens.

Suggs offered that the sports soccer, rowing, golf and lacrosse have seen the most growth since 1987, but the majority of those athletes identify racially as White. In looking at Table 5.5 to women's golf as an example of what can be deduced, one can see that racial demographics have been slowly shifting over roughly the last decade to include less White (–122) and Black (–22) athletes and more Asian (+174), Hispanic/Latino (+22) and multiracial (+22) women. While women's college golf is still overwhelmingly White (2,203 in 2018) versus women of color (713 total in 2018), if the numbers of growth and decline remain the same, racial demographics within women's golf could be close to 50/50 in two to three decades. For women's rowing, there has also been a significant decline in White (–226) athletes, as well as small declines for Black (–7) and Asian (–9) athletes. Meanwhile, the Hispanic/Latino (+114) and multiracial (+219) numbers of collegiate female rowers is on the rise from 2008. Similar to women's golf, women's rowing remains overwhelmingly White (4,348 in 2018) versus women of color (879 in 2018), but it will take much longer than a couple of decades to reach a 50-50 racial demographic within the sport of women's rowing at the current rates of change. This mean that there absolutely must be increased intentional initiatives created to funnel more women of color into the sport of rowing. And according to Table 5.5 racial demographic data on women's lacrosse, similar drastic interventions need to be made in the sport to increase the number of women of color as student-athletes in lacrosse. Even though the number of women of color college athletes playing lacrosse at the Division I & II levels increased

Table 5.5   Women's NCAA Division I and II Coaches and Student-Athlete Racial Demographics from Eight Sports (2008–2018)

Sport	Position at Institution	Racial Identity	Gender	2008	2018	Change over 10 years (+/-)
Basketball	Head Coaches	White	Male	219	227	+8
			Female	266	268	+2
		Black	Male	44	54	+10
			Female	68	86	+18
		Hispanic/ Latino	Male	4	8	+4
			Female	1	4	+3
		Asian	Male	1	3	+2
			Female	2	3	+1
		Multiracial	Female	1	1	—
	Assistant Coaches	White	Male	306	324	+18
			Female	598	557	-41
		Black	Male	154	195	+41
			Female	338	463	+125
		Hispanic/ Latino	Male	13	16	+3
			Female	10	20	+10
		Asian	Male	2	9	+7
			Female	10	13	+3
		Multiracial	Male	1	3	+2
			Female	3	20	+17
		Am. Indian/ Alaska Native	Male	2	0	-2
			Female	2	3	+1
	Student-Athletes	White	Female	4,314	3,909	-405
		Black	Female	3,763	3,960	+197
		Hispanic/ Latino	Female	243	320	+77
		Asian	Female	118	108	-10
		Multiracial	Female	47	607	+560

(continued)

Table 5.5   (continued)

Sport	Position at Institution	Racial Identity	Gender	2008	2018	Change over 10 years (+/-)
		Am. Indian/ Alaska Native	Female	45	67	+22
Field Hockey	Head Coaches	White	Male	9	13	+4
			Female	85	84	-1
		Black	Male	0	1	+1
			Female	2	0	-2
		Hispanic/ Latino	Male	0	1	+1
			Female	1	3	+2
		Asian	Female	2	1	-1
		Multiracial	Female	1	2	+1
	Assistant Coaches	White	Male	27	23	-4
			Female	125	146	+21
		Black	Male	3	1	-2
			Female	2	6	+4
		Hispanic/ Latino	Male	1	2	+1
			Female	4	3	-1
		Asian	Female	3	0	-3
		Multiracial	Male	0	1	+1
			Female	0	3	+3
		Am. Indian/ Alaska Native	Female	1	0	-1
	Student- Athletes	White	Female	2,125	2,020	-105
		Black	Female	38	56	+18
		Hispanic/ Latino	Female	31	49	+18
		Asian	Female	34	33	-1
		Multiracial	Female	4	66	+62

Table 5.5   (*continued*)

Sport	Position at Institution	Racial Identity	Gender	2008	2018	Change over 10 years (+/-)
		Am. Indian/ Alaska Native	Female	1	6	+5
Golf	Head Coaches	White	Male	173	223	+50
			Female	162	195	+33
		Black	Male	12	5	-7
			Female	0	2	+2
		Hispanic/ Latino	Male	0	2	+2
			Female	3	3	—
		Asian	Male	3	3	—
			Female	4	2	-2
		Multiracial	Male	1	3	+2
			Female	0	2	+2
		Am. Indian/ Alaska Native	Male	1	0	-1
	Assistant Coaches	White	Male	83	160	+77
			Female	91	135	+44
		Black	Male	4	2	-2
			Female	1	0	-1
		Hispanic/ Latino	Male	2	4	+2
			Female	0	2	+2
		Asian	Male	2	1	-1
			Female	5	13	+8
		Multiracial	Male	0	1	+1
			Female	1	3	+2
		Am. Indian/ Alaska Native	Female	0	1	+1
	Student- Athletes	White	Female	2,325	2,203	-122
		Black	Female	113	91	-22

(*continued*)

Table 5.5   *(continued)*

Sport	Position at Institution	Racial Identity	Gender	2008	2018	Change over 10 years (+/-)
		Hispanic/ Latino	Female	142	164	+22
		Asian	Female	165	339	+174
		Multiracial	Female	9	101	+92
		Am. Indian/ Alaska Native	Female	12	18	+6
Gymnastics	Head Coaches	White	Male	34	23	-11
			Female	34	37	+3
		Black	Male	3	3	—
		Hispanic/ Latino	Male	0	1	+1
			Female	1	1	—
		Asian	Male	2	2	—
			Female	0	2	+2
		Multiracial	Female	0	2	+2
	Assistant Coaches	White	Male	55	54	-1
			Female	56	58	+2
		Black	Male	4	2	-2
			Female	1	6	+5
		Hispanic/ Latino	Male	2	2	—
			Female	1	2	+1
		Asian	Male	0	1	+1
			Female	1	0	-1
	Student-Athletes	White	Female	950	859	-91
		Black	Female	63	106	+43
		Hispanic/ Latino	Female	39	53	+14
		Asian	Female	83	79	-4
		Multiracial	Female	3	91	+88

Table 5.5   (*continued*)

Sport	Position at Institution	Racial Identity	Gender	2008	2018	Change over 10 years (+/-)
		Am. Indian/ Alaska Native	Female	6	4	-2
Ice Hockey	Head Coaches	White	Male	21	22	+1
			Female	8	8	—
		Am. Indian/ Alaska Native	Male	1	0	-1
	Assistant Coaches	White	Male	23	29	+6
			Female	42	37	-5
		Asian	Male	0	1	+1
			Female	0	2	+2
	Student-Athletes	White	Female	665	560	-105
		Black	Female	3	2	-1
		Hispanic/ Latino	Female	6	7	+1
		Asian	Female	12	6	-6
		Multiracial	Female	2	15	+13
		Am. Indian/ Alaska Native	Female	7	3	-4
Lacrosse	Head Coaches	White	Male	20	31	+11
			Female	100	168	+68
		Black	Male	0	2	+2
			Female	2	5	+3
		Hispanic/ Latino	Female	1	3	+2
		Asian	Male	0	1	+1
			Female	0	2	+2
		Multiracial	Female	0	2	+2
	Assistant Coaches	White	Male	32	45	+13
			Female	160	300	+140

(*continued*)

Table 5.5   *(continued)*

Sport	Position at Institution	Racial Identity	Gender	2008	2018	Change over 10 years (+/-)
		Black	Male	1	1	—
			Female	3	9	+6
		Hispanic/ Latino	Male	0	2	+2
			Female	0	2	+2
		Asian	Male	2	0	-2
			Female	1	1	—
		Multiracial	Male	0	1	+1
			Female	0	2	+2
	Student-Athletes	White	Female	2,939	5,071	+2,132
		Black	Female	50	222	+172
		Hispanic/ Latino	Female	45	188	+143
		Asian	Female	33	68	+35
		Multiracial	Female	5	181	+176
		Am. Indian/ Alaska Native	Female	8	39	+31
Rowing	Head Coaches	White	Male	61	60	-1
			Female	34	38	+4
		Black	Male	1	1	—
		Hispanic/ Latino	Male	1	0	-1
		Asian	Male	1	3	+2
		Multiracial	Female	0	1	+1
	Assistant Coaches	White	Male	49	65	+16
			Female	146	164	+18
		Black	Male	2	1	-1
			Female	0	2	+2
		Hispanic/ Latino	Male	0	1	+1
			Female	1	3	+2

Table 5.5 (continued)

Sport	Position at Institution	Racial Identity	Gender	2008	2018	Change over 10 years (+/-)
		Asian	Male	0	2	+2
			Female	2	1	-1
		Multiracial	Male	0	4	+4
			Female	1	2	+1
	Student-Athletes	White	Female	4,574	4,348	-226
		Black	Female	133	126	-7
		Hispanic/Latino	Female	207	321	+114
		Asian	Female	204	195	-9
		Multiracial	Female	18	237	+219
		Am. Indian/Alaska Native	Male	26	31	+5
Softball	Head Coaches	White	Male	170	173	+3
			Female	294	337	+43
		Black	Male	25	17	-8
			Female	21	20	-1
		Hispanic/Latino	Male	7	4	-3
			Female	4	7	+3
		Asian	Male	4	4	—
			Female	2	9	+7
		Multiracial	Male	0	1	+1
			Female	1	7	+6
		Am. Indian/Alaska Native	Male	1	1	—
			Female	0	4	+4
	Assistant Coaches	White	Male	190	235	+45
			Female	570	724	+154
		Black	Male	20	21	+1
			Female	35	38	+3

(continued)

Table 5.5   *(continued)*

Sport	Position at Institution	Racial Identity	Gender	2008	2018	Change over 10 years (+/-)
		Hispanic/ Latino	Male	14	19	+5
			Female	21	53	+32
		Asian	Male	7	6	-1
			Female	13	15	+2
		Multiracial	Male	4	7	+3
			Female	1	15	+14
		Am. Indian/ Alaska Native	Male	2	1	-1
			Female	2	2	—
	Student-Athletes	White	Female	7,897	8,811	+914
		Black	Female	798	843	+45
		Hispanic/ Latino	Female	668	1,173	+505
		Asian	Female	203	236	+33
		Multiracial	Female	57	721	+664
		Am. Indian/ Alaska Native	Female	83	107	+24

Source: Data sample from the NCAA Demographics Database collected for 2008 and 2018, which can be found at http://www.ncaa.org/about/resources/research /ncaa-demographics-database.

almost five times the amount from 2008, the overall increase in White female players (+2,132 from 2008 to 2018) over the decade is more than 3x the total number of women of color playing college lacrosse (698 in 2018). While not a sport included in Table 5.5 within this text, according to the NCAA Demographic Database, women's collegiate soccer players still remain overwhelmingly White (11,585 in 2018) while the total players of color (3,491 in 2018) equates to about 30 percent of the total number of White female soccer players. It appears that NCAA women's soccer has more work to do as well if it strives for more equally distributed racial representation.

A couple other crucial points of data to note at the NCAA women's college level regard the multiracial population and the racial and gender identities of coaches. Just as the NCAA men's racial demographics revealed between 2008 and 2018, the multiracial student-athlete population for women's college athletics is universally on the rise. In terms of coaching, NCAA women's athletics, there is high representation of men in coaching overall. In every sport listed in the demographics database, there is male representation in head and assistant coaching in NCAA women's college sport; this is *not* the case for NCAA men's sports coaching. This encroachment by men into women's college sport started to become evident as early as the 1980s. Historian Susan Ware shares in the introduction of *Title IX: A Brief History of Documents*:

> In 1973, women had coached 92 percent of women's teams, but by 1984 this had dropped to 53.8 percent and by 2002 it was only 44 percent. Even though there has been an increase in the absolute numbers of coaching opportunities because of the dramatic growth in women's teams, most of these new opportunities have gone to men...In part because of Title IX, jobs coaching women's teams became better compensated and more attractive to men; since the 1970s, the gap between men's and women's coaching salaries has widened, not shrunk, in large part because of skyrocketing salaries paid to high-profile football and basketball coaches. A similar decline in positions for women administrators in athletics departments was also apparent . . . [as] most institutions merged the previously separate men's and women's athletic departments, invariably ending up with men in charge. (15)

The gendered coaching aspect of NCAA women's athletics is important to couple with research on race because for every White male identifying coach that is hired, there is also one less qualified female of color that could be coaching in collegiate athletics. Fortunately, there are initiatives like the Racial and Gender Report Card from The Institute for Diversity and Ethics in Sport (TIDES) that help to keep the public informed about and hold a mirror to sports organizations to the gender and racial inequities at the collegiate and professional levels of sport.

For NCAA athletes, irrespective of gender and racial identity, the question of socioeconomic earning power has been a contentious topic in the last few decades. The NCAA is a multimillion-dollar industry and even spilled into the billion dollar category in revenue generation during the 2016–2017 school year. The NCAA makes the majority of their money off the success of its athletic programs, which understandably, means their student-athlete talent. Many times, the NCAA makes money off the use of its athletes' name, image, or likeness (e.g., video games and broadcast deals). Yet, NCAA athletes are considered amateurs and according to the NCAA website's rules about amateurism and the promoting or endorsing commercial products or services, "after student-athletes enroll at an NCAA school, they may no longer promote or endorse a product or allow their name, image or likeness to be used for commercial or promotional purposes" and they certainly cannot be financially compensated for it. As early as 2009 and several times since then, former and current college athletes have filed lawsuits or even attempted to unionize to fight back against the NCAA's rules of amateurism. In 2009, former UCLA men's basketball player, Ed O'Bannon, somewhat successfully sued the NCAA in an antitrust lawsuit. Case 14-17068, "Edward O'Bannon Jr. v. NCAA," with the U.S. Court of Appeals for the Ninth Circuit summarizes O'Bannon's initial litigation from 2009 and details the appeal argued and submitted on March 17, 2015:

In 2008, Ed O'Bannon, a former All-American basketball player at UCLA, visited a friend's house, where
his friend's son told O'Bannon that he was depicted in
a college basketball video game produced by Electronic
Arts (EA), a software company that produced video
games based on college football and men's basketball
from the late 1990s until around 2013. The friend's son
turned on the video game, and O'Bannon saw an avatar of himself—a virtual player who visually resembled
O'Bannon, played for UCLA, and wore O'Bannon's jersey number, 31. O'Bannon had never consented to the
use of his likeness in the video game, and he had not been
compensated for it.

In 2009, O'Bannon sued the NCAA and the Collegiate
Licensing Company (CLC), the entity which licenses the
trademarks of the NCAA and a number of its member
schools for commercial use, in federal court. The grava-
men of O'Bannon's complaint was that the NCAA's amateurism rules, insofar as they prevented student-athletes
from being compensated for the use of their NILs, were
an illegal restraint of trade under Section 1 of the Sher-
man Act, 15 U.S.C. § 1. (12)

The United States Court of Appeals for the Ninth Circuit left
O'Bannon and the NCAA unhappy. The NCAA was unhappy
because the appeals court agreed with Federal District Court
Judge Claudia Wilkens ruling that the NCAAs compensation
rules were an "illegal restraint of trade." O'Bannon's team was
left unhappy because two of the three judges concluded that
preserving amateurism was paramount; thus, compensation
rules were mostly upheld. Both sides appealed to the Supreme
Court, but the case was turned down.

A decade later, however, a monumental piece of legislation
has been passed in the state of California related to college
athletics, student-athlete compensation and representation.
On September 30, 2019, California governor Gavin Newsom

signed into law Senate Bill 206, also referred to as the Fair Pay to Play Act. According to the Legislative Counsel's Digest section of Senate Bill 206:

> Existing law, known as the Student Athlete Bill of Rights, requires intercollegiate athletic programs at 4-year private universities or campuses of the University of California or the California State University that receive, as an average, $10,000,000 or more in annual revenue derived from media rights for intercollegiate athletics to comply with prescribed requirements relating to student athlete rights.
>
> This bill would prohibit California postsecondary educational institutions except community colleges, and every athletic association, conference, or other group or organization with authority over intercollegiate athletics, from providing a prospective intercollegiate student athlete with compensation in relation to the athlete's name, image, or likeness, or preventing a student participating in intercollegiate athletics from earning compensation as a result of the use of the student's name, image, or likeness or obtaining professional representation relating to the student's participation in intercollegiate athletics. The bill also would prohibit an athletic association, conference, or other group or organization with authority over intercollegiate athletics from preventing a postsecondary educational institution other than a community college from participating in intercollegiate athletics as a result of the compensation of a student athlete for the use of the student's name, image, or likeness. The bill would require professional representation obtained by student athletes to be from persons licensed by the state. The bill would specify that athlete agents shall comply with federal law in their relationships with student athletes. The bill would prohibit the revocation of a student's scholarship as a result of earning compensation or obtaining legal representation as authorized under these provisions. The bill would

prohibit a student athlete from entering into a contract providing compensation to the athlete for use of the athlete's name, image, or likeness if a provision of the contract is in conflict with a provision of the athlete's team contract. The bill would prohibit a team contract from preventing a student athlete from using the athlete's name, image, or likeness for a commercial purpose when the athlete is not engaged in official team activities, as specified.

These provisions would become operative on January 1, 2023.

This bill would require the Chancellor of the California Community Colleges to convene a community college athlete name, image, and likeness working group composed of individuals appointed on or before July 1, 2020, as specified. The bill would require the working group to review various athletic association bylaws and state and federal laws regarding a college athlete's use of the athlete's name, image, and likeness for compensation and, on or before July 1, 2021, submit to the Legislature and the California Community College Athletic Association a report containing its findings and policy recommendations in connection with this review. (2019)

This bill means that in 2023, U.S. society might witness a small group of collegiate athletes in the state of California making tens of thousands of dollars—if not more—while also playing college sport. And many of these athletes are likely to be athletes of color, considering the most financially lucrative NCAA sports are men's basketball and football (both sports are majority student-athletes of color, according to Table 5.4). The possibility of taking away the socioeconomic struggles for student-athletes is definitely beneficial, considering the rising costs of college tuitions in the United States, but what will be the socioeconomic impact on student-athletes of any race who are not deemed "marketable" by the companies willing to utilize California's NCAA athletic talent? In addition, it's unclear how the vague language in the part of the bill that states, "The bill would prohibit a student athlete from entering into a contract providing compensation to the athlete for use of the athlete's name, image, or likeness if a provision of the contract is in conflict with a provision of the athlete's team contract," will pan out. What determines that—and who decides when—"a provision of the contract is in conflict with a provision of the athlete's team contract"? The NCAA Board of Governors has also officially responded to Governor Newsom in a letter addressing California Senate Bill 206 that warns, "If the bill becomes law and California's 58 NCAA schools are compelled to allow an unrestricted name, image and likeness scheme, it would erase the critical distinction between college and professional athletics and, because it gives those schools an unfair recruiting advantage, would result in them eventually being unable to compete in NCAA competitions" (Members of the NCAA Board of Governors, 2019). No matter how this legislation plays out in collegiate athletics, it's guaranteed that the student-athletes are the most vulnerable people in the situation and likely that those student-athletes of color will have the most to gain *and* to lose.

Race and Sport: Professional Level

The most comprehensive resource for data on race and sport at the professional level is in the annual Racial and Gender Report Card (RGRC) published by the Institute for Diversity and Ethics in Sport (TIDES). According to the Executive Summary of "The 2018 Complete Sport Racial and Gender Report Card," TIDES "believes in the importance of diversity and inclusion on and off the playing field. With the release of each RGRC and the compilation of all report cards, TIDES aims to educate and emphasize the value of diverse and inclusive hiring practices to all professional leagues and college sport" (Lapchick, 2019). While Lapchick has been releasing the "report cards" since 1988, the rapid advances in technology and increased use in social media may be a huge reason why the U.S. professional sport industry is making the largest strides in the last decade to improve and amend policies and hiring practices related to racial and gender diversity and inclusivity. Within a matter of days, sometimes even hours, mistakes and criticisms of professional sports organizations can "go viral" nationwide and worldwide. The hope is that those in power and in the front offices of these professional and collegiate sports organizations have the best intentions with regards to racial and gender equity in sport, but it doesn't hurt to have the Racial and Gender Report Card to hold these organizations accountable either.

Table 5.6 represents the overall grades that were given to the following professional sports organizations: the Women's National Basketball Association, the National Basketball Association, the National Football League, Major League Baseball, and Major League Soccer. For most people who have grown up in U.S. society, simply looking at the grades for each of these organizations may read very simply: an A+ is the best grade, and anything below that means there's room for improvement. This is the genius of the "report card" model because even if one doesn't take the time to learn *how* these grades are given to sporting organizations, one can still deduce the general meaning behind the grade. However, it's absolutely worth understanding how grades are calculated for each RGRC and Dr. Lapchick and his team at TIDES always include this information, along with their methodology in each report:

> Federal affirmative action policies state the workplace should reflect the percentage of the people in the racial group in the population. When we first published the Racial and Gender Report Card in the late 1980s, approximately 24 percent of the population was comprised of people of color. Thus, an **A** was achieved if 24 percent of the positions were held by people of color, **B** if 12 percent of the positions were held by people of color, **C** if it had 9 percent, a **D** if it was at least 6 percent and **F** for anything

Table 5.6 2018 Racial and Gender Report Card Grades for Professional Sport

Overall Grades by League	WNBA	NBA	NFL	MLB	MLS
	A+	A	B	B-	B+
Racial Grade by League	A+	A+	A-	B+	A
Gender Grade by League	A+	B	C	C	C+

Source: Data from the 2018 Complete Racial and Gender Report Card (RGRC) from The Institute for Diversity and Ethics in Sport (TIDES), https://43530132-36e9-4f52-811a-182c7a91933b.filesusr.com/ugd/7d86e5_b9332a76bbf342c2b44d40cb47e09f79.pdf.

below 6 percent. The change in the nation's demographics has been dramatic with the most recent census making all people of color and minorities closer to 35 percent. To be fair in transition to the organizations and sports we examine in the Racial and Gender Report Cards, we decided to increase the standards in two steps. . . . To get an A for race, the category now needs to have 30 percent people of color and to get an A for gender, 45 percent is needed. . . . All data for the college sport report was collected by the research team at The Institute for Diversity and Ethics in Sport in the University of Central Florida's DeVos Sport Business Management Graduate Program. All data for the professional sports leagues was collected by the respective professional league offices and passed on to the research team at The Institute for Diversity and Ethics in Sport. The findings were compared to data from previous years. After evaluating the data, the report text was drafted and compared changes to statistics from previous years. The report draft was then sent to the respective organizations to be reviewed for accuracy. In addition, updates were requested for personnel changes that had occurred during or after the seasons being reported. (Lapchick, 2019, 30)

In looking to Table 5.6 at the grades given to five major professional sports organizations in the United States, it becomes more clear what areas these organizations need to improve in so that they are meeting federal affirmative action policies related to the workplace. The efforts of TIDES and the RGRC appear to be having an effect. For example, Major League Baseball has initiated a campaign called "The Diversity Pipeline Program," which seeks to develop and grow the number of qualified female and underrepresented racial groups for employment in the MLB organization. Moreover, since 2014, the NBA has hired a number of female coaches—such as Becky Hammon, Kristi Toliver, Kara Lawson, Nancy Lieberman, Lindsay Gottlieb and others—to improve their gender grade, and the NFL followed suit in 2015 with the hire of coach Jen Welter by the Arizona Cardinals. The progress of all professional sports organizations toward racial and gender equity may be slow-going, but it *is happening* and that should not be lost on anyone.

Race and Sports Data: Looking toward the Future

So much controversy and criticism is—and has been—directed at athletes, coaches, sports organizations, marketing executives, and sports fans for bringing in conversations on race in the realm of sport. Punishments have been dealt out, and some careers have even ended. Perhaps worst of all, talented athletes who speak out against racial and other injustices have been accused of being unpatriotic—accused of not sounding "American" or in support of the U.S. government. The racism within U.S. sport and beyond, however, has not gone unnoticed by the U.S. government. On April 2, 2019, Resolution 283, "Condemning Racism in Sports," was introduced in the House of Representatives in the first session of the 116th Congress. This resolution, introduced by Representative Adriano Espaillat (D-NY-13), acknowledged much of the troubling information about racism within sport, such as the following: the historically racist infrastructure of the sports industry; the existence of covert and overt racism by sports fans; the role the

forty-fifth president of the United States has negatively escalated the issue of racism in sports to a national discussion; data
on the increased instances of racist acts in sports since previous
years; punishments being dealt out to athletes for responding
to racist incidents; the media's role in the perpetuation of racist ideologies and expectations of athletes; and the continued
problem of sports teams with racist mascots and names against
Native Americans. At the end of Resolution 283, Rep. Espaillat
then shifts to the real power the sports realm has in improving
race relations and understanding differences, and he reminds
the House of Representatives that sport is "based on the principle of a level playing field" and that "there is still more work
to be done around altering the public discourse on race and
racism." To end, Rep. Espaillat left the House of Representatives to sit with weighty considerations:

> Now, therefore, be it *Resolved*, that it is the sense of the
> House of Representatives that—
>
> (1) athletes have the right to exercise their constitutionally
> protected right to freedom of speech;
>
> (2) racism in sports must be combatted and unequivo-
> cally condemned; and
>
> (3) public officials should use their platform to encour-
> age diversity in sport and highlight role models for young
> members of minority communities. (H.Res.283—116th
> Congress: Condemning Racism in Sports, 2019, 4–5)

DOCUMENTS

Blackhorse v. Pro-Football, Inc. (2014)

The Blackhorse v. Pro-Football, Inc. *decision of the Trademark
Trial and Appeal Board (TTAB or "Board") resolved the joint petition filed at the U.S. Patent and Trademark Office (USPTO) by
five Native Americans, who sought cancellation of six federal registrations for trademarks that include the term "Redskins," on June*

18, 2014. The TTAB determined that the Blackhorse petition-
ers established that the term "Redskins" was disparaging of Native
Americans when used in relation to professional football services.
Thus, in accordance with applicable law, the federal registrations
for the "Redskins" trademarks involved in this proceeding must be
cancelled. This full document also presents the legal knowledge to
understand why the NFL's Washington team owner had still been
allowed to use it.

OVERVIEW

Petitioners, five Native Americans, have brought this cancellation proceeding pursuant to Section 14 of the Trademark Act
of 1946, 15 U.S.C. § 1064(c). They seek to cancel respondent's registrations issued between 1967 and 1990 for trademarks consisting in whole or in part of the term REDSKINS
for professional football-related services on the ground that the
registrations were obtained contrary to Section 2(a), 15 U.S.C.
§ 1052(a), which prohibits registration of marks that may disparage persons or bring them into contempt or disrepute. In its
answer, defendant, Pro-Football, Inc., asserted various affirmative defenses including laches.

As explained below, we decide, based on the evidence properly before us, that these registrations must be cancelled because
they were disparaging to Native Americans at the respective
times they were registered, in violation of Section 2(a) of the
Trademark Act of 1946, 15 U.S.C. § 1052(a). This decision
concerns only the statutory right to *registration* under Section
2(a). We lack statutory authority to issue rulings concerning
the right to *use* trademarks.

[. . .]

[T]he Board noted that the test for disparagement comprises
a two-step inquiry:

a. What is the meaning of the matter in question, as it appears
    in the marks and as those marks are used in connection
    with the goods and services identified in the registrations?

b. Is the meaning of the marks one that may disparage Native Americans?

[. . .]

CONCLUSIONS

As noted above, as was found in the *Harjo* case, both by the Board and the District Court, and conceded by respondent, "the meaning of the matter in question," retains the core meaning Native American when used as the name of respondent's sports team. More specifically, the term "redskin(s)" as used by respondent in its registered marks when used in connection with professional football retains the "likely meaning" Native Americans. Much of respondent's evidence is directed to the first part of the test. Respondent's argument regarding "secondary meaning" in the sense that it has "a secondary or alternate meaning" denoting a football team, is not persuasive in that the "secondary meaning" has not stripped the word "redskins" of its "ethnic" meaning. *See Squaw Valley*, at 1282 [emphasis added] (Squaw Valley ski resort meaning of squaw is "likely meaning" "*rather than* the meaning of Native American woman or wife").

We turn then to the second question, "was the meaning one that may have disparaged" a substantial composite, which need not be a majority, of Native Americans, at the times of the registrations. The crux of this case is whether or not this record supports petitioners' contention that the answer to that question is yes.

Respondent contends that it does not and characterizes the record as, at most, showing a handful of individuals (the *Harjo* petitioners, the current petitioners, the letter writers, a few individuals from various organizations) who have their own individual opinion. Such a characterization, however, ignores, and is contradicted by the substantial evidence of record.

NCAI Resolution 93-11 represents the views of a substantial composite of Native Americans. NCAI consists of member tribes from across the United States and they voice their collective opinion through the Executive Council by resolutions. A resolution from the oldest Native American organization composed of tribes from across the United States and structured in a manner to represent the collective opinion of its membership through resolutions is strong evidence of the views of Native Americans. The NCAI members throughout the relevant time period represent approximately 30 percent of Native Americans.

[. . .]

The record establishes that, *at a minimum*, approximately thirty percent of Native Americans found the term REDSKINS used in connection with respondent's services to be disparaging at all times including 1967, 1972, 1974, 1978 and 1990. Section 2(a) prohibits registration of matter that disparages a substantial composite, which need not be a majority, of the referenced group. Thirty percent is without doubt a substantial composite. To determine otherwise means it is acceptable to subject to disparagement 1 out of every 3 individuals, or as in this case approximately 626,095 out of 1,878,285 in 1990. There is nothing in the Trademark Act, which expressly prohibits registration of disparaging terms, or in its legislative history, to permit that level of disparagement of a group and, therefore, we find this showing of thirty percent to be more than substantial.

[. . .]

In view of the above, petitioners have shown by a preponderance of the evidence that a substantial composite of Native Americans found the term REDSKINS to be disparaging in connection with respondent's services during the relevant time frame of 1967–1990. Accordingly, the six registrations must be cancelled as required under Sections 2(a) and 14(3) of the Trademark Act.

Source: United States Patent and Trademark Office. https://www.uspto.gov/about-us/news-updates/blackhorse-v-pro-football-inc-decision

Stolen Identities: The Impact of Racist Stereotypes on Indigenous People (2011)

On May 5, 2011, the United States Senate Committee on Indian Affairs held a hearing called "Stolen Identities: The Impact of Racist Stereotypes on Indigenous People." The full hearing is lengthy and immensely informative. The opening statement of the hearing, made by U.S. Senator Tom Udall from New Mexico, is presented below. Politicians, educators, activists, and cultural heritage leaders are some of the witnesses, committee members, and creators of statements presented at the hearing.

Senator Udall. Thank you all for being here today. I call the meeting to order.

Unfortunately, Chairman Akaka had a minor accident at home that precludes him from being at the hearing today. I know that he really wished to be here. On his behalf, I would like to welcome you to our hearing entitled Stolen Identities: The Impact of Racist Stereotypes on Indigenous Peoples.

In this hearing, we will explore how Indian mascots, common caricatures and prevalent mis-portrayals of Native people have far-reaching impacts on the identity and sense of self-worth of Native peoples, and negatively impacts how all of our Nation's people perceive and relate to each other. It is my hope that this hearing will help bring more understanding about the real impacts of these common mis-portrayals to light, so that we can as a Nation resolve these concerns.

I would especially like to thank Ms. Charlene Teters for being here today, a professor from the Institute of American Indian Arts in my State of New Mexico. The Institute is a great asset to young Native artists and to the Nation as a whole. I appreciate Ms. Teters' work and the work of the Institute to create beauty, retain cultural knowledge and move aggressively in a new era of technology and creativity. It is my hope that the young artists coming out of IAIA will brandish strong and creative talents that can help to wash away the ugly stereotypes and perceptions of the past.

In the last couple of days, most of us in this room have heard the news reports on the association of Geronimo being used as a code word associated with the successful mission to kill Osama bin Laden. It goes without saying that all of us feel a tremendous sense of relief and pride toward our military personnel, intelligence community, and Commander In Chief, both past and present, for accomplishing this mission. This is especially relevant for Native Americans, who historically have the highest per capita rate of military service of any ethnic group. Tens of thousands of Native Americans serve in our military today, defending their homeland, just as Geronimo did.

Here today we also have the President of the Navajo Nation, Ben Shelly. Ben and I both know that 11 Navajos have died in military service since 9/11. Just last night, our local New Mexico news stations, KOAT-7, interviewed Geronimo's great-grandson, Joseph Geronimo, who explained the offense he feels based on the report's of his ancestor's name being used. My office has tried to get clarification about the code name from the Department of Defense. Their protocol prohibits the release of information regarding operation names. As a result, the details of how Geronimo's name was used are unclear.

I find the association of Geronimo with bin Laden to be highly inappropriate and culturally insensitive. It highlights a serious issue and the very issue we have come here to discuss today: a socially ingrained acceptance of derogatory portrayals of indigenous people.

I hope that we can use this hearing as an opportunity to communicate to the Nation the importance of recognizing and rejecting derogatory stereotypes. And since no other members of the Committee have joined us quite yet, I think there will be others here, some of them may give opening statements. I may interrupt based on schedules and things. But at this point, we are going to go directly to the panel.

[. . .]

First, I would like to welcome the Honorable Tex Hall, the Chairman of the Mandan, Hidatsa and Arikara. Chairman Hall also serves as the Chairman of the Great Plains Tribal Chairman's Association and is joining us from New Town, North Dakota.

We will also hear from Suzan Harjo, President of the Morning Star Institute, who is here in Washington. I think, Suzan, you have had a long acquaintance with these issues, and I believe you have written articles and books. We are very happy to have you here today.

And as I mentioned earlier, our final witness on the panel will be Charlene Teters, a professor with the Institute of American Indian Arts in Santa Fe, New Mexico.

Welcome to everyone. Chairman Hall, we are ready to go with you and then we will just go down the line. Great to have you here today.

Source: Hearing before the Committee on Indian Affairs, United States Senate, 112th Congress, 1st Session. May 5, 2011. Washington, D.C.: Government Printing Office, 2011. https://www.govinfo.gov/content/pkg/CHRG-112shrg66994/html/CHRG-112shrg66994.htm

Flood v. Kuhn (1972)

Flood v. Kuhn *arose from a challenge by Major League Baseball player Curt Flood. The St. Louis Cardinals' outfielder refused to be traded to the Philadelphia Phillies after the 1969 season. Flood sought relief from the reserve clause, which prevented him and other players from negotiating with other teams. Although Flood lost his case, it would eventually lead to free agency for professional baseball players and other athletes. An excerpt from this important case is provided below.*

II

The Petitioner

The petitioner, Curtis Charles Flood, born in 1938, began his major league career in 1956 when he signed a contract with the Cincinnati Reds for a salary of $4,000 for the season. He had no attorney or agent to advise him on that occasion. He was traded to the St. Louis Cardinals before the 1958 season. Flood rose to fame as a center fielder with the Cardinals during the years 1958–1969. In those 12, seasons he compiled a batting average of .293. His best offensive season was 1967, when he achieved .335. He was .301 or better in six of the 12 St. Louis years. He participated in the 1964, 1967, and 1968 World Series. He played errorless ball in the field in 1966, and once enjoyed 223 consecutive errorless games. Flood has received seven Golden Glove Awards. He was co-captain of his team from 1965–1969. He ranks among the 10 major league outfielders possessing the highest lifetime fielding averages.

Flood's St. Louis compensation for the years shown was:

1961 $13,500 (including a bonus for signing)
1962 $16,000
1963 $17,500
1964 $23,000
1965 $35,000
1966 $45,000
1967 $50,000
1968 $72,500
1969 $90,000

These figures do not include any so-called fringe benefits or World Series shares. But, at the age of 31, in October, 1969, Flood was traded to the Philadelphia Phillies of the National League in a multi-player transaction. He was not consulted about the trade. He was informed by telephone and received formal notice only after the deal had been consummated. In December, he complained to the Commissioner of Baseball and asked that he be made a free agent and be placed at liberty to strike his own bargain with any other major league team. His request was denied.

Flood then instituted this antitrust suit in January, 1970, in federal court for the Southern District of New York. The defendants (although not all were named in each cause of action) were the Commissioner of Baseball, the presidents of the two major leagues, and the 24 major league clubs. In general, the complaint charged violations of the federal antitrust laws and civil rights statutes, violation of state statutes and the common law, and the imposition of a form of peonage and involuntary servitude contrary to the Thirteenth Amendment and 42 U.S.C. § 1994, 18 U.S.C. § 1581, and 29 U.S.C. §§ 102 and 103. Petitioner sought declaratory and injunctive relief and treble damages.

Flood declined to play for Philadelphia in 1970, despite a $100,000 salary offer, and he sat out the year. After the season was concluded, Philadelphia sold its rights to Flood to the Washington Senators. Washington and the petitioner were able to come to terms for 1971 at a salary of $110,000. Flood started the season but, apparently because he was dissatisfied with his performance, he left the Washington club on April 27, early in the campaign. He has not played baseball since then.

III

The Present Litigation

Judge Cooper, in a detailed opinion, first denied a preliminary injunction observing on the way:

"Baseball has been the national pastime for over one hundred years, and enjoys a unique place in our American heritage. Major league professional baseball is avidly followed by millions of fans, looked upon with fervor and pride, and provides a special source of inspiration and competitive team spirit, especially for the young."

"Baseball's status in the life of the nation is so pervasive that it would not strain credulity to say the Court can take judicial notice that baseball is everybody's business. To put it mildly and with restraint, it would be unfortunate indeed if a fine sport and profession, which brings surcease from daily travail and an escape from the ordinary to most inhabitants of this land, were to suffer in the least because of undue concentration by any one or any group on commercial and profit considerations. The game is on higher ground; it behooves every one to keep it there."

Flood's application for an early trial was granted. The court next deferred until trial its decision on the defendants' motions to dismiss the primary causes of action, but granted a defense motion for summary judgment on an additional cause of action.

Trial to the court took place in May and June, 1970. An extensive record was developed. In an ensuing opinion, Judge Cooper first noted that:

"Plaintiff's witnesses in the main concede that some form of reserve on players is a necessary element of the organization of baseball as a league sport, but contend that the present all-embracing system is needlessly restrictive, and offer various alternatives which, in their view, might loosen the bonds without sacrifice to the game. . . ."

" * * * *"

"Clearly, the preponderance of credible proof does not favor elimination of the reserve clause. With the sole exception of plaintiff himself, it shows that even plaintiff's witnesses do not contend that it is wholly undesirable; in fact, they regard substantial portions meritorious. . . ."

He then held that *Federal Baseball Club v. National League*, and *Toolson v. New York Yankees, Inc.*, were controlling; that it was not necessary to reach the issue whether exemption from the antitrust laws would result because aspects of baseball now are a subject of collective bargaining; that the plaintiff's state law claims, those based on common law as well as on statute, were to be denied because baseball was not "a matter which admits of diversity of treatment," that the involuntary servitude claim failed because of the absence of "the essential element of this cause of action, a showing of compulsory service," and that judgment was to be entered for the defendants. Judge Cooper included a statement of personal conviction to the effect that "negotiations could produce an accommodation on the reserve system which would be eminently fair and equitable to all concerned," and that "the reserve clause can be fashioned so as to find acceptance by player and club."

On appeal, the Second Circuit felt "compelled to affirm." It regarded the issue of state law as one of first impression, but concluded that the Commerce Clause precluded its application. Judge Moore added a concurring opinion in which he predicted, with respect to the suggested overruling of *Federal Baseball* and *Toolson*, that "there is no likelihood that such an event will occur."

We granted certiorari in order to look once again at this troublesome and unusual situation.

Source: *Flood v. Kuhn*, 407 U.S. 258 (1972).

Clay v. United States (1971)

The United States Supreme Court case, Clay v. United States *(1971) reversed boxer Muhammad Ali's—formerly legally named Cassius Clay—conviction for refusing to be inducted into the Selective Service by the United States armed forces. The judgment of reversal was unanimous. Two years later, on June 30, 1973, the United States formally ended the draft and began to rely upon an all-volunteer army.*

Petitioner appealed his local draft board's rejection of his application for conscientious objector classification. The Justice Department, in response to the State Appeal Board's referral for an advisory recommendation, concluded, contrary to a hearing officer's recommendation, that petitioner's claim should be denied, and wrote that board that petitioner did not meet any of the three basic tests for conscientious objector status. The Appeal Board then denied petitioner's claim, but without stating its reasons. Petitioner refused to report for induction, for which he was thereafter tried and convicted. The Court of Appeals affirmed. In this Court the Government has rightly conceded the invalidity of two of the grounds for denial of petitioner's claim given in its letter to the Appeal Board, but argues that there was factual support for the third ground. Held: Since the Appeal Board gave no reason for the denial of a conscientious objector exemption to petitioner, and it is impossible to determine on which of the three grounds offered in the Justice Department's letter that board relied, petitioner's conviction must be reversed.

[. . .]

The petitioner was convicted for willful refusal to submit to induction into the Armed Forces. The judgment of conviction was affirmed by the Court of Appeals for the Fifth Circuit. We granted certiorari to consider whether the induction notice was invalid because grounded upon an erroneous denial of the petitioner's claim to be classified as a conscientious objector.

I

The petitioner's application for classification as a conscientious objector was turned down by his local draft board, and he took an administrative appeal. The State Appeal Board tentatively classified him I-A (eligible for unrestricted military service) and referred his file to the Department of Justice for an advisory recommendation, in accordance with then-applicable procedures. The FBI then conducted an "inquiry" as required by the statute, interviewing some 35 persons, including members of the petitioner's family and many of his friends, neighbors, and business and religious associates.

There followed a hearing on "the character and good faith of the [petitioner's] objections" before a hearing officer appointed by the Department. The hearing officer, a retired judge of many years' experience, heard testimony from the petitioner's mother and father, from one of his attorneys, from a minister of his religion, and from the petitioner himself. He also had the benefit of a full report from the FBI. On the basis of this record the hearing officer concluded that the registrant was sincere in his objection on religious grounds to participation in war in any form, and he recommended that the conscientious objector claim be sustained.

Notwithstanding this recommendation, the Department of Justice wrote a letter to the Appeal Board, advising it that the petitioner's conscientious objector claim should be denied. Upon receipt of this letter of advice, the Board denied the petitioner's claim without a statement of reasons. After various further proceedings which it is not necessary to recount here, the petitioner was ordered to report for induction. He refused to take the traditional step forward, and this prosecution and conviction followed.

II

In order to qualify for classification as a conscientious objector, a registrant must satisfy three basic tests. He must show that he is conscientiously opposed to war in any form. He must show that this opposition is based upon religious training and belief, as the term has been construed in our decisions. And he must show that this objection is sincere. In applying these tests, the Selective Service System must be concerned with the registrant as an individual, not with its own interpretation of the dogma of the religious sect, if any, to which he may belong.

In asking us to affirm the judgment of conviction, the Government argues that there was a "basis in fact," for holding that the petitioner is not opposed to "war in any form," but is only selectively opposed to certain wars. Counsel for the petitioner, needless to say, takes the opposite position. The issue is one that need not be resolved in this case. For we have concluded that even if the Government's position on this question is correct, the conviction before us must still be set aside for another quite independent reason.

III

The petitioner's criminal conviction stemmed from the Selective Service System's denial of his appeal seeking conscientious objector status. That denial, for which no reasons were ever given, was, as we have said, based on a recommendation of the Department of Justice, overruling its hearing officer and advising the Appeal Board that it "finds that the registrant's conscientious-objector claim is not sustained and recommends to your Board that he be not [so] classified." This finding was contained in a long letter of explanation, from which it is evident that Selective Service officials were led to believe that the Department had found that the petitioner had failed to satisfy each of the three basic tests for qualification as a conscientious objector.

As to the requirement that a registrant must be opposed to war in any form, the Department letter said that the petitioner's expressed beliefs "do not appear to preclude military service in any form, but rather are limited to military service in the Armed Forces of the United States. . . . These constitute only objections to certain types of war in certain circumstances, rather than a general scruple against participation in war in any form. However, only a general scruple against participation in war in any form can support an exemption as a conscientious objector under the Act.

As to the requirement that a registrant's opposition must be based upon religious training and belief, the Department letter said: "It seems clear that the teachings of the Nation of Islam preclude fighting for the United States not because of objections to participation in war in any form but rather because of political and racial objections to policies of the United States as interpreted by Elijah Muhammad. . . . It is therefore our conclusion that registrant's claimed objections to participation in war insofar as they are based upon the teachings of the Nation of Islam, rest on grounds which primarily are political and racial."

As to the requirement that a registrant's opposition to war must be sincere, that part of the letter began by stating that "the registrant has not consistently manifested his conscientious-objector claim. Such a course of overt manifestations is requisite to establishing a subjective state of mind and belief." There followed several paragraphs reciting the timing and circumstances of the petitioner's conscientious objector claim, and a concluding paragraph seeming to state a rule of law - that "a registrant has not shown overt manifestations sufficient to establish his subjective belief where, as here, his conscientious-objector claim was not asserted until military service became imminent.

In this Court the Government has now fully conceded that the petitioner's beliefs are based upon "religious training and belief," as defined in *United States v. Seeger*, supra: "There is no dispute that petitioner's professed beliefs were founded on basic tenets of the Muslim religion, as he understood them, and derived in substantial part from his devotion to Allah as the Supreme Being. Thus, under this Court's decision in *United States v. Seeger*, his claim unquestionably was within the 'religious training and belief' clause of the exemption provision." This concession is clearly correct. For the record shows that the petitioner's beliefs are founded on tenets of the Muslim religion as he understands them. They are surely no less religiously based than those of the three registrants before this Court in *Seeger*.

The Government in this Court has also made clear that it no longer questions the sincerity of the petitioner's beliefs. This concession is also correct. The Department hearing officer—the only person at the administrative appeal level who carefully examined the petitioner and other witnesses in person and who had the benefit of the full FBI file—found "that the registrant is sincere in his objection." The Department of Justice was wrong in advising the Board in terms of a purported rule of law that it should disregard this finding simply because of the circumstances and timing of the petitioner's claim.

Since the Appeal Board gave no reasons for its denial of the petitioner's claim, there is absolutely no way of knowing upon which of the three grounds offered in the Department's letter it relied. Yet the Government now acknowledges that two of those grounds were not valid. And, the Government's concession aside, it is indisputably clear, for the reasons stated, that the Department was simply wrong as a matter of law in advising that the petitioner's beliefs were not religiously based and were not sincerely held.

This case, therefore, falls squarely within the four corners of this Court's decision in *Sicurella v. United States.* There as here the Court was asked to hold that an error in an advice letter prepared by the Department of Justice did not require reversal of a criminal conviction because there was a ground on which the Appeal Board might properly have denied a conscientious objector classification. This Court refused to consider the proffered alternative ground:

> "[W]e feel that this error of law by the Department, to which the Appeal Board might naturally look for guidance on such questions, must vitiate the entire proceedings at least where it is not clear that the Board relied on some legitimate ground. Here, where it is impossible to determine on exactly which grounds the Appeal Board decided, the integrity of the Selective Service System demands, at least, that the Government not recommend illegal grounds. There is an impressive body of lower court cases taking this position and we believe that they state the correct rule."

The doctrine thus articulated 16 years ago in *Sicurella* was hardly new. It was long ago established as essential to the administration of criminal justice. In *Stromberg* the Court reversed a conviction for violation of a California statute containing three separate clauses, finding one of the three clauses constitutionally invalid. As Chief Justice Hughes put the matter, "[I]t is impossible to say under which clause of the statute the conviction was obtained." Thus, "if any of the clauses in question is invalid under the Federal Constitution, the conviction cannot be upheld."

The application of this doctrine in the area of Selective Service law goes back at least to 1945, and Judge Learned Hand's opinion for the Second Circuit in *United States v. Cain.* It is a doctrine that has been consistently and repeatedly followed by the federal courts in dealing with the criminal sanctions of the selective service laws. In every one of the above cases the defendant was acquitted or the conviction set aside under the *Sicurella* application of the Stromberg doctrine.

The long established rule of law embodied in these settled precedents thus clearly requires that the judgment before us be reversed.

It is so ordered.

Source: *Clay v. United States,* 403 U.S. 698 (1971).

H. Res. 77 Encouraging the Development of Best Business Practices to Fully Utilize the Potential of the United States (2017)

House Resolution 77 was presented in the House of Representatives of the Fifteenth Congress, First Session, on January 31, 2017. This resolution calls for U.S. corporate, academic, and social entities, regardless of size or field of operation, to develop an internal rule for recruiting and interviewing modeled after a successful business practice, such as the Rooney Rule (developed for the National Football League) or the RLJ Rule (developed by the founder of Black Entertainment Television).

RESOLUTION

Encouraging the development of best business practices to fully utilize the potential of the United States.

Whereas the Rooney Rule, formulated by Daniel Rooney, chairman of the Pittsburgh Steelers football team in the National Football League (referred to in this preamble as the "NFL"), requires each NFL team with a job opening for a coach or general manager position to interview at least 1 minority candidate for that position;

Whereas the Rooney Rule has been successful in increasing minority representation in higher leadership positions in professional football, as shown by the fact that, in the 80 years between the hiring of Fritz Pollard as coach of the Akron Pros and the implementation of the Rooney Rule in 2003, only 7 minority head coaches were hired but, since 2003, 15 minority head coaches have been hired;

Whereas the Rooney Rule has demonstrated that once highly qualified and highly skilled diversity candidates are given exposure during the hiring process, the abilities of those diversity candidates can be better utilized;

Whereas the RLJ Rule, formulated by Robert L. Johnson, founder of Black Entertainment Television (commonly known as "BET") and The RLJ Companies, and based on the Rooney Rule from the NFL, similarly encourages companies to voluntarily establish a best practices policy to identify minority candidates and minority vendors by implementing a plan to interview—

(1) not fewer than 2 qualified minority candidates for each managerial opening at the director level and above; and

(2) not fewer than 2 qualified minority-owned businesses before approving a vendor contract;

Whereas, according to Crist-Kolder Associates, as cited in the Wall Street Journal, at the top 668 companies in the United States, less than 10 percent of Chief Financial Officers are African-American, Hispanic, or of Asian descent;

Whereas underrepresented groups contain members with the necessary abilities, experience, and qualifications for any position available;

Whereas business practices such as the Rooney Rule or the RLJ Rule are neither employment quotas nor Federal law but rather voluntary initiatives instituted by willing entities to provide the human resources necessary to ensure success;

Whereas experience has shown that people of all genders, colors, and physical abilities can achieve excellence;

Whereas the increased involvement of underrepresented workers would improve the economy of the United States and the experience of the people of the United States; and

Whereas ensuring the increased exposure, and resulting increased advancement, of diverse and qualified candidates would result in gains by all people of the United States through stronger economic opportunities: Now, therefore, be it

Resolved, That the House of Representatives encourages each corporate, academic, and social entity, regardless of size or field of operation, to—

(1) develop an internal rule modeled after a successful business practice, such as the Rooney Rule or RLJ Rule, and, in accordance with title VII of the Civil Rights Act of 1964 (42 U.S.C. 2000e et seq.), adapt that rule to specifications that will best fit the procedures of the individual entity; and

(2) institute the individualized rule described in paragraph (1) to ensure that the entity will always consider candidates from underrepresented populations before making a final decision with respect to selecting a business vendor or filling a leadership position.

Source: H.Res.77, 115th Congress (2017–2018). https://www.congress.gov/bill/115th-congress/house-resolution/77/text.

References

Clay v. United States. 1971. Eagan, MN: FindLaw.com.

Flood v. Kuhn. 1972. Justia.com: U.S. Supreme Court.

House of Representatives. 2017. House—Education and the Workforce. H.Res.77—Encouraging the Development of Best Business Practices to Fully Utilize the Potential of the United States (January 31).

Kelley, Bruce, and Carl Carchia. 2013. "Hey, Data Data— Swing!" *ESPN The Magazine* (July 11).

Lapchick, Richard. 2019. "The 2018 Complete Sport Racial and Gender Report Card." Edited by Lee Bowman Brittany Barber, Meaghan Coleman, Yeehang Fan, Nate Harvey, Daniel Martin, Miranda Murphy, William Thomas II, and David Zimmerman. Orlando, FL: The Institute for Diversity and Ethics in Sport. https://43530132-36e94f52811a182c7a91933b.filesusr.com/ugd/7d86e5_b9332a76bbf342c2b44d40cb47e09f79.pdf.

Laws, Rachel Gayle. 2012. "South African & U.S. Black Female Athletes Compared: A Critical Ethnography Focused on Image, Perceptions, and Narratives." Doctor of Philosophy Theses, African American & African Studies, Michigan State University.

Lytle, James. 2016. "The NCAA's Hidden Influence on High Schools." *Education Week* 35 (18): 25.

Members of the NCAA Board of Governors. 2019. "NCAA responds to California Senate Bill 206." NCAA.org (September 11).

Rep. Espaillat, Adriano. 2019. H.Res.283—116th Congress: Condemning Racism in Sports. Edited by House-Judiciary. Congress.gov: Library of Congress.

Schutte, Gerard. 1995. *What Racists Believe: Race Relations in South Africa and the United States*. Thousand Oaks, CA: SAGE Publications, Inc.

Steele, C. M., and J. Aronson. 1995. "Stereotype Threat and the Intellectual Test Performance of African Americans." *Journal of Personality and Social Psychology* 69 (5): 797–811.

Suggs, Welch. 2001. "Left Behind." *The Chronicle of Higher Education* (November 30): A35.

"Time in U.S. History." Release number CB18-41 (March 13). https://www.census.gov/newsroom/press-releases/2018/cb18-41-population-projections.html.

United States Census Bureau. 2018. "Older People Projected to Outnumber Children for First."

United States Courts Opinions. 2015. 14-17068 Edward O'Bannon, Jr. v. NCAA, et al. Edited by Judicial Publications. govinfo.gov: U.S. Government Publishing Office.

United States Patent and Trademark Office. 2014. Trademark Trial and Appeal Board. *Blackhorse v. Pro-Football Inc.* (June 18).

Ware, Susan. 2007. *Title IX: A Brief History with Documents.* 1st ed. Long Grove, IL: Waveland Press Inc.

Wendling, Elodie. 2018. "Youth Athletes' Sustained Involvement in Elite Sport: An Exploratory Examination of Elements Affecting Their Athletic Participation." *International Journal of Sports Science & Coaching* 13 (5): 658–73.

Zarrett, Nicole, Philip Veliz, and Don Sabo. (2018). *Teen Sport in America: Why Participation Matters.* East Meadow, NY: Women's Sports Foundation.

6 Resources

Introduction

Race and sports as an area of academic focus has only been in existence since the 1970s. Race and sports is discussed through a multitude of mediums: books, articles, film, reports, and internet sites. These resources often give insight into a host of related issues, including the economics, policy and organizational structure, and intersectionality. This chapter can list only a limited number of the numerous publications now available on this topic. These resources include publications in one of four categories: books, articles, film, and reports and internet sites.

The majority of items listed in this chapter are devoted exclusively or primarily to the topic of race and sports. However, a number of athlete and coach memoirs and autobiographies exist that discuss race related experiences within the realm of sports. In addition, a number of films—especially documentaries—have been made to visually deliver valuable facts and historical experiences on the topic of race and sports. Lastly, this annotated bibliography also provides some texts dedicated to race theory more generally so that future researchers might also have a starting reference for combining important theories on race with events and individuals in the realm of sports.

Two members of the University of Tennessee women's 4x100 relay team compete at the 2011 Penn Relays in Philadelphia, Pennsylvania. The Penn Relays, founded in 1895, is the oldest and largest track and field competition in the United States. (Aspenphoto/Dreamstime.com)

Books

Anthony, K. H. 2009. *Unfavorable Odds: The Story of UCLA's First African-American Female Gymnastics Champion*. Mustand, OK: Tate Publishing & Enterprises.

> Kim Hamilton Anthony was the first African American gymnast offered an athletic scholarship to attend the University of California Los Angeles (UCLA). Hamilton Anthony offers an autobiography that unearths her challenges with family, drugs, violence, socioeconomic instability, and racism. Hamilton Anthony's fourth chapter entitled "Little Black Girl in a White Girl's World" gives particular attention to the relationship between race and gymnastics for African American girls during the late 1980s and 1990s. This text is 277 pages and twenty-five chapters.

Ashe, Arthur R. 1988. *A Hard Road to Glory: A History of the African-American Athlete since 1946*. New York: Warner Books, Inc.

> This text is the third in a three-series volume by tennis legend Arthur Ashe. Ashe toiled for a decade to research for his three-volume historiography of the African American athlete. This particular volume is valuable to research on the topic of race and sport because it gives readers the history of Blacks in baseball. From baseball's infancy in Black colleges to the late 1980s, it covers the establishment of both major leagues and the Negro Leagues, Jackie Robinson's reintegration of professional sports, and Curt Flood's struggle to establish a free agency.
>
> The format is the same for all three volumes: there are chapters on each major sport; historical information is presented from the African American perspective; key players, teams, and events are featured in chronological order; and analyses of the sports and the players, as well as interpretations of their influence on U.S. life are presented. In

addition, each volume has statistics of teams, individual players, and awards given.

Baker, A. 2006. *Contesting Identities: Sports in American Film.* Champaign: University of Illinois Press.

This 162-page text analyzes roughly ninety movies about sports that represent certain social identities—race, sexual orientation, gender, and class. Baker includes four chapters in addition to an introduction and conclusion. Baker states in the introduction that he "hope[s] that the analysis of sports films in this book will critique the powerful mythology of self-determination by illustrating some of the values and practices that inform social identities" (p. 5).

Baker, C. A. 2008. *Why She Plays: The World of Women's Basketball.* Lincoln: University of Nebraska Press.

This source provides information on women's basketball from the youth level through to the WNBA. The author focuses her periodization on the thirty-five years that had elapsed since Title IX was established in 1972. Statistics and trends, and exclusive interviews with players, coaches, and other women within the sports industry are presented.

Bass, A. 2002. *Not the Triumph but the Struggle: The 1986 Olympics and the Making of the Black Athlete.* Minneapolis: University of Minnesota Press.

Author Amy Bass presents a deep look into the political landscape in the United States and globally that made a deep impression on Black athletes in the 1960s. Bass provides a nuanced account of the Olympic Project for Human Rights (OPHR), the Black athletes involved in the organization, and Dr. Harry Edwards's role in leading these young Olympic-qualifying student-athletes. Topics such as Black consciousness, South African apartheid, and patriotism are discussed as well. This work is formatted into seven chapters and is 464 pages in length.

Bass, A. 2005. *In the Game: Race, Identity and Sports in the Twentieth Century*. New York: Palgrave Macmillan.
  This source is great for the researcher on race and sports who wants to learn more beyond the United States and about race relations beyond Black and White. Eleven contributors present essays that focus on topics of race in sport such as Native Americans and mascots, Black culture in the 1970s NFL experience, race and cricket in the West Indies, and how race plays out in Argentine soccer. This resource is 284 pages in length.

Baylor, E. 2018. *Hang Time: My Life in Basketball*. New York: Houghton Mifflin Harcourt.
  This autobiography is written by former NBA All-Star turned NBA general manager (GM) Elgin Baylor. Baylor, who is considered one of the greatest players all-time, recounts to readers his role in helping break down racial barriers in the sport of basketball. The author also recounts his 1964 boycott of that year's All-Star game and twenty-two years spent as GM for the LA Clippers under Donald Sterling—Sterling being a documented racist towards African Americans. This resource consists of ten chapters and 336 pages.

Bennett, Michael, and David Zirin. 2018. *Things That Make White People Uncomfortable*. Chicago, IL: Haymarket Books.
  This thirteen-chapter source is part memoir and part manifesto on life as a professional Black athlete who is unafraid to discuss racism in the United States and its sporting structure. This text is written by Super Bowl champion Michael Bennett and sports journalist and author Dave Zirin. Bennett discusses racism, police brutality, Black athletes' place in the NCAA and the NFL, and

the responsibilities of athletes as activists against oppression and injustice.

Bennett, Robert A., III, Samuel R. Hodge, David L. Graham, and James L. Moore III, eds. 2015. *Black Males and Intercollegiate Athletics: An Exploration of Problems and Solutions.* Diversity in Higher Education. Bingley, UK: Emerald Group Publishing Limited.

This resource comprises fourteen essays that address topics such as identity, mental health, economic realities of athletic competition, academic support programs, and the differences between the NCAA's principles and goals and the lived realities of its student-athletes. This text stands out in research on race and sport due to the fact that the effort is made to also highlight Black male experience in sport as coaches, academic support staff, and administration. This resource is 384 pages in length.

Billings, Andrew C., and Jason Edward Black. 2018. *Mascot Nation: The Controversy over Native American Representations in Sports.* Urbana: University of Illinois Press.

This 256-page resource comprises eight chapters that discuss various aspects of the controversy over Native American representations in sports, specifically mascots. What is unique about this resource compared to others that address the mascot debate is that the authors go far beyond the surface-level issues. Chapters presented focus on the visual, ritualistic, textual and performative aspects of sports mascots. Qualitative data is merged with cultural analysis to offer an approach to understanding the different perspectives, issues, and stakes of mascot debates.

Bryant, H. 2002. *Shut Out: A Story of Race and Baseball in Boston.* New York: Routledge.

This resource, written by sports journalist Howard Bryant, focuses specifically on the city of Boston, racism, and the sport of major league baseball (MLB). Specifically, Bryant focuses on the Boston Red Sox ownership decision not to sign African American Jackie Robinson in 1945 and the subsequent rejection of African American Willie Mays four years later. Both Jackie Robinson and Willie Mays went on to become prolific Black players in the major leagues. This source is broken up into seventeen chapters, with an introduction and epilogue and a dozen black-and-white photographs.

Bryant, H. 2018. *The Heritage: Black Athletes, a Divided America, and the Politics of Patriotism.* Boston, MA: Beacon Press.
This 272-page text, written by Howard Bryant, focuses on what Bryant refers to as "the heritage." What Bryant refers to and presents as the heritage is the historical and present-day return of athlete-activism in public spaces—Black athletes in particular. This text is broken up into three parts with ten total chapters. Some Black athletes given strong attention and analysis are Paul Robeson, Muhammad Ali, Jackie Robinson, O. J. Simpson, LeBron James, Colin Kaepernick, Carmelo Anthony, Tiger Woods, and Michael Jordan.

Cahn, S. K. 1994. *Coming on Strong: Gender and Sexuality in Twentieth-Century Women's Sport.* Cambridge, MA: Harvard University Press.
This 298-page resource focuses centrally on women's athletic history. Racial politics surrounding African American female track and field stars is given its own chapter. Other chapters in this text discuss sexual orientation and gendered stereotypes as well as other important social aspects to the female experience in sport. This source contains robust notes, an index, and photographs for researchers.

Carlos, John D. Z. 2013. *The John Carlos Story: The Sports Moment that Changed the World.* Chicago, IL: Haymarket Books.

This primary source memoir is written by John Carlos, the Black track and field Olympian who historically raised his fist alongside Tommie Smith atop the 1968 Mexico City podium. This work is eight chapters and illuminates how John Carlos both arrived at the historical moment in Mexico City and also how life for him played out after his politically charged gesture. Carlos's story builds a case for the importance of civic-minded athletes and sports-minded citizens who care about social issues that affect lived experiences.

Cole, Cheryl, and Susan Birrel, eds. 1994. *Women, Sport, and Culture*. Champaign, IL: Human Kinetics.

This resource is a collection of essays written by various contributors, several of whom are not typically cited or sighted in sport studies literature. Two chapters specifically address race in their titles: "African-American Women and Competitive Sport, 1920–1960" and "Visible Difference and Flex Appeal: The Body, Sex, Sexuality, and Race in *Pumping Iron* Films." In addition, the index specifies ten locations where racism is mentioned in this resource.

Collins, Patricia Hill, and Margaret L. Anderson, eds. 2004. *Race, Class, and Gender: An Anthology*. Belmont, CA: Wadsworth/Thomson Learning.

This anthology offers sixty-four essays pertaining to race, class, and gender, written by various contributors. Some essays pertain to the United States, and others are focused on other global nations. The index offers ten different page references to "Athletics" that consider race, class, sexual orientation, and gender dynamics. This resource has 576 pages and offers suggested readings beyond what is offered within the anthology itself.

Colton, L. 2000. *Counting Coup: A True Story of Basketball and Honor on the Little Big Horn*. New York: Warner Books, Inc.

This 420-page book follows the struggles of Sharon La-Forge, a Native American teenager of the Crow tribe from Montana, as she tries to make the most of her basketball talents in high school. This source gives a glimpse into the Native American experience with race and sport when the Native American is coming from life on a reservation. This book also showcases the racism within the non-Native community of Hardin, Montana. Former professional baseball player–turned-journalist Larry Colton spent fifteen months with the Crow community while capturing LaForge's life.

Conyers, James L., ed. 2014. *Race in American Sports Essays*. Jefferson, NC: McFarland & Company.

This 288-page volume is a collection of essays edited by professor James Conyers, Jr. These essays examine race and sport through an interdisciplinary perspective, emphasizing that race and sport are combined to influence many aspects of the American lived experience and mindset. Essay topics focus on Title IX, media and sports journalism, Native American mascots, Asian American athlete influence, and much more.

Crenshaw, K. 1996. *Critical Race Theory: The Key Writings That Formed the Movement*. New York: The New Press.

This resource focuses on understanding racial injustice and identifying the intersections between race, gender, sexual orientation, and class in society. Along with Crenshaw's book, this work is edited by the leading theoreticians of the critical race theory movement. Nineteen of the movement's most important essays are included in the 528-page reader.

Entine, J. 2000. *Taboo: Why Black Athletes Dominate Sports and Why We're Afraid to Talk about It*. New York: PublicAffairs.

This 400-page resource attempts to answer the question: Is there a genetic reason that African Americans dominate professional sports? Entine discusses the history of sports and race science, racial breeding and eugenics, the segregation and integration of sports, and sports and IQ. The author takes the writing form of an argument, presenting his conclusion first as a case to be proved in the body of the work using selected evidence.

Fenelon, J. V. 2017. *Redskins? Sports Mascots, Indian Nations and White Racism.* New York: Routledge.
This resource is 172 pages in length and is structured into seven chapters. These chapters explore the origin of team names in institutional racism and U.S. society's denial of the impact of four centuries of colonial conquest. Controversies over professional sports teams—in the NFL and MLB specifically—are addressed.

Garrison, Z. 2001. *Zina: My Life in Women's Tennis.* Berkeley, CA: Frog, Ltd.
This autobiography is written by Zina Garrison, the first African American woman to reach a Grand Slam final—in 1990 at Wimbledon—since Althea Gibson in 1958. Garrison relives her personal experiences with racism in the majority White world of professional tennis, as well as battles with bulimia and depression. This source is particularly valuable for researchers interested in how race, sport, and class intersect in a predominantly White, upper-class dominated sport like tennis. This book is 211 pages and is formatted into eighteen chapters on Garrison's life.

González, Christopher, and Frederick Luis Aldama. 2013. *Latinos in the End Zone: Conversations on the Brown Line in the NFL.* New York: Palgrave Pivot.

This resource focuses specifically on the sport of professional football and its history of Latino athlete participation. Periodization begins in the early twentieth century into the twenty-first century. Issues discussed include omission of prominent Latino names honored within the Pro Football Hall of Fame; why Latinos have utilized the Canadian Leagues to prove themselves to White Americans; and racial prejudice. This text is 122 pages in length.

Harper, S. R., ed. 2017. *Scandals in College Sports*. New York: Routledge.

This edited collection of twenty-one essays present an array of controversies that have occurred in college sports. Categorized into "Four Quarters," editor Shaun Harper and his contributors' essays focus on the following sections: Recruitment and Compensation Scandals; Competition Schemes, Academics, and Unfair Advantages; Abuse and Harm to Student Athletes; and Sexual Misconduct and Gender Discrimination. Each contributor details the specifics of each dilemma, explains what the dilemma meant in a sociocultural context, and offers an alternative solution as a pathway to guide future practices that serve collegiate student athletes.

Hawkins, B. 2010. *The New Plantation: Black Athletes, College Sports, and Predominantly White NCAA Institutions*. London: Palgrave Macmillan.

This resource is comprised of ten chapters that focus on aspects of the African American experience in college athletics. Chapters included discuss topics such as the sociocultural experiences of Black athletes on predominantly White college campuses; racists ideologies tied to Black athletic bodies; and the economics of college sports with predominantly Black athletes. In addition,

Hawkins provides a chapter that offers ideas for athletic reform.

Hawkins, Billy J., Akilah Carter-Francique, and J. Kenyatta Cavil, eds. 2015. *The Athletic Experience at Historically Black Colleges and Universities: Past, Present, and Persistence.* Lanham, MD: Rowman & Littlefield.

A resource comprising eleven edited essays that attempts to showcase the athletic experience at Historically Black Colleges and Universities (HBCUs). There are a range of topics covered in this resource, such as: Black female athlete experience at HBCUs; the culture of revenue-producing sports at HBCUs, the origin and perseverance of HBCU Classic football games; and financial and academic challenges. This 282-page volume provides the narrative of the Black experience in sport within academic institutions designed specifically to serve Black people.

Hawkins, Billy J., Akilah R. Carter-Francique, and Joseph N. Cooper, eds. 2017. *Critical Race Theory: Black Athletic Sporting Experiences in the United States.* New York: Palgrave Macmillan.

Edited by Billy J. Hawkins, Akilah R. Carter-Francique, and Joseph N. Cooper, this 330-page volume of collected essays, written by various contributors and the editors themselves, examines race and racism in sport through use of critical race theory. According to the editors, the ultimate goal of this volume "is to examine the crucial role race occupies in sporting practices and how sport has been and continue to be a platform that reflect and reinforce ideas about race, as well as a platform where resistance is forged against dominant racial ideologies" (p. 3). This resource is presented in four parts: Part I, Theoretical Practices, Reform and Advocacy; Part II, Academic Experiences, Challenges and Legislation; Part III, Athletic Representation and Leadership; and Part IV, Best Practices and Leadership.

Holway, J. B. 2008. *BlackBall Tales: Rollicking, All New, True Adventures of the Negro Leagues by the Men Who Lived and Loved Them*. Springfield, VA: Scorpio Books.

This text is one that gives valuable perspectives of dozens of baseball stars from the Negro Leagues. There are valuable statistics that prove the athletic success of the Negro League players when they were segregated from playing in Major League Baseball. Holway weaves together interviews with former Negro League players to recreate major historical experiences. There are seventeen chapters and 225 pages in this work.

Jacobs, B. 2007. *Across the Line: Profiles in Basketball Courage: Tales of the First Black Players in the ACC and SEC*. Guilford, CT: The Lyons Press.

This text focuses on the 1960s and 1970s, when Black basketball players began gaining admittance to the Atlantic Coast (ACC) and Southeastern Conferences (SEC) most cherished historically White schools. Jacobs presents the perspectives of Black players from eighteen schools across the ACC and SEC. Readers of this text will encounter narrative on the civil rights struggles on campus and within the larger community, enriched by the perspective of players, their families, teammates and opponents, and coaches. This book is formatted into three parts—Vanguard; Changing of the Guard; Rear Guard—with a total of fourteen chapters.

Kendi, I. X. 2016. *Stamped form the Beginning: The Definitive History of Racist Ideas in America*. New York: Nation Books.

This work does not merge the topic of race and sports. However, this text offers readers a comprehensive history of how racist ideology was created and spread throughout the United States.

Kendi's work is separated into five parts and thirty-seven chapters. The five parts are actually named for the life stories of major American intellectuals he uses to drive this history: Puritan minister Cotton Mather, Thomas Jefferson, abolitionist William Lloyd Garrison, W.E.B. Du Bois, and legendary activist Angela Davis. This work will give researchers on the topic of race and sports the tools needed to reveal racist thinking in the realm of sports.

King, C. R., ed. 2006. *Native Athletes in Sport and Society: A Reader*. Lincoln: University of Nebraska Press.

This eleven-chapter reader features essays by editor C. Richard King and other academics who've chosen to highlight the achievements of, and explore what these accomplishments have meant to, Native American athletes and Indigenous athletes in Canada and the fans who support them. Many lesser-known Indigenous athletes are discussed in sports like golf and baseball. In addition, beyond the professional level, stories on amateurs, coaches, activists, and athletes who have fallen from stardom are present in this resource.

King, C. R., ed. 2017. *Asian American Athletes in Sport and Society*. Routledge Research in Sport, Culture and Society. New York: Routledge.

These edited essays are presented under the subheadings of Society and Celebrity. Essay contributors probe topics such as: Chinese American women's experience of sport; women's basketball in Japanese American society; the Jeremy Lin phenomenon; and the presence of the "Model Minority" in college sports. There are eleven essays included in this 204-page volume.

Lanctot, N. 2004. *Negro League Baseball: The Rise and Ruin of a Black Institution*. Philadelphia: University of Pennsylvania Press.

Historian Neil Lanctot offers an expansive history of Negro League baseball in the United States. This work covers the initial African American response to segregation, the challenge to establish separate and successful sporting initiatives, and what happened as integration began to occur. This resource is particularly valuable for a researcher seeking to gain more knowledge about professional baseball, as well as the business of sport and its history with race and racism. Lanctot breaks this book into two parts: "Separate but Equal?" and "Integration." There are eleven chapters, a list of abbreviations, and black-and-white photographs provided.

Lansbury, J. H. 2014. *A Spectacular Leap: Black Women Athletes in Twentieth-Century America*. Fayetteville: University of Arkansas Press.

This text focuses on the experience of race and sport through the stories of six Black female athletes. Starting with Alice Coachman and moving on to Ora Washington, Althea Gibson, Wilma Rudolph, Wyomia Tyus, and Jackie Joyner-Kersee, author Jennifer Lansbury presents readers with how these women confronted racism, sexism, and classism all within varying sociopolitical landscapes in history. The focus on these six athletes, however, does limit the sporting scope of this text to two sports: track and field, and tennis. The book is presented in six chapters and is 300 pages in length.

Lapchick, R. 2001. *Smashing Barriers: Race and Sport in the New Millennium*. Lanham, MD: Madison Books.

This five-part, twenty-one-chapter resource contains stories about racially diverse sports figures like Tiger Woods, Muhammad Ali, Tony Elliot, Roberto Clemente, and Venus and Serena Williams. In addition, this updated edition describes the changing face of diversity in sport, addressing the dangers of new racial stereotypes, the value of youth athletic programs, the importance of improving the student-athlete experience, and social responsibility. This resource is 352 pages in length.

Leonard, David J. 2017. *Playing While White: Privilege and Power on and off the Field.* Seattle: University of Washington Press.

Author David Leonard attempts to identify how Whiteness is central to the commodification of athletes and the sports industry overall. Leonard offers analysis of a number of White athletic stars along with sectors of sports that remain predominantly White: Jordan Spieth, Josh Hamilton, NASCAR, Lance Armstrong, Marshall Henderson, and extreme sports. Some of the themes and trends discussed have to do with racial dynamics of sports traditions, the reception and media portrayals of specific White athletes, and perceptions about White athletes compared to athletes of color. This resource is 320 pages in length.

Lomax, M. E., ed. 2011. *Sports and the Racial Divide: African American and Latino Experience in an Era of Change.* Jackson: University Press of Mississippi.

This collection of nine edited essays explore the sporting experiences of Latinos and African Americans in post–World War II America. Athletes like Roberto Clemente and Muhammad Ali are highlighted, as are the topics of cultural nationalism, Black Power, and Title IX. This resource is 262 pages in length and provides valuable quantitative data on race and sport.

Mahiri, Jabari, and Derek Van Rheenen. 2010. *Out of Bounds: When Scholarship Athletes Become Academic Scholars.* New York: Peter Lang Publishing Inc.

This book focuses on the challenges and possibilities of athletes who worked to become professional scholars. The authors helped to document and analyze the life stories of six informants who were successful scholarship athletes who went on to become academic scholars. Chapter 3, "Slaves of Sport," is particularly insightful into research on the relationship between race and sport as it presents the stories of two Black men, Ernest and Malo. A strength of this work "is that its description and analyses are across time, race, class, and gender as well as across different levels or sport and school practices" (p. 21). This chapter is thirty-four pages in length, and the whole book consists of five total chapters and 139 pages.

Maraniss, A. 2016. *Strong Inside: Perry Wallace and the Collision of Race and Sports in the South*. Nashville, TN: Vanderbilt University Press.

Over the course of thirty chapters, sports journalist Andrew Maraniss presents a biography of Perry Wallace, the first Black basketball player in the Southeastern Conference (SEC) Maraniss builds this biography off more than eighty interviews, revealing Wallace's experiences on the Vanderbilt University campus and in the racially hostile gyms of the deep South. Wallace's encounters with civil rights leaders and his activism on the Vanderbilt campus are also presented. This resource is 480 pages in length.

Martin, C. H. 2010. *Benching Jim Crow: The Rise and Fall of the Color Line in Southern College Sports, 1890–1980*. Urbana: University of Illinois Press.

In nine chapters, along with introductory and concluding chapters, the author chronicles the rise and slow decline of segregation in Southern American college athletics. While Martin focuses on the sports of basketball and football, he does so in a way that highlights how the racism present in Southern schools had effects on colleges and universities nationwide. Martin also discusses how many of the Southern teams were focused on national recognition but hindered themselves through standing by Jim Crow policies that prevented their competing against racially integrated teams. Martin relies on original research, existing arguments, and documentation on the integration of college sports as well as previously unpublished primary source papers and correspondence of college administrators and athletic directors to inform this text.

Martin, L. L. 2015. *White Sports/Black Sports: Racial Disparities in Athletic Programs*. Santa Barbara, CA: ABC-CLIO, LLC.
Author Lori Martin attempts to refute the claim that American society is "postracial" in this 209-page book. Martin documents that racial stereotypes with deep historical roots are still present—albeit covertly—in society today. In addition, this work examines how race and sports are both powerful social constructions that are assigned value. Sport in particular is presented as a space that can be both liberating and oppressive, depending on the circumstances.

McRae, D. 2002. *Heroes without a Country: America's Betrayal of Joe Louis and Jesse Owens*. New York: HarperCollins Publishers Inc.
Author Donald McRae presents the intertwined events and coincidences that had boxer Joe Louis and track and field superstar Jesse Owens, crossing paths from the late 1930s through to 1970. This work is 389 pages in length and is formatted into seventeen chapters. Both Louis and Owens found athletic success on a global scale in the face of widely accepted national and global White supremacist ideology.

Milner, Adrienne, and Jomills H. Braddock II, eds. 2017. *Women in Sports: Breaking Barriers, Facing Obstacles*. Santa Barbara, CA: Praeger.

This edited, two-volume text comprises the work of over a dozen contributors. The framework of the work is a sociological one, where experiences of race, class, sexual orientation, religion, physical size, and other social constructs that affect women athletes are explored. The volume also highlights specific areas that should be changed on both the individual and structural levels in order to gain gender equity and fairness within sport. A few of the contributing essays mention race; specifically, see chapters 4 and 5.

Mooney, K. C. 2014. *Race Horse Men: How Slavery and Freedom Were Made at the Racetrack*. Cambridge, MA: Harvard University Press.

Historian Katherine Mooney presents a history of American horse-racing through the lens of its race relations. In nineteenth-century horse racing in the Southern United States, Black men were often employed as jockeys, trainers, and grooms. Mooney showcases how White resentment of Black success in the sport grew so much that it ultimately ousted Blacks from the sport of horse racing completely. This source is structured into seven chapters and is 336 pages in length.

Morris, W. 1992. *The Courting of Marcus Dupree*. Jackson: University Press of Mississippi.

Author Willie Morris presents one perspective of the 1980s Deep South town of Philadelphia, Mississippi, and its prized Black high school quarterback, Marcus Dupree. Morris follows Dupree starting in the summer before his senior year and through each game of Dupree's senior season. The athletic recruitment experience for NCAA Division I level football is addressed; Morris talks with college recruiters, the high school coach and principal, some community members, and Dupree and his family. This resource is 464 pages in length.

Myers, R. L. 2016. "African American Female Athletic Image: What We Should Take Away from the London 2012 Olympic Games." In *Race Still Matters: The Reality of African American Lives and the Myth of Postracial Society*, edited by Y. Kiuchi, 321–341. Albany: State University of New York Press.

> This book chapter aims to show how structural racism and internalized racism are still persistent in U.S. society through the lens of sport. In order to prove this claim, the author focuses on the 2012 London Olympic Games and incidents surrounding several Black female athletes: gymnast Gabby Douglas and track and field hurdlers, Lolo Jones, Kelli Wells, and Dawn Harper. This book chapter is twenty pages in length, including notes.

Ogden, David C., and Joel Nathan Rosen, eds. 2008. *Reconstructing Fame: Sport, Race, and Evolving Reputations*. Jackson: University Press of Mississippi.

> This edited book provides eight chapters from nine different contributors. These essays attempt to clarify the stories of athletes of color—Jackie Robinson, Roberto Clemente, Paul Robeson, Bill Russell, Curt Flood, Tommie Smith, and John Carlos—and their places as twentieth-century icons by analyzing the myths that surround them. All of the athletes included have had their careers affected by racism.

Rhoden, W. C. 2006. *Forty Million Dollar Slaves: The Rise, Fall, and Redemption of the Black Athlete*. New York: Three Rivers Press.

> Sports journalist William Rhoden causes readers to tense as he presents the argument in this book that Black athletes in the United States have simply landed in figurative plantations from their historical roots in slavery. Rhoden highlights the impact that the multibillion-dollar industry of sport has on the everyday lives of the Black athletes who continue to make the industry profitable. In the end,

Rhoden posits that the Black athletes of the early 2000s were less prepared to deal with the racial realities that exist in America than any preceding generation. This text became a *New York Times* bestseller, is 286 pages in length, and provides over a dozen black-and-white images.

Robinson, J. 2003. *I Never Had It Made: An Autobiography of Jackie Robinson*. New York: Harper Perennial.

This autobiography, written by Jackie Robinson, recalls what it took for Robinson to become the first Black man in history to play MLB. Robinson discusses the highs and lows of his life after baseball, his political activism, his friendships with MLK Jr., William Buckley Jr., Nelson Rockefeller, and Malcolm X. This autobiography has twenty-five chapters and is 304 pages long.

Salamone, F. A., ed. 2015. *The Native American Identity in Sports: Creating and Preserving a Culture*. Lanham, MD: Rowman and Littlefield.

This collection of essays, edited by Frank Salamone, brings to light the untold and underemphasized contributions of Native Americans throughout sports in the United States. The majority of the collection's twelve essays share stories of specific athletes; mascot controversies; the sports of wrestling, tennis, and track and field; and important history on experiences in former Indian Schools. Additional essays explore obesity in Native American communities, the Seminoles' commercialization of alligator wresting, and more. This resource is 222 pages in length and is great for researchers interested in the impact sports has on race and culture.

Schilling, V. 2016. *Native Athletes in Action!* Summertown, TN: 7th Generation.

This revised text features thirteen biographies of Native American athletes—two more than the original edition. Some of the sports discussed are figure skating, basketball, ice hockey, and wrestling. This 128-page resource describes the hard work, determination, and education it took to accomplish each Native American athlete's dreams to become the successes they were/are.

Shropshire, K. 1998. *In Black and White: Race and Sports in America*. New York: New York University Press.

Author Kenneth Shropshire confronts claims of color-blindness and reverse racism in the world of sports, characterizing these claims as self-serving and a way to distract others from the real issues. Shropshire focuses this work on the front offices of the sports industry, which are overwhelmingly comprised of White ownership and management. This resource offers strategies for bringing more people of color into the coaching and business of sports. There are seven chapters in this book.

Smith, E. 2013. *Race, Sport and the American Dream*. Durham, NC: Carolina Academic Press.

This text presents the findings of a research project that investigated the scope and consequences of the relationship between the realm of sport and Black males. The author approaches his research to show how sport has come to influence schooling, the Black family, and economic opportunities. This third edition provides updated empirical data, an expanded discussion on conference realignment, continued discussion of leadership, and a new chapter on instances of male athletes inflicting violence on women. This resource is 322 pages in length.

Spickard Prettyman, Sandra, and Brian Lampman, ed. 2010. *Learning Culture through Sports: Perspectives on Society and Organized Sports*. Lanham, MD: Rowman & Littlefield Publishers, Inc.

This edited volume contains nineteen essays that address a particular issue in sport: youth and sport; gender and sexuality; race and ethnicity; sport, media, and big business; and international perspectives on sport and participation. This resource provides its readers with an understanding of the tremendous influence sport has in people's lives and global society. This second edition includes more contemporary research data on controversies and issues in sport.

Suggs, W. 2005. *A Place on the Team: The Triumph and Tragedy of Title IX*. Princeton, NJ: Princeton University Press.

This text does not focus on race and sport specifically. Rather, it provides the history of Title IX and its evolution since it passed in 1972. This work chronicles the successes and failures in sporting communities since the passing of Title IX, which does include issues related to race. This resource is structured into twelve chapters and includes nine appendixes. In addition, it includes a list of landmark Title IX lawsuits.

Tatum, B. D. 1997. *Why Are All the Black Kids Sitting Together in the Cafeteria: And Other Conversations about Race*. New York: Basic Books.

This resource is focused on race and racism from a psychological framework and lens. Chapters in this work focus on defining the terms of racism and identity; understanding Blackness in a White context; understanding Whiteness in a White context; understanding identity development for races beyond Black and White (e.g., Native, Multiracial, Asian and Pacific Islander, Latinx); and the importance of cross-racial dialogue. This work is 464 pages in length and formatted into ten chapters.

Thangaraj, Stanley I., Constancio R. Arnaldo, and Christina B. Chin, ed. 2016. *Asian American Sporting Cultures*. New York: New York University Press.

This edited volume focuses on the history of Asian American sporting culture, concerning itself with how identities and communities are negotiated through sport. Boxing, basketball, wrestling, and even spelling bees are examined in connecting Asian American identity formation. This work incorporates essays on Southeast Asian Americans, East Asian Americans, Pacific Islanders, and South Asians; explores how sports are gendered within the Asian American community; and explores the role sport plays in the process of citizen making, illuminating how marginalized communities perform their "American-ness" in sporting spaces.

Thomas, E. 2018. *We Matter: Athletes and Activism*. Brooklyn, NY: Edge of Sports.

This primary source is written by former eleven-year NBA player Etan Thomas. Thomas aims to show the powerful influence professional athletes can have when they use sports as a platform to discuss hard societal issues: race, civil rights, and politics. Thomas conducted over fifty interviews with athletes, journalists, family members of unarmed Black men who were shot and killed, and media figures. Some of the individuals interviewed are Jemele Hill, Anquan Boldin, Jamal Crawford, Juwan Howard, Ray Jackson, Shannon Sharpe, James Blake, John Carlos, Laila Ali, Michael Eric Dyson, Jahvaris Fulton (brother of Trayvon Martin), Emerald Snipes (daughter of Eric Garner), and Allysza Castile (sister of Philando Castile).

Veazey, K. 2012. *Champions for Change: How the Mississippi State Bulldogs and Their Bold Coach Defied Segregation*. Charleston, SC: The History Press.

This seven-chapter text offers a unique perspective of race and the sport of basketball. Author Veazey focuses on a historic basketball game in the early 1960s where Mississippi State's all-White basketball team defied a formerly statewide respected stance of not competing in athletic competitions against integrated programs. This resource showcases how Whites, not necessarily for the pursuit of racial equality, sought to push societal racial norms when it encroached on their sporting experience and potential success. The final chapter of this text discusses what happened in the years that followed the decision of Mississippi State's 1963 basketball team and its coach, Babe McCarthy.

Vennum, Thomas, Jr. 1994. *American Indian Lacrosse: Little Brother of War*. Washington, D.C.: Smithsonian Institution Press.

Late author Thomas Vennum Jr. wrote this book as the first comprehensive history of the game of lacrosse. Although only 6 of the 360 pages explicitly mention racism, the topic of race and sport runs throughout this work. Native Americans invented the game of lacrosse, which holds deep cultural meaning, yet it was White men who adopted and changed the rules of the game to suit White western cultural norms. Vennum Jr. starts in the year 1637 and brings this work to a close in the year 1991, showcasing everything from individual athletes, equipment, playing fields, Native American traditions, and the move to youth, collegiate, and international levels of lacrosse. This work features rare archival illustrations as well as over a dozen black-and-white images.

Ware, S. 2007. *Title IX: A Brief History with Documents*. Long Grove, IL: Waveland Press, Inc.

This source is focused on Title IX legislation. Specifically, this book provides insight into the passage of and early years of Title IX, strides toward gender equity, and consequences and aspirations for the future. In addition, twenty-six primary source documents provide perspective, including the following: "Back Story," "Early Years of Title IX," the debate over gender equity, and "Title IX and American Culture." This resource is 185 pages and contains multiple pages that discuss minority athletes and their participation opportunities and participation rates.

Wiggins, D. K. 1997. *Glory Bound: Black Athletes in a White America*. Syracuse, NY: Syracuse University Press.
This resource is 324 pages long and chronicles some of the reasons Black athletes have experienced a turbulent relationship with mainstream White America. Wiggins, a sports scholar, provides eleven essays that address topics such as Blacks in baseball, Jesse Owens and the 1936 Olympic Games, and the Black sporting press. The periodization of this text spans from the nineteenth century through the mid-1990s.

Wiggins, D. K., ed. 2018. *More Than a Game: A History of the African American Experience in Sport*. The African American Experience Series. Lanham, MD: Rowman & Littlefield.
This eight-chapter text discusses how Black women and men in the United States sought to participate in sport and what that participation meant to them. This text recognizes the reality that many young Black athletes do not find overwhelming success in sport, and these athletes' experiences reflect and can change views of race. This work spans the era of slavery all the way through to the protests of former NFL quarterback Colin Kaepernick.

Wiggins, David K., and Patrick B. Miller. 2005. *The Unlevel Playing Field: A Documentary History of the African American Experience in Sport*. Champaign: University of Illinois Press.
This collection of primary sources presents the history of Africans American and sport between 1810 and the early 2000s. More than one hundred documents are included, and authors Wiggins and Miller use the introductions and headnotes to place each document in context. Some

of the athletes highlighted are Jesse Owens, Tiger Woods, Michael Jordan, Althea Gibson, Venus and Serena Williams, and Muhammad Ali. A bibliographical essay by the authors concludes this text.

Wigginton, R. T. 2006. *The Strange Career of the Black Athlete: African Americans and Sports.* Westport, CT: Praeger Publishers.
This five-chapter text presents the historical rise of the Black athlete in the United States, spanning the years 1892–2005. Chapters included explore the role of Black athletes in the civil rights era, the role of Black female athletes, and the experiences of Black athletes in predominantly White sports (e.g., hockey, tennis, golf). The author takes a mostly biographical approach to his writing, which makes this text accessible to readers at all levels, as it concentrates on a few Black athletes from three different eras.

Willard, Michael N., and John Bloom, eds. 2002. *Sports Matters: Race, Recreation and Culture.* New York: New York University Press.
This edited volume includes fifteen essays from various contributors, including editors John Bloom and Michael Willard. Though some of the essays focus on race and sport during specific historical moments (e.g., the 1968 Olympic Games), other essays focus on the experiences of racial groups (e.g., African Americans, Native Americans, Mexican Americans). Some of the sports examined are golf, track and field, baseball, and football.

Willms, N. 2007. *When Women Rule the Court: Gender, Race, and Japanese American Basketball.* New Brunswick, NJ: Rutgers University Press.
This five-chapter resource explores the importance of the sport of basketball in Japanese American life—specifically the communities tied to the highly organized Japanese

American leagues in California. The author utilizes interviews and observations to inform this work. This resource is 258 pages in length.

Wu, F. H. 2002. *Yellow: Race in America beyond Black and White*. New York: Basic Books.

This resource by law professor Frank Wu is valuable in understanding where Asian Americans fit into discussions of race. In eight chapters, Wu discusses the following topics: the "model minority" stereotype; "perpetual foreigner" syndrome; affirmative action legislation as it affects Asian Americans; assimilation and multiculturalism; intermarriage and the mixed-race movement; and coalition building. The author blends his personal experiences as a lens to discuss these important topics in understanding Asian American racial identity and racial politics.

Zirin, D. 2005. *What's My Name, Fool?: Sports and Resistance in the United States*. Chicago, IL: Haymarket Books.

In ten chapters, author David Zirin recounts moments of resistance within the sports world. Zirin especially takes care to explain the business of sport in relation to all constituencies involved in the play and prosperity within the sports world. Chapters 2, 3, 4, and 7 all discuss athletes and issues related to race and sports. Other topics center on journalism, sexism, homophobia, unions and sports, administration, and ownership. This text is 293 pages long and contains roughly a dozen photos in black and white.

Zirin, D. 2008. *A People's History of Sports in the United States: 250 Years of Politics, Protest, People, and Play*. New York: The New Press.

Author David Zirin provides a historiography of sports through a political lens in this text. Zirin critically examines the political forces and power at work in the world of sports. The work is dedicated to all "rebel athletes" who wouldn't allow themselves to be exploited by those who financially control the world of sports. This text is 302 pages in length and provides a helpful index; the word "race" and other subheadings can be easily found throughout the text using the index.

Articles

Beamon, K. 2014. "Racism and Stereotyping on Campus: Experiences of African American Male Student-Athletes." *The Journal of Negro Education* 83 (2): 121–134.

> This article shares on a study that was conducted to examine the perception of racism by twenty former Division I athletes on Division I-A campuses. The data narratives presented by former student-athletes discuss race and sport, as well as the role that racism played in their athletic careers. This study seeks to answer the following research questions: What are the experiences of high-profile African American student-athletes concerning racism on predominantly White campuses? Does the status of "athlete" serve as a buffer to racism?

Beamon, Krystal, and Chris Messer. 2014. "Professional Sports Experiences as Contested Racial Terrain." *Journal of African American Studies* 18 (2): 181–191.

> This resource is valuable for those looking to learn more about the experiences of race and sport for the thousands of Black male athletes who don't necessarily reach fame and economic fortune. A review of literature is provided, with particular attention paid to the sports of basketball and football. The authors use mostly used qualitative research methods when analyzing data from fourteen Black male respondents who played varying levels and types of professional sports. Three themes emerged from the data about areas of "contested racial terrain" in sport: politics, lack of control (over one's destiny), and lack of respect.

DaSilva, M. 2018. "What It Means to Be Black in This Sport: Lacrosse Star Joey Coffy '14 Sounds Off." *Hotchkiss Magazine* (Summer): 68–69.

In this two-page article, found in the Summer 2018 issue of the Hotchkiss School's—an elite New England boarding school—magazine, readers get a glimpse of the racialized experience of a Black Ivy League lacrosse player. Former Cornell University player Joey Coffy addresses teammates' use of the N-word, being the only Black person in the room, and hearing racism from opponents' parents. Joey Coffy attended the Hotchkiss School, graduating in 2014, before attending Cornell.

Hauser, C. 2019. "Maine Just Banned Native American Mascots. It's a Movement That's Inching Forward." *The New York Times*, May 22.

Hauser's article covers the historic piece of legislation that the state of Maine passed, effectively banning Native American mascots statewide in public schools and colleges. The article discusses the increasing support of Native American tribes and culture in the state of Maine. In addition, this source provides a snapshot of how similar steps have been taken by other U.S. states and educational institutions since 2010. The article ends with some background of how Native American representation has been handled at the professional level with sports teams.

Hersh, P. 2016. "Simone Biles and Gabby Douglas are Latest and Greatest Heroes in a Storied History of African-American Gymnasts." *TeamUSA.org News*.

This article was published before the success of Black gymnasts Simone Biles and Gabby Douglas before the 2016 Rio Olympic Games (where the team won the Olympic gold medal). The author goes through a history of successful Black male and female gymnasts at the Olympic and collegiate levels. For researchers on race and sport, this article is significant in understanding how Black gymnasts have experienced the sport as racial minorities.

Hoyer, M. 2018. "The Psychological Toll of That Name." *The Washington Post*. Washington, D.C.
    Published in the "Opinions" section of the *Washington Post* in October 2018, this article is written by the grandson of a Menominee Indian. The author highlights important statistics and personal experiences about what happens when negative stereotypes about Native Americans are internalized by the Native Americans themselves. Although sport—specifically the NFL's controversially named Washington team—is the primary focus, important statistical information is linked to this article regarding the overall well-being of Native Americans more generally.

Korver, K. 2019. "Privileged." *The Players' Tribune*.
    This primary source article is written by White NBA player Kyle Korver. Korver writes this article to share with readers about his own uncomfortable and awakening journey in understanding White privilege. Korver also encourages readers who are White to truly examine their own privilege and to speak out and act when they see discrimination occurring against people of color.

Lomax, M. E. 2002. "Revisiting 'The Revolt of the Black Athlete': Harry Edwards and the Making of the New African-American Sport Studies." *Journal of Sport History* 29 (3): 469–479.
    This article is mainly a review of Harry Edwards's 1968 book, *The Revolt of the Black Athlete*. Author Michael Lomax summarizes the main points of Edwards's narrative and then takes things further by discussing what other scholars have researched since then. Lomax recognizes that "Edwards established a high standard for

research and analysis throughout his narrative and paved the way for intellectual respectability for the sport history and sport sociology fields" (p. 476).

O'Neal, L. 2018. "Say It Loud! Black, Female and Proud." *ESPN Magazine* 21: 52–58.

This article, found in the tenth installment of ESPN's *Body Issue*, discusses some of the history of Black female athletes and the coping mechanisms they've come up with to endure and succeed in sport. Specifically, the author references the findings of a new study by Morgan State University and includes numerous quotes from Black female athletes and coaches. This article is six pages in length and includes color photos of prolific Black female athletes like Serena Williams, Gabbie Douglas, and Simone Manuel.

Reynolds, G. 2016. "Hoping Olympic Gold Might End a Racial Divide." *The New York Times*: 1.

This article focuses on the sport of swimming and the impact of Simone Manuel, the first African American woman to win an Olympic gold medal in the sport. This article discusses the reasons why African Americans are underrepresented in the sport of swimming and also offers statistics on this topic. Initiatives that are being implemented to increase Blacks participation in swimming are also provided.

Sailes, G. A. 1991. "The Myth of Black Sports Supremacy." *Journal of Black Studies* 21 (4): 480–487.

This eight-page article presents significant background on the myth that Blacks are superior at sport. Some of the reasons discussed are grounded in science, and others are not. This resource is crucial for someone wanting to learn more about scientific racism and racial stereotypes surrounding the bodies of athletes.

Sigelman, L. 1998. "The African American Athletic Fixation." *Social Science Quarterly* 79 (4): 892–897.

In this article, social scientist Lee Sigelman confronts the assertion by Hoberman in his 1997 text, *Darwin's Athletes: How Sport Has Damaged Black America and Preserved the Myth of Race*, that African Americans are fixated on sport. Instead, Sigelman makes a case to show that athletic fixation is "American" and not a fixation of any specific racial group. This article is six pages in length.

The Undefeated. 2018. "State of the Black Athlete." *ESPN*: 48–84.

Various writers from *The Undefeated*—ESPN'S multi-platform content initiative exploring the intersections of sports, race and culture—as well as athletes and academics contribute articles or letters in the February 5, 2018, issue's section on the "State of the Black Athlete." Contributing authors include Kevin Merida, Lonnae O'Neal, Marc J. Spears, Jemele Hill, Claudia Rankine, Howard Bryant, Kevin Durant, Martellus Bennett, Chiney Ogwumike, John Wall, and Chris Archer. Some of the topics discussed include the politicization of the Black athlete, athletes Maya Moore and Cam Newton, the impact of Black family members on Black athletes, and the NFL anthem protest. The "State of the Black Athlete" section spans the last thirty-six pages of the eighty-four-page issue.

Weiner, M. 2016. "Onondaga Nation's Oren Lyons Invited to Eulogize Muhammad Ali." https://www.syracuse.com/news/2016/06/onondaga_nations_oren_lyons_invited_to_eulogize_muhammad_ali.html.

This article provides a glimpse into the coalition building that has occurred among athletes of color—in this case between Native Americans and African Americans. Oren Lyons is a Native American lacrosse legend and activist who had a strong friendship with Muhammad Ali.

Specifically, the "Longest Walk," a 3,600-mile protest from San Francisco to Washington, D.C., in the name of Native American rights is where the two athlete-activists met for the first time.

Wright, J. 2016. "Be Like Mike?: The Black Athlete's Dilemma." *Spectrum: A Journal on Black Men* 4 (2): 1–19.

This essay uses the success of former NBA basketball champion Michael Jordan to showcase the "modern Black athlete dilemma: to be or not be like Mike?" This essay explores this dilemma in three ways: (1) it compares other Black athletes post-Jordan as iconic figures, (2) it challenges opinion that Black athletes have to be representatives of the entire race on issues concerning Blacks, and (3) it critiques Jordan's historical significance in the Black community. This article posits that Black athletes of today no longer have to step up in the ways that Black athletes of the Civil Rights era did in fighting societal injustices.

Yamashita, A. 2019. "How Will We Talk about Asian American Athletes." *The Seattle Globalist*.

This article is written by an Asian American journalist, Andy Yamashita, and focuses on how Americans will talk about a new wave of Asian American professional athletes. Yamashita talks about the historical stereotypes that exist about Asian Americans and takes a look at how fans and media have already begun to talk about them. The author also compares how Black athletes have been negatively stereotyped with the stereotypes around Asian American athletes in order to show how these similar racialized experiences may land on the Asian American athletes.

Films

Burns, K. 2004. *Unforgiveable Blackness: The Rise and Fall of Jack Johnson*. Hollywood, CA: PBS Home Video, 224 minutes.

This PBS documentary, directed by Ken Burns, tells the story of Jack Johnson in two parts. The first part of the documentary focuses on his early life and how he got into the sport of boxing. The second half of the documentary focuses on Johnson's heavyweight champion status—he was the first African American to win this title in the history of boxing—and the aftermath. Viewers will see how racism played a major role in Johnson's experience inside and outside the sport of boxing.

Fuqua, A. 2019. *What's My Name: Muhammad Ali*. HBO, SpringHill Entertainment, 2 hours 45 minutes.

In *What's My Name: Muhammad Ali*, director Antoine Fuqua uses interviews, fight footage, and home movies from Ali's life to tell his story. This film shows Ali grow from a reserved Olympic medalist to a notorious wordsmith against opponents—Ali made his bouts seem personal by insulting his opponents. The film also highlights when Ali took a turn toward activism, befriending Malcolm X and joining the Nation of Islam. Ali's refusal to be drafted into Vietnam isn't given substantial screen time, but footage of other Black athletes—including Jackie Robinson—criticizing Ali for his political stances is presented.

Hock, J. 2011. *Off the Rez*. New York: FilmBuff, 86 minutes.

Director Jonathan Hock's documentary *Off the Rez* focuses on the story of Native American basketball player Shoni Schimmel and her mother Ceci Moses during Schimmel's senior year of high school. Once a basketball star in her own right, Schimmel's mom is convinced she was passed over by college scouts because of her Native American ethnicity, and she wants better for her talented daughters, Shoni and Jude. Viewers follow the Schimmel family from their home on Oregon's Umatilla Indian Reservation to Portland, Oregon, in hopes of increasing Shoni's opportunity to earn an athletic scholarship.

James, Lebron, and Maverick Carter. 2018. *The Shop: Uninterrupted.* HBO, 30 minutes/episode.

An unscripted series, *The Shop* is a collaboration between the NBA's LeBron James and his friend Maverick Carter's joint enterprise *Uninterrupted* and the HBO network. Available only through HBO, each episode features LeBron James and his business partner Maverick Carter talking with celebrities from the world of sports and entertainment about sports, music, pop culture, world events, business, and other cultural topics. The majority of the celebrities from the sports and entertainment industry are people of color, and race is often discussed. The intention of the barbershop atmosphere experienced in each episode is to model a space from James's childhood where opinions were able to be expressed freely. There are currently two seasons of *The Shop* available.

James, S. 1994. *Hoop Dreams.* New York: Fine Line Features, 170 minutes.

This documentary gives intimate focus on two young African American boys who play basketball for the same predominantly White Catholic high school outside of Chicago, Illinois. In pursuit of becoming professional basketball players, this documentary spans five years of filming and is the result of over 250 hours of footage. *Hoop Dreams* shines a light on race, socioeconomic status, education, and value systems within the United States and around sports.

Klores, D. 2008. *Black Magic.* Santa Monica, CA: ESPN Films, 224 minutes.

This ESPN Films documentary, directed by Dan Klores, takes viewers on a historical journey of the Black athlete and the National Basketball Association (NBA). When the NBA was founded in 1949, there were no Black players. *Black Magic* explores how and where Black male basketball player legends emerged and the changes that happened in society over time into the early 2000s. This documentary is narrated by actor Samuel L. Jackson and jazz musician Wynton Marsalis.

Real Sports with Bryant Gumbel. 1995–. HBO, 60 minutes/episode.

This HBO network documentary series began airing in 1995 and continues to air today. Although journalist Bryant Gumbel is the main host, there are several other journalists who work on episodes that are directed and produced by various individuals in the film industry. Each episode shares four stories throughout the hour, and all stories are about famous athletes, society and sports, or various conflicts affecting sports. At times, the episodes can feature investigative reporting and exclusive interviews about things traditional sports networks don't bother covering. This resource is ideal for the research of race and sports because it is less concerned with athletic performance and more concerned with how individuals are experiencing sport in connection with society and other stimuli.

Rhoden, W. C. 2008. *Breaking the Huddle: The Integration of College Football.* HBO Sports, 60 minutes.

This documentary chronicles the history of college football in the South and the pathways that led to the end of segregation and major players that helped integrate Southern college teams. A major theme that emerges in this documentary is that racial progress had less to do with an embrace of civil rights and more to do with what coaches needed to win: Black players. This resource is brief at only sixty minutes in runtime.

Rhoden, W. C., and Leslie D. Farrell. 1996. *The Journey of the African American Athlete.* HBO Films, 119 minutes.

Narrated by African American actor Samuel L. Jackson, this documentary covers over one hundred years of racial barrier breaking and challenges faced by Black athletes. Sports such as horse racing, cycling, basketball, boxing, baseball, track and field, tennis, football, and golf are examined by scholars, coaches, and athletes. Many of the social, political, and economic aspects are discussed as well as the influence various historical movements had on the arena of sport in the United States. Some of the athletes featured include Jack Johnson, Joe Louis, Muhammad Ali, Jackie Robinson, Jim Brown, Bill Russell, Arthur Ashe, Julius Erving, Jesse Owens, Wilma Rudolph, Wyomia Tyus, Tommie Smith, and John Carlos.

30 for 30. 2009. ESPN, 60 minutes/episode.

ESPN Films' *30 for 30* is a documentary series that features stories about sports and culture from various directors. The storytellers come from within and outside of the sports world, with each of the series' films bringing to life a compelling story. Some of the episodes that connect directly to the topic of race and sports are: "Muhammad and Larry," "The U," "Straight Outta L.A.," "Goose," "Broke," "Ghosts of Ole Miss," "Bernie and Ernie," and "Benji." Currently, a total of ninety-eight episodes of *30 for 30* have been made.

Reports and Internet Sites

"NCAA Diversity Research Archive." 2001–present. *NCAA*. NCAA.org.

The Diversity Research Archive can be found through the NCAA.org website. This catalog of data holds the NCAA Student-Athlete Ethnicity Archive, Athletic Administrators and Coaches Archive and Conference Office Personnel Archive. Each of those subheadings contains data spanning somewhere between the years 1994 and 2010.

This internet site is helpful for researchers that want to gather and analyze data on race and sports at the collegiate level from the athlete, coaching, and administrative perspectives.

"The Players' Tribune." 2014. New York: The Players' Tribune. https://www.theplayerstribune.com/en-us.

The Players' Tribune is a media company founded by former New York Yankee Derek Jeter that publishes first-person stories from athletes. These stories can take the form of video series, short-form stories, and podcasts. By using this platform's search feature, researchers on race and sport can access twenty-four articles related to "racism" that are written or produced by current or former professional athletes. The Players' Tribune also features pieces written by athletes that are not from the United States.

"TIDES: The Institute for Diversity and Ethics in Sport." 2001. *TIDES*. https://www.tidesport.org/.

This source is the University of Central Florida's TIDES (The Institute for Diversity and Ethics and Sport) website. This website provides four tabs: "Home," "About Us," "Reports," and "Current News." The "Reports" and "Current News" tabs are particularly helpful, as they allow researchers on race and sport to access the Racial and Gender Report Cards issued for NCAA and professional sports organizations, Super Bowl ad studies, and reports of college graduation rates. The "Current News" tab provides weekly updates on human trafficking in sport, athlete activism and protests, homophobia in sport, racism in sport, refugees in sport, and sexuality in sport. This website covers both domestic and international issues in sport related to diversity and equity.

The chronology on race and sports presented here is unique. This chronology is unique in that it does not solely provide the "first" and "founded" references. This chronology also references the moments when race and sports in the United States collided to cause division, collective solidarity, or patriotism on a national and/or global scale.

1890   George Dixon becomes the first African American world boxing champion.

1899   Marshall "Major" Taylor becomes the first African American world cycling champion.

1903   Major League Baseball (MLB) is founded.

1908   African American boxer Jack Johnson defeats Tommy Burns to become the first Black heavyweight champion.

1910   The National Collegiate Athletic Association. The NCAA formulates and enforces rules and eligibility criteria for intercollegiate athletics, functions as a general legislative and administrative authority for intercollegiate athletics, and supervises regional and national intercollegiate athletic competitions.

1912   Jim Thorpe becomes the first Native American to win an Olympic gold medal, winning the decathlon and pentathlon in the Stockholm Games.

Heavyweight boxing champion, Jack Johnson. Johnson became the first African American to win the title after defeating Jim Jeffries, the "Great White Hope," in July of 1910. (Library of Congress)

1914   U.S. Football Association (USFA) granted full membership in Federation Internationale de Football Association (FIFA) on June 24.

1917   National Hockey League (NHL) founded.

1920   National Football League (NFL) founded.

Negro National League (NNL) created by Black entrepreneurs to market and support Black baseball players and teams.

1921   Fritz Pollard becomes the first African American head coach in the NFL, coaching the Akron Pros.

1922   The National Football League had a team completely made up of Native American players: the Oorang Indians. The team was organized by Walter Lingo, owner of the Oorang Dog Kennels in LaRue, Ohio. Lingo's sole purpose of the team was to advertise his dogs and kennels; the pregame and halftime entertainment opportunities were more important than the actual games to Lingo. The team only won three games in two years, officially folding after the 1923 season. Former Olympic gold medalist and fellow Native American Jim Thorpe served as the head coach of the team.

1924   During the Summer Games in Paris, William DeHart Hubbard is the first Black athlete to win an Olympic gold medal in an individual event (long jump).

1936   Jesse Owens wins four gold medals in the 1936 Olympic Games track and field events. His victories ruin Adolf Hitler's intentions to use the Games as a show of Aryan supremacy.

1943   All American Girls Professional Baseball League is formed under Chicago White Sox owner Philip Wrigley due to the void left by male players enlisting in the war. Women of color are not allowed to play in the league, which plays its last season in 1954.

1945   MLB baseball is integrated when Jackie Robinson plays first base against the Boston Braves at Ebbets Field in Brooklyn, New York. Robinson played for the Brooklyn Dodgers for ten seasons.

1948   At the 1948 London Olympics, high jumper Alice Coachman takes gold in the event, becoming the first Black woman to win Olympic gold and the only American woman that year to win.

At the 1948 London Olympics, ten-meter platform diver Sammy Lee earns gold, becoming the first Asian American to win one. Lee goes on to repeat as gold medal winner in the 1952 Games in Helsinki.

1949   National Basketball Association (NBA) organized.

1950   Football player Earl Lloyd is the first African American to play in the NBA.

1954   *Brown v. Board of Education* ruling by the Supreme Court overturns the *Plessy v. Ferguson* ruling that "separate but equal" educational facilities are adequate. This decision paves the way for integration in schools and eventually all facilities.

1956   African American, Arthur Mitchell, becomes the only Black dancer in the New York City Ballet. Mitchell will go on to be the director of the Dance Theatre of Harlem.

1957   Althea Gibson becomes the first Black female tennis player to play in, and win, the Wimbledon women's singles title.

1958   NHL gains its first African American ice hockey player in Willie O'Ree.

1960   African American track and field star Wilma Rudolph becomes the first woman in Olympic history to earn three gold medals in a single Olympics.

1961   Wendell Scott becomes the first African American to start a NASCAR race. Scott wins his first event two years later in 1963 at Jacksonville's Speedway Park.

Syracuse University football player Ernie Davis becomes the first African American to win the Heisman Trophy.

Stewart Udall, former President John F. Kennedy's interior secretary, threatens to take away the stadium of the Washington football team due to owner George Preston Marshall's refusal to sign a Black player. Marshall begrudgingly signs a handful of Black players for the 1962 season. Washington, D.C., was the last team in the NFL to integrate.

1962   Jackie Robinson becomes the first African American inducted into the National Baseball Hall of Fame.

Golfer Charlie Sifford becomes the first African American PGA tour member.

1964   Native American distance runner Billy Mills wins the 10,000m race in Olympic record time at the Tokyo Games. No American had ever won the 10,000m before in an Olympic competition.

1966   Bill Russell becomes the first Black coach of an NBA team (Boston Celtics).

Texas Western coach Don Haskins starts five Black players and defeats the all-White Kentucky University basketball team for the NCAA basketball championship. No college coach had ever started five Black players before. Texas Western is currently known as the University of Texas at El Paso—UTEP.

1967   The first Black person is inducted into the NFL Hall of Fame: Emlen Tunnell (New York Giants and Green Bay Packers).

At age twenty-five, boxing heavyweight champion of the world Muhammad Ali appears at his scheduled induction into the U.S. military and refuses to step forward when his name is called. Accepting immediate arrest, Ali never goes into the military. Ali stays out of prison while his case is appealed, but he is also stripped of his title, and his license to box is suspended. Ali remains unable to obtain a boxing license for the next three years.

1968   Track and field athletes John Carlos and Tommie Smith give the Black Power salute during medal ceremony at the Mexico City, Olympics.

1970   Nine members of the Syracuse University football team—Greg Allen, John Godbolt, Bucky McGill, Duane Walker,

John Lobon, Ron Womack, Dana Harrell, Richard Bulls, and Al Newton—all walk out of a spring practice to protest racial discrimination on SU's campus. The young men, incorrectly dubbed "The Syracuse 8," are condemned by teammates and administration. It is not until 2006 that Syracuse University officially recognize the nine players for their courageous stand.

MLB player Curt Flood challenges the leagues reserve clause, which prevented players from changing teams unless they were traded. Flood likens his current state to that of "property to be bought and sold." Although Flood loses his case, he opens the door for the free agency that has existed in MLB since 1975.

1972   Title IX of the Education Amendments Act of 1972 is passed. In relation to athletics, Title IX requires equitable opportunities for men and women to play sports, requires equitable scholarships to be offered, and requires equal provisions (i.e., coaching, locker rooms, recruitment, access to tutoring, publicity, housing, etc.) for male and female sports teams.

1973   Tina Sloan Green becomes named the first African American women's college lacrosse coach at Temple University. Green coaches there until 1992.

1975   Golfer Lee Elder is the first Black to play in the Masters Tournament at Augusta, Georgia.

Arthur Ashe wins the tennis singles title at Wimbledon, becoming the first Black man to win a major singles championship.

1978   Syracuse University drops its "Saltine Warrior" mascot after Native American students condemned the mascot as demeaning and racist.

The International Charter of Physical Education and Sport is adopted by UNESCO (United Nations Educational Scientific and Cultural Organization). This charter addressed the importance of facilities, support for youth sports and for those with disabilities, adequate coaching development, positive media promotion of sport, and the importance of social and cultural respect of individuals in sports participation.

President Jimmy Carter signs the Amateur Sports Act of 1978. The Act established the U.S. Olympic Committee and provided for national governing bodies for each Olympic sport. The act also guarantees certain due process rights, including hearings and appeals, for U.S. athletes.

1986 The NCAA adopts Proposition 48, which required incoming student-athletes to have minimally earned a GPA of 2.0 and an SAT score of 700 or a score of 15 on the ACT. If the athlete failed to reach this minimum requirement, there would be an automatic year of ineligibility. Between 1986 and 1990, there was a marked drop in African American participation in NCAA sports.

1988 NFL player Doug Williams becomes the first Black quarterback to win a Super Bowl.

1989 LA Raiders coach Art Shell becomes the second-ever African American NFL coach.

Asian American tennis player Michael Chang becomes the youngest and only Asian American man to win the French Open.

1991 The largest democratic education organization of its kind in the world, the National Education Association (NEA) passes resolutions in 1991 and 1992 that denounce the use of ethnic-related sports team nicknames, symbols, and mascots. In 2001, the NEA passes another resolution reaffirming their stance from the early 1990s.

1992 The first Asian American to win a gold medal in Olympic women's figure staking is Kristi Yamaguchi in Albertville, France.

Native American activist Suzan Shown Harjo, along with six other Native Americans, file the landmark case *Harjo et al. v. Pro-Football, Inc.* The case was against the Washington football team's disparaging name.

Mexican American boxer Oscar De La Hoya wins Barcelona Olympic gold in the lightweight division. Over a sixteen-year career, De La Hoya wins multiple world titles in six different weight classes.

The Black Women in Sport Foundation (BWSF) is founded by Tina Sloan Green, Dr. Nikki Franke, Dr. Alpha Alexander, and Linda Greene, Esq. in Philadelphia, PA. The nonprofit organization's mission is to increase the involvement of Black women and girls in all aspects of sport: playing, coaching, and administration.

1994   Both Marquette University and St. John's University change their mascots. Marquette goes from the "Warriors" to "Golden Eagles," and the St. John's "Redmen" become the "Red Storm."

1995   Black female basketball player, Sheryl Swoopes becomes the first female athlete to have an athletic shoe named after her.

1996   Amy Chow becomes the first Asian American gymnast to medal at the Atlanta Olympics, winning team gold and earning a silver medal on bars.

Dominique Dawes becomes the first African American gymnast to win an individual Olympic medal, winning team gold and earning bronze on the floor exercise.

African American NBA player Mahmoud Abdul-Rauf, of the Denver Nuggets, sits during the anthem of a game because he views the flag as a symbol of oppression and racism. The act earns him a suspension from the NBA Commissioner at the time, David Stern. Supported by the players' union, Abdul-Rauf reaches a compromise with the league and is allowed to bow his head in Islamic prayer during the anthem as long as he still stood. Ultimately, his protest costs him money, playing time, and eventually his career by the time he turns twenty-nine years old in 1998.

1997   Inaugural season of the Women's National Basketball Association (WNBA).

Tiger Woods becomes the first African American to win the Masters Golf Tournament.

The NCAA enacts Proposition 16, which raises the required GPA of prospective student-athletes to 2.5 from the original

2.0 in Proposition 48. This causes legal issues against the NCAA from African American student-athletes (see *Pryor v. NCAA* and *Cureton v. NCAA*).

1998 The NCAA's Minority Opportunities and Interests Committee concludes that mascots that depict Native Americans as caricature and mimic ceremonial rites are in conflict with the NCAA's commitment to ethnic student welfare.

1999 Dat Nguyen is drafted by the Dallas Cowboys, making him the first Vietnamese American player in the NFL.

At age ten, Asian American golfer Michelle Wie is the youngest player to qualify for a USGA amateur championship. She turns professional at age sixteen.

The U.S. Patent and Trademark Office rules that the word "Redskins" is a term disparaging to Native Americans and tends to bring them shame and disrespect. The decision has the potential to strip the NFL's Washington team of trademark protections, but that proves difficult, as the Washington team still uses the word for their organization presently.

2000 The National Women's Football League (WNFL) is formed.

2002 Ozzie Newsom becomes the first African American general manager of an NFL team (Baltimore Ravens).

Oscar De La Hoya founds Golden Boy Promotions, a combat sport promotional firm. This makes De La Hoya the first Mexican American to own a national boxing promotional firm.

Swimmer Maritza Correia, wins the 50- and 100-yard freestyle events at the NCAA Championships, making her the first African American woman to win an NCAA Championship.

2003 The National Football League adopts the "Rooney Rule," a policy requiring league teams to interview minority candidates for head coaching administrative positions before those vacancies are filled. The push for the policy came after two African American head coaches were fired from the

NFL—despite having winning success in their tenures—in 2002. Pittsburgh Steelers owner Dan Rooney spearheads an effort to put the policy in place.

2004   Entrepreneur Robert L. Johnson becomes the first African American to own a major league sports franchise in North America (Charlotte Bobcats).

At the Summer Olympic Games in Athens, Maritza Correia becomes the first African American woman to make the U.S. Olympic swim team and to win a medal (a silver in the 400 freestyle relay).

2005   Florida State University is granted a waiver by the NCAA to continue using its "Seminoles" nickname and iconography, mostly thanks to support from the Seminole Tribe of Florida, which keeps a friendly relationship with the university.

2006   Speed skater Shani Davis becomes the first Black person to win a gold medal in an individual event at the Winter Olympic Games in Turin, Italy.

2010   Jeremy Lin becomes the first American of Chinese or Taiwanese descent to play in the NBA. While playing with the New York Knicks in 2012, his amazing play helped create a winning streak for the team and a following for Lin dubbed "Linsanity."

2012   Gymnast Gabby Douglas becomes the first African American to win the individual all-around event at the 2012 London Olympics.

In response to the shooting death of unarmed African American teenager Trayvon Martin, members of the NBA's Miami Heat wore hoodies in response to demonstrate what it looks like to be racially profiled as Black men in America. Trayvon Martin was shot and killed in his own neighborhood by an unfamiliar neighbor, George Zimmerman, who felt afraid because of what Martin looked like. Zimmerman was found not guilty for murder or manslaughter in Martin's death in July 2013.

2013 The University of Louisville women's basketball team, thanks to Native American sisters Shoni and Jude Schimmel, make it to the championship game of the NCAA Women's Basketball Tournament. The Cardinals would fall to the University of Connecticut, but Jude and Shoni brought massive attention to Native Americans and the current state of Native reservations.

The Oneida Indian Nation launches the first ads in its "Change the Mascot" campaign, which call for the Washington Redskins to end their use of the dictionary-defined racial slur "Redskins" as their mascot.

2014 In December, after the summertime death of unarmed, nonresisting Eric Garner due to a chokehold by police officers as Garner said, "I can't breathe," a number of NBA players voice their outrage by wearing shirts that read, "I Can't Breathe."

A group of the NFL's St. Louis Rams players take the field in a "hands up, don't shoot" gesture in support of the Black Lives Matter protests in Ferguson, Missouri after the shooting death of unarmed Michael Brown by police in August.

2015 Thirty Black players from the University of Missouri, with support from their White coaches and teammates, pledge to boycott the 2015 season. This helps to strengthen demonstrations for the ouster of the university president and his handling of the school's racial tensions, and he resigns two days later. The entire 2015 University of Missouri football team receives the ESPN Enspire Award at the Sports Humanitarian of the Year Awards held in Los Angeles in July 2016.

Ross Initiative in Sports for Equality (RISE) is founded by NFL Miami Dolphin's owner, Stephen M. Ross. The goal of RISE is to use sport as a platform to improve race relations and drive social progress in the United States.

2016 Swimmer Simone Manuel becomes the first African American woman to win a gold medal in an individual swimming event at the Rio Olympics, setting Olympic and U.S. records with her 100 m freestyle time.

Simone Biles, an African American woman, becomes the most decorated American gymnast of all time after collecting five medals—four gold and one bronze—at the Rio Olympics.

In July, the WNBA's Minnesota Lynx players all don T-shirts that read "Change starts with us. Justice & Accountability" in support of the Black Lives Matter movement and justice for shooting deaths of unarmed Philando Castile (St. Paul, MN) and Alton Sterling (Baton Rouge, LA) by police officers.

In mid-August, Colin Kaepernick, quarterback of the San Francisco 49ers NFL team, begins to sit in protest during the national anthem before games. Kaepernick explains that he is sitting as an act of protest against police brutality and the continued oppression of people of color in the United States.

The NCAA enacts a new academic policy that shifts emphasis from standardized test scores on to GPA: it's referred to as "2.3 Or Take a Knee."

2018 The Cleveland Indians MLB team announce that they'll be phasing out the Chief Wahoo logo, a cartoonish and ultimately racist depiction of Native Americans.

The image of Florida State University's first Black head football coach, Willie Taggart, is used by an FSU football fan in a social media post that depicts Taggart being lynched. The image is condemned by FSU's president and the man who posted the image was fired from his job.

During the 2018 US Women's Open Championship match between Naomi Osaka and Serena Williams, Williams and match referee, Carlos Ramos, noticeably argue. The heated dispute begins when Williams is losing to Osaka two games into the second set after Ramos says he witnessed a code violation for coaching—Williams's coach, Patrick Mouratoglou, had given her a thumbs up—and gives Williams a warning. Serena Williams goes on to break a racquet and refer to Ramos as a "thief" after losing a point due to penalties. Osaka, who identifies racially as Japanese and Black, goes on to win the title, becoming the first Japanese American woman to do so.

LeBron James opens the I Promise School in Akron, Ohio.

2019   Former NFL quarterback Colin Kaepernick settles collusion case against the NFL. Specifics of the settlement were not disclosed, ending the eighteen-month standoff over claims by Kaepernick and Eric Reid, former teammates with the San Francisco 49ers, that they had been denied jobs in the league because they knelt through the national anthem before games. They accused the NFL's thirty-two teams of colluding to keep them out of the sport.

African American gymnast Simone Biles (at age twenty-two) becomes the most decorated gymnast of all time after capturing her twenty-fourth and twenty-fifth world championship medals.

Devontae Shuler, an African American sophomore guard for the University of Mississippi men's basketball program, leads seven teammates in taking a knee during the national anthem on a February day when White supremacists march through the campus.

With tensions high between mainland China and Hong Kong, and as NBA players travel to China to play preseason games, Houston Rockets GM Daryl Morey tweets a message of support for Hong Kong protesters. Mainland China immediately responds contentiously. Chinese sponsors dump the Rockets and NBA. The NBA is then criticized by politicians, media, and fans for appearing too appeasing to China by condemning Morey's stance. The NBA later change their statement and support Morey.

Colin Kaepernick privately works out for eight NFL teams but still remains unsigned over three years after he first started his kneeling protest during the national anthem in 2016.

After the Pan American Games in Peru, two U.S. athletes—White male fencer Race Imboden and Black female hammer thrower Gwen Berry—are disciplined after making separate silent protests on the medal podiums. Both athletes were silently supporting the Black Lives Matter movement and protesting acts of social injustice in the United States broadly. The U.S. Olympic Committee places both athletes on twelve months' probation.

2020   A historic collective bargaining agreement (CBA) is made between players in the WNBA and the league. The eight-year CBA includes increased player compensation (the league's top players have potential to earn up to $500,000), mental health resources, fully paid maternity leave, and travel and accommodation upgrades. Many of the addressed issues have stemmed from public comments made by women of color in the WNBA.

Retired African American NBA All-Star Kobe Bryant (age forty-one) and his daughter Gianna (age thirteen) die in a tragic helicopter crash in Calabassas, California. Seven other lives are lost in the crash, and the United States mourns collectively.

In March, for the first time in history, collegiate and professional sports competitions in the United States (as well as many athletic events globally) are suspended due to COVID-19, a highly communicable strain of coronavirus that rapidly became a pandemic after first emerging in China in December 2019. For example, in the United States, the entire NCAA men's and women's basketball tournaments were canceled, the NBA suspended its season, and MLB canceled spring training. And globally, the 2020 Tokyo Olympic Games were postponed to take place in the summer of 2021.

Glossary

Affirmative Action   Proactive measures for remedying the effect of past discrimination and ensuring the implementation of equal employment and educational opportunities. Affirmative action is undertaken only for certain protected groups of individuals: females, Blacks, Latinos/Hispanics, Asians, American Indians, people with disabilities, and covered veterans.

Ally   Someone who makes the commitment and effort to recognize their privilege (based on gender, class, race, sexual identity, etc.) and work in solidarity with oppressed groups in the struggle for justice. Allies commit to reducing their own complicity or collusion in oppression of those groups and invest in strengthening their own knowledge and awareness of oppression.

Assimilationist   One who expresses the racist idea that a racial group is culturally or behaviorally inferior and supports cultural or behavioral enrichment programs to develop that racial group.

Athlete   A person who practices and competes in any organized sport.

Biracial   A person who identifies as coming from two races and whose biological parents are of two different races.

Black Lives Matter   A political movement to address systemic and state violence against African Americans. This movement was created in 2013 by Alicia Garza, Patrisse Cullors and

Opal Tometi in response to the acquittal of Trayvon Martin's murderer, George Zimmerman.

Coach   A person who is responsible for teaching and training the athletes to improve their skills.

Critical Race Theory   Considers many of the same issues as conventional civil rights and ethnic studies but places them in a broader perspective that includes economics, history, and even feelings and the unconscious. Unlike traditional civil rights, which embraces incrementalism and step by step progress, critical race theory questions the very foundations of the liberal order, including equality theory, legal reasoning, enlightenment rationalism, and principles of constitutional law.

Heteronormativity   A cultural norm that assumes that heterosexuality is the only normal and acceptable sexual orientation.

Implicit/Unconscious Bias   Social stereotypes about certain groups of people that individuals form outside their own conscious awareness. Everyone holds unconscious beliefs about various social and identity groups, and these biases stem from one's tendency to organize social worlds by categorizing.

Institutional Racism   Refers specifically to the ways institutional policies and practices create different outcomes for different racial groups. While the institutional policies may never explicitly mention any racial group, their effect is to create advantages for Whites and oppression and disadvantage for people from groups classified as people of color.

Internalized Racism   The situation that occurs in a racist system when a racial group oppressed by racism supports the supremacy and dominance of the dominating group by maintaining or participating in the set of attitudes, behavior, social structures and ideologies that undergird the dominating group's power.

Interpersonal Racism   Occurs between individuals. Once people bring their private beliefs into their interactions with others, racism is now in the interpersonal realm.

LGBTQ A shorthand description of sexual orientations and gender identities/expressions typically included when discussing lesbian, gay, bisexual, transgender, questioning or queer issues.

Microaggression The everyday verbal, nonverbal, and environmental slights, snubs, or insults, whether intentional or unintentional, that communicate hostile, derogatory, or negative messages to target persons based solely upon their marginalized group membership.

Model Minority A term used to describe the Asian community as being able to overcome oppression because of their cultural values. This term creates an understanding of ethnic groups, including Asian Americans, as a monolith or as a mass whose parts cannot be distinguished from each other. The model minority myth can be understood as a tool that White supremacy uses to pit people of color against each other in order to protect its status.

Multiracial An individual that comes from more than one race (and likely more than two).

NCAA (or N.C.A.A.) The National Collegiate Athletic Association is a member-led organization dedicated to the well-being and lifelong success of college athletes in the United States.

Oppression The systematic subjugation of one social group by a more powerful social group for the social, economic, and political benefit of the more powerful social group.

People of Color The preferred collective term for referring to non-White racial groups.

Race A grouping of human beings based on a shared geographic origin, common history, nationality, ethnicity, distinct physical characteristics that are genetically inherited, or genealogical lineage.

Racism Racism involves one group having the power to carry out systematic discrimination through the institutional policies and practices of the society and by shaping the cultural beliefs and values that support those racist policies and practices.

Rooney Rule   Named after former NFL owner of the Pittsburgh Steelers, Dan Rooney, this policy was adopted in 2003 by the NFL. This policy requires teams to interview ethnic-minority candidates for head coaching jobs. Since then, the Rooney Rule has been expanded to include general manager jobs as well.

Stereotype   A positive or negative set of beliefs held by an individual about the characteristics of a certain group.

Tokenism   A term used when a perfunctory effort or symbolic gesture toward the accomplishment of a goal, such as racial integration; the practice of hiring or appointing a token number of people from underrepresented groups in order to deflect criticism or comply with affirmative action rules.

Whiteness   The term White, referring to people, was created by Virginia slave owners and colonial rules in the seventeenth century, replacing terms like "Christian" and "Englishman" to distinguish European colonists from Africans and Indigenous peoples. Whiteness was established as a legal concept after Bacon's Rebellion in 1676; the creation of "Whiteness" meant giving privileges to some while denying them to others with the justification of biological and social inferiority. Whiteness itself refers to the specific dimensions of racism that serve to elevate White people over people of color.

White Supremacy   The ideology that White people and the ideas, thoughts, beliefs, and actions of White people are superior to people of color and their ideas, thoughts, beliefs, and actions. White supremacy is present in institutional and cultural assumptions that assign value, morality, goodness, and humanity to the White group while casting people and communities of color as bad, worthless (worth less), immoral, and undeserving. White supremacy also refers to a political or socioeconomic system where White people enjoy structural advantage and rights that other racial and ethnic groups do not, both at a collective and an individual level.

Index

About the Author

Rachel Laws Myers currently serves as director of equity and inclusion and English department faculty at Choate Rosemary Hall, an independent boarding school in Connecticut. Prior to Choate, she served as the inaugural director of diversity and inclusion at the Hotchkiss School. A competitive youth gymnast turned basketball player, as an undergraduate at Binghamton University, Rachel Laws Myers earned a BA in Africana Studies with a minor in sociology while playing four years of NCAA Division I basketball. She went on to earn a PhD in African American and African Studies with a concentration in English from Michigan State University. In 2016, she was inducted into Binghamton University's Athletic Hall of Fame. Dr. Myers is a published scholar who has focused her scholarship on the experience of Black female athletes, race and sport, media representation in sport, and conceptions of masculinity in sport.